The Logic of Poverty

First published in 1981, *The Logic of Poverty* consists of eight essays that share at least one assumption: that Northeast Brazil provides a startling example of inhumane economic development. The contributors have all worked in the area, and know it at first hand. They look at rural structure and the role of the unemployed 'reserve army', the state of the sugar industry, the ineffectiveness of the irrigation schemes, the stagnation in the fishing sector, the lack of credit available to peasants and the role of SUDENE, the first development agency in the region. Together they paint a picture of poverty and of the factors that allow it to continue, and they place that poverty in the context of the wider economy of Brazil, relating it to the extraordinary transformation that has been called 'the Brazilian miracle'. This book will be of interest to students of geography, anthropology, economics and sociology.

The Logic of Poverty

The Case of the Brazilian Northeast

Edited by Simon Mitchell

Routledge
Taylor & Francis Group

First published in 1981
By Routledge & Kegan Paul Ltd.

This edition first published in 2024 by Routledge
4 Park Square, Milton Park, Abingdon, Oxon, OX14 4RN
and by Routledge
605 Third Avenue, New York, NY 10017

Routledge is an imprint of the Taylor & Francis Group, an informa business

Publisher's Note
The publisher has gone to great lengths to ensure the quality of this reprint but points
out that some imperfections in the original copies may be apparent.

Disclaimer
The publisher has made every effort to trace copyright holders and welcomes
correspondence from those they have been unable to contact.

A Library of Congress record exists under ISBN: 0710006373

ISBN: 978-1-032-76259-3 (hbk)
ISBN: 978-1-003-47827-0 (ebk)
ISBN: 978-1-032-76378-1 (pbk)

Book DOI 10.4324/9781003478270

THE LOGIC OF POVERTY
The case of the Brazilian Northeast

Edited by
SIMON MITCHELL
Institute of Latin American Studies
University of Glasgow

ROUTLEDGE DIRECT EDITIONS

ROUTLEDGE & KEGAN PAUL
London, Boston and Henley

First published in 1981
by Routledge & Kegan Paul Ltd
39 Store Street,
London WC1E 7DD,
9 Park Street,
Boston, Mass. 02108, USA and
Broadway House,
Newtown Road,
Henley-on-Thames,
Oxon RG9 1EN
Printed in Great Britain by
Thomson Litho Ltd, East Kilbride
© Routledge & Kegan Paul 1981

British Library Cataloguing in Publication Data

The logic of poverty.
  1. Brazil, Northeast - Social conditions - Congresses
  I. Mitchell, Simon
  309.1'81.'306   HN282   80-41332

  ISBN 0 7100 0637 3

CONTENTS

TABLES

CONTRIBUTORS

D.E. Goodman
University of London

Jaime Reis
Universidade Nova, Lisbon

Colin Henfrey
University of Liverpool

Regis de Castro Andrade
University of Glasgow

Simon Mitchell
University of Glasgow

Anthony Hall
Field Director of Oxfam

Francisco de Oliveira
CEBRAP (Centro Brasileiro de Analise e Planejamento),
São Paulo, Brazil

PREFACE

This collection of papers originated from a conference held at the University of Glasgow in April 1975, at which students working in the UK on Northeast Brazil presented papers under the broad unifying themes of perennial problems of the area and, in particular, the poverty of its population.

The essays (including one offered by de Oliveira) together constitute something of a fruit salad; but this was difficult to avoid, given the interests of the few people who have worked in the region. They do, however, share a set of common assumptions; that Northeast Brazil is in a bad state, that contemporary growth in Brazil has been skewed, and that the Northeast itself provides a startling example of inhumane economic development.

Editorial thanks are offered to the Nuffield Foundation for making the conference financially possible, and to the Carnegie Trust and the University of Glasgow for providing a guarantee against publication costs. Thanks are also given to all who came to the conference, to the contributors to this volume who waited with great patience for the editor to get the book together, and above all to Regis de Castro Andrade who fastidiously translated de Oliveira's paper and was a constant source of encouragement throughout some dark periods when it looked as though the book would never materialise.

Glasgow, 1979

Chapter 1

INTRODUCTION

The Northeast of Brazil, the region of that enormous country which forms the 'bulge' of Latin America, contains some of the poorest people in the western hemisphere. Their degree of extreme poverty is (at first sight) surprising because the region is politically and economically part of a comparatively rich country in Latin-American terms, and one which has developed very rapidly over the last decade. The Northeast is in some ways analogous to the Italian Mezzogiorno, but the material misery of most of its people is far greater, and the contrast of their condition compared with that of richer Brazilians in the state capitals and the cities of the Centre-South is very extreme. A reasonably successful doctor earns much more than fifteen times the official govern-mentally determined minimum salary. (This minimum salary is notional, since a great many of those who are salaried are paid less, and those paid more are persuaded to think that any extra is a high favour). The elite are fabulously rich; the majority have children suffering from malnutrition.

The Northeast is traditionally defined as the area encompassed by the nine coastal states between Maranhão and Bahia. (1) It covers an area larger than Italy, Spain and Portugal combined, and has a population of approximately 32 million, about a third of Brazil's total. It is also the most heavily populated under-developed area of the country.

The poverty of the majority of Northeasterners is partly explained by the region's history, patterns of settlement and organisation since Portuguese colonisation in the sixteenth century. From the start social organisation ensured extreme social-economic differences between people. Most of the population were to be 'pre-political' (to use Furtado's expression) and be economically excluded from the benefits of the land. Enormous land grants were given by the Portuguese crown to donatarios, prominent political men, who, in turn, handed out extensive tracts known as capitanias hereditárias to individual colonisers. Latifúndios were thus established from the beginning, and one of their effects was to produce a polarised, highly inegalitarian class system, based by the 1530s on slave labour. Many of the effects of this organisation are still immediately recognisable in the present day.

The first area to be settled, the narrow fertile coastal strip
called the zona da mata (forest zone) approximately 100 kilometres
wide and running parallel to the littoral from Paraíba to Bahia,
was almost entirely monopolised by plantations devoted to the
production of sugar cane. Monocrop agriculture on the plantations
was so extreme that worry was expressed by the Dutch, who held
Pernambuco between 1630 and 1654, and by a few Brazilian observers
that insufficient foodstuffs were being grown to feed the local
population.

Until the mid-seventeenth century the sugar planters thrived,
but from that time onwards, with competition from other sugar-
producing areas, the industry declined. It enjoyed a brief upsurge in the late nineteenth century with the introduction of
sugar-refining factories and an improved type of cane, but again
declined from the early years of this century.

Many features of colonial organisations remain in the zona da
mata. Sugar-growing latifúndios, whose products continue to be
heavily subsidised by the state, continue to be the primary units
in the countryside, and the conditions of sugar workers remain
as wretched as they were in the past. Hall's essay in this
volume describes some aspects of the industry's organisation.
Reis's paper focuses upon the nutrition of the workers.

The zona da mata is the most densely populated sub-region of
the Northeast. It occupies 7 per cent of the total area but
contains over 27 per cent of the region's population. The largest
cities, and nearly all the state capitals, are sited on the coast,
with their numbers swollen by constant migration from the interior.
The countryside contains far too many people, given its present
economy.

The sub-region adjacent to the zona da mata, known as the
agreste, occupies about 11 per cent of the Northeast's area. It
is a transitional zone between the well-watered coastal zone and
the extensive semi-arid interior, the sertão. With reasonable
rainfall and fairly good soils it has been used for the cultivation
of cereals, fruit and cotton, and for cattle raising. The past
patterns of settlement have resulted in a rather more complicated
land tenure system than the other sub-regions. The agreste was
partly populated by people migrating from the zona da mata during
the long decline of the sugar industry, by runaway slaves, and by
ex-slaves after abolition. These people were able to exist in the
agreste on a subsistence economy in a way which was not possible
in the coastal area. At the same time others established large
estates which were primarily devoted to the raising of cattle.
The owners of these estates allowed landless families to clear the
land and grow food crops or cotton in exchange for grazing rights
or rent, or for a share of the cotton production, or for one or
two days of free labour each week. These relationships were, and
are, highly exploitative of the landless who, having no advantages with which to negotiate and with minimal legal rights, are
forced to accept very harsh contracts to remain on the land.
While the agreste has a certain amount of minifundios and some
middle-sized farms, the greater part of it, as in the zona da mata,
is in the hands of owners with fairly large estates who, with
state incentives, are tending to intensify cattle raising and are

expelling landless families from their properties. The situation
in some areas of the agreste is not unlike that of Scotland during
the Highland clearances.

A third physical sub-region, the sertão, covers approximately
half the total Northeast. Most of this region is semi-arid and
suffers from erratic rainfall, but also from periodic droughts
which have been appalling in their effect upon people and livestock. There are a few scattered humid areas, but nearly all the
region is a harsh and desiccated environment covered naturally by
low xerophytic vegetation.

The sertão was occupied, as was the agreste, by men moving
westward in search of land for stock raising. Huge cattle ranches
were established and, since each animal required about ten hectares
for its support and also required very little tending, the area
for three hundred years was very thinly populated. When droughts
occurred, cattle died, but the low population density allowed men
and their families to survive the crises.

In the nineteenth century, however, a most unfortunate innovation occurred. It was discovered that cotton grew well in the
sertão, and this resulted fairly quickly in migrants arriving from
other sub-regions in hope of employment. Cotton production was
stimulated in the latter half of the century by the USA's inability to provide sufficient quantities for the European market,
and the boom tempted even more families to move from other regions
to find permanent employment. Estate owners contracted out land
to sharecroppers to grow cotton, and used their crop stubble as
feed for their own cattle. As in the agreste these contracts have
always been very harsh, favouring the landowner at the expense
of the worker and his family. Sharecroppers, as a result, were,
and are, forced to grow subsistence crops to keep themselves alive,
and this in an extremely hostile environment always liable to
suffer from a critical shortage of water. Given the pattern of
land tenure, the ecology and the precarious economy of almost all
its inhabitants, the sertao with the growth of its population
became, in effect, a massive trap; a severe drought in 1877-8
is estimated to have been responsible for the deaths of half a
million people and many more cattle; but even this catastrophe did
not check the rising population. In 1970 the area contained about
46 per cent of the Northeast's population with about 14 people per
square kilometre. Improvements in communication have helped to
allow flagelados, those fleeing from the effects of the droughts,
to move to the coastal regions or to the Centre-South; but
successive droughts have continued to have appalling consequences
for the people of the region.

From the turn of the century federal administrations have
financed programmes attempting to counteract the effects of the
droughts. These schemes have had little effect in eliminating
the hardship caused to sharecroppers and those tenuously living
by subsistence agriculture, but they did change the political and
physical face of parts of the sertão. Federal money gave considerable powers of patronage to those administering the funds,
and much of the money actually spent was devoted to the building
of dams which were of direct benefit to landowners and their
cattle, but did nothing for over 95 per cent of the sertão's

population. The abuse of funds, the corruption and the in-
effectuality of the schemes led to this 'aid' being popularly
referred to as 'The Drought Industry'.

More recently federal money has been applied to irrigation
schemes (Hall's essay in this book is concerned with three projects of this kind), yet they also have made no significant impact
on the region. It is true that the effects of the most recent
droughts have been alleviated by work fronts instituted by the
government and by emergency relief measures, but nothing has
been done to solve the basic man-land problem. The most recent
crises of 1970 and 1976 have resulted in the traditional pattern
of starving sertanejos fleeing for the nearest town or the coast,
in shops being looted by desperate families, in deaths by the
hundred of adults and children. There is high irony, given the
sorry history of the government's role, in a Brazilian president,
Medici, flying up to see the effects of the 1970 drought and
announcing to the rest of Brazil how horrified he personally was
by its social consequences. The threat remains: that of a large
population without resources in the face of recurring natural
calamity. No Brazilian government has yet attempted, with serious
and honest concern, to come to grips with the problem.

The fourth sub-region, comprising 22 per cent of the Northeast
and known as the Meio-Norte (Middle North), is composed of the
state of Maranhão and part of Piauí. Both soil and rainfall are
reasonable in this area but little commercial development has
taken place up to the present time. The region is lightly populated, having about 13 people per square kilometre, and is an
obvious potential spill-over area for the other sub-regions.
SUDENE, the once powerful aid agency set up in 1959, planned
initially to persuade families from other places in the Northeast
to colonise the Meio-Norte, but attempts so far at settling new
migrants have been on a small scale and have encountered considerable problems. Castro Andrade's paper in this volume
describes the present economic conditions of a group living in
this sub-region.

In all the sub-regions the same man-made characteristic is
present: an extreme inequality of land tenure which has, from its
beginning, shaped a rural structure in which there is an equally
extreme social inequality between classes untempered by any
significant sense of noblesse oblige or humanism on the part of
landowner to those working the land. Table 1.1 shows the land
tenure situation in 1972; it is almost certainly not accurate,
but if taken as a rough approximation, serves our purposes. The
situation is, if anything, likely to be more extreme than the
table suggests.

Given this kind of structure, the countryside, with the exception of the Meio-Norte, is overpopulated; too many families
have too few resources with which to maintain a minimal standard of
living. The dependency ratio, the proportion of the young to those
working, is high; and there are no feasible alternatives for
employment. The cities are packed with a vast semi- or unemployed
'reserve army' of poor whose condition of life is as appalling
as that of their country counterparts.

TABLE 1.1 Land holding in Northeast Brazil

Size of property (ha.)	No. of properties	Area (ha.)
1 - 10	363,776	1,573,149
10 - 50	362,785	8,632,177
50 - 100	115,859	7,961,478
100 - 500	129,319	26,042,086
500 +	27,209	41,821,384

Note: It is also worth observing that there are 15 latifundios
in the Northeast of more than 100,000 hectares, which
occupy 2,659,135 hectares, considerably more land than
that occupied by 363,776 small properties.

Source: INCRA Estatisticas Cadastrais No. 1, 1972.

The class structure of the cities always was, and remains,
rather more complicated than that in the countryside. In rural
areas a class structure evolved in which there was a dearth of
anything resembling a middle class; professionals always practised
from towns or cities, priests were so few as to make no impact,
communications were extremely poor, and all sophisticated
activities occurred in the cities. Nevertheless, a class structure
developed in which there was very limited social mobility and in
which an abyss separated the material conditions of the bourgeoisie
and the extensive urban poor. An aspiring petit bourgeoisie came
into being, but from early on Northeast Brazil, and in differing
degrees the rest of Brazil, became in effect a country of two
nations. And so it has remained to the present day.

The physical appearance of cities reflects this class structure.
The larger city centres and their surrounding middle-class suburbs
can confuse the visitor who looks no further. They have an
affluent, modern, even elegant appearance with handsome public
buildings, well-ordered apartment blocks and leafy suburbs with
opulent villas. But all the cities have around their core extensive slums of makeshift huts built of cardboard, corrugated
iron, wattle, thatch or wood in which the majority of the urban
population live.

The numbers of those who live in urban squalor have risen very
swiftly, partly because of intensive rural out-migration over the
last few decades. In about 1950 about 25 per cent of the Northeast's population lived in towns or cities; in 1980, according
to recent projections, the figure must be nearer to 50 per cent.
Towns and cities have, in general, made little effort to cope
with migrant families; (2) most migrants are poor and the urban
authorities have always given very low priority to the poorest
sectors. The earth roads in the slums are usually pot-holed and
flooded in winter, sanitation is appalling, and electricity often
absent. The new houses, pitifully few, which have been built for
low-income workers have been little more than dog kennels con-
structed far from the city centres; they are reminiscent of the

most depressing South African townships, and symbolise vividly
the disparity between the classes. Indeed, the size of these
houses and the environments in which they have generally been
placed tell one a great deal about Brazilian society; planners
with set cultural assumptions have designed houses for entire
families which are only a little larger than a single maid's
quarters in a middle-class apartment.

   The condition of the majority of families in cities of the
Northeast is not only extreme. There is no sign that things are
getting better, despite official claims to the contrary. Open
unemployment is surprisingly low, taking official figures, (3)
but veiled unemployment is rife. There are very few jobs indeed
which are reasonable in terms of either hours of work or salary,
and it is only with ingenuity and the most careful planning that
many are able to survive from day to day. It has only become
clear from empirical research during the last few years just how
appalling the situation of urban workers really is. It was
estimated, for example, in 1970 that in each of the nine Northeast
states a third of all urban wage-earners subsisted on monthly
incomes of US$32, and that two-thirds survived with monthly
incomes of US$64 or less. (4)

   During the last quarter of 1972 a full 40 per cent of the urban
labour force earned less than half the minimum salary, that is to
say less than US$34 a month, and this during the period of Brazil's
dynamic growth, the much publicized Brazilian 'miracle'. (5) This
40 per cent, moreover, did not include only the marginally self-
employed, the sellers of combs and plastic trinkets, the crab
catchers, small artisans and odd-job men, but also people being
paid by commercial organisations. No comfort is afforded by
supposing that the cost of living was low at this period or in
more recent times; the cost of food and essentials was considerable, and has steadily increased up to the present. These
wages were at near-starvation level.

   Nor may comfort be gained by supposing that individual salaries
are not a direct indicator of what a family unit earns. In the
same period, of 2.5 million urban families, 22 per cent were sur-
viving on a half, or less, of the minimum salary, 26.6 per cent
on between a half and one single minimum salary, and 25.1 per cent
on between one and two minimum salaries. (6) Cold print and
figures cannot adequately describe the misery: beggars, homeless
people sleeping under bridges, in pipes and on pavements, hungry
children of all ages, the numb daily struggle of desperate
parents, widespread disease, and much of it made worse by malnutrition.

   The Brazilian government has claimed that in the late 1960s or
early 1970s a period of development and improving economic welfare
occurred. There are no signs that this development has touched
the lives of most Nordestinos. What appears to have happened
between roughly 1965 and the present day has been a worsening of
the situation in two senses: the poorest sectors have become poorer
in absolute terms; and the difference, always extreme, between
the richest and poorest has widened still further. The effects of
economic growth have benefited only a tiny portion of the population, and the unhappy class structure, already polarised, has,

through maldistribution of income, become still more extreme. In 1969-70 the poorest 30 per cent of the urban population received 6 per cent of the urban income, while the richest 30 per cent received 71 per cent. (7) Another graphic finding in the same year was that the richest 10 per cent of the urban population of Maranhão and Piauí gained 44 per cent of the urban income; in Ceará, Rio Grande do Norte, Paraíba, Pernambuco and Alagoas the same proportion gained 50 per cent, and in Bahia and Sergipe 48 per cent. In contrast, the share of the poorest 50 per cent of the population was 17, 13 and 15 per cent respectively. (8) We have no evidence since 1970 that this grotesque pattern of distribution has become any more equitable.

Why, apart from the historical factors very briefly described above and the physical disadvantages of the sertao, has Brazil's Northeast remained in such a poor state?

Two types of argument, which are not mutually exclusive, have been put forward. The first would maintain that the region experienced four centuries of an agriculturally based export economy in which capitalist and pre-capitalist sectors evolved, the two existing symbiotically, with the former feeding off the latter. The type of industrialisation which has developed in more recent times has permitted these two sectors to continue in being, the pre-capitalist sector providing cheap food and reserve labour army for the capitalist sector. Moreover, the Northeast is a quasi-colony within Brazil, a region dependent upon the more developed Centre-South of the country, and a victim of capitalist forces controlled by the Centre-South and by multi-national companies operating in Brazil.

A second line of argument would focus upon the incompetence and irresponsibility of planners in SUDENE and other development agencies, federal and local. Fiscal incentives offered to industrialists to create industries and employment have been badly monitored, with the result that too much capital-intensive, rather than labour-intensive plant has been established, giving companies from the South handsome profits but doing little for people in the region. Planners have also, it is argued, been squeamish about undertaking any actions of a politically delicate nature; land reform has not been touched; taxes, always a useful instrument to redress distortion, have not been employed properly; planning consultants, planners, bankers and civil servants responsible for development plans have failed again and again to follow through their own theoretical schemes. One credit scheme after another, designed to help small-holders and those most vulnerable to crisis, has foundered and has ultimately helped those who least need help. It is as though avowedly technocratic 'apolitical' planners for the last fifteen years have been determined to see that nothing actually changes.

Both arguments would seem in broad terms to be correct. The plight of the Northeast cannot possibly be understood without reference to the rest of Brazil and the wider mercantile system. The Northeast has provided and continues to provide cheap labour guaranteed by a surplus labour force. The region offers fiscal incentives to large-scale entrepreneurs, and landowners are subsidized by the government. Interests outside the Northeast without doubt make profits from the area, but, as Goodman has pointed out, we lack knowledge about resources and financial flows to show the extent to which the region is being milked by external agents.

But is is also certainly true that the highly anti-social forms of capitalist organisation established in the past have been strengthened rather than weakened by government planners. The regional aid agency, SUDENE, has permitted the establishment of industrial concerns which have not shared their profits with their work-force nor resolved the problem of urban or rural unemployment. Since 1964, despite endless numbers of schemes on paper, no loans for investment have been offered to small-holders, sharecroppers or renters of land; these people are left to fall back on their own resources, borrowing high-interest loans from the owners whose land they work or from professional money lenders. The bene-ficiaries of public money given for low interest have been the landowners and those already economically established. The common excuse for this abuse of funds is usually made by the staff of banks, that, as executives of the scheme, they must insist on rigorous guarantees before loans are given. The planners, the civil servants, do not interfere because, it seems legitimate to assume, they do not care enough about the practical operation of the schemes. The bureaucracy of aid flounders on; regiments of economists, agronomists, sociologists and technicians make a great deal of money evaluating, measuring and planning; very little changes. There are no pressures from this aid technocracy to advocate serious land reallocation, to ensure that credit schemes and fiscal measures should be properly monitored, or to lessen the extreme inequality in the distribution of wealth.

The effects of capitalism have been very ugly in Northeast Brazil. De Oliveira's paper in this collection offers a salutory interpretative antidote to the conventional assumption that governments and aid agencies are trying genuinely to improve people's conditions. State employees and the Brazilian bourgeoisie in general have highly under-developed social consciences, and the priorities of the federal government since 1964 have given little indication of any concern for the total polity. Cynical in its application of Orwellian slogans, heartless in its pursuit of efficiency objectives, hell-bent on economic growth at the expense of the majority, it has been, especially since 1967, one of the most inhumane administrations anywhere in the world. 'Growth before distribution' has been its idée fixe, even if the present generation do not have enough to eat. Brazil under its hand has become a capitalist's paradise; strikes are forbidden, wages are kept to subsistence level, the country's resources are enormous.

The Northeast, always problem-ridden, shows in more stark relief than other parts of the country the administration's concern for untempered capitalist development, its preference for large-scale enterprises, its neglect of social welfare and its unwillingness to undertake financial or structural changes to ensure greater equality between people. Exporting latifundios flourish, sub-sidised by federal funds. Lightly taxed enterprises expand and make high profits, but 95 per cent of the Northeast's population are excluded from any benefits accruing from their economic success. Even the money supply for regional development in the

region has decreased over the last decade, as the government
has turned its interest to the Amazon. The government has,
moreover, done little to check the growth of new latifundios in
the frontier regions. The Northeast, with the appalling social
effects of its archaic structures, appears to have taught them
no lessons.

NOTES

1 The states of Bahia, Sergipe, Alagoas, Pernambuco, Paraíba,
   Rio Grande do Norte, Ceará, Piauí and Maranhão.
2 Many writers have observed that cities are unable to cope
   with the quantity of incoming migrants. This supposed inability is open to question, since urban authorities have
   shown minimum inclination to offer significant help to poor
   immigrants.
3 The IBGE *Censo Demográfico 1970* (Tabulações Especiais)
   estimates rates of open unemployment in 100 urban municipios
   to be in the range of 4 to 7 per cent.
4 IBGE Censo Demográfico 1970, op.cit.
5 Cf. D.E. GOODMAN, The Brazilian Economic 'Miracle' and Regional
   Policy: Some Evidence from the Urban Northeast, in *Journal of
   Latin American Studies*, vol. 8, pt 1, May 1976.
6 IBGE - PNAD *Pesquisa de Rendimentos*, 2, 4° Trimestre de 1972,
   vol. 3 (Rio de Janeiro, 1972).
7 GOODMAN, op.cit., p.16.
8 ibid.

Chapter 2

RURAL STRUCTURE, SURPLUS MOBILISATION AND MODES OF PRODUCTION IN A PERIPHERAL REGION: THE BRAZILIAN NORTHEAST

D. E. Goodman

INTRODUCTION

The Brazilian Northeast region (1) has achieved a fairly rapid growth rate of agricultural production since the 1940s, notably of food staples for local internal consumption. In broad terms, and with the obvious exception of the periodic drought years in the semi-arid interior, it is agreed that the rising urban demand for foodstuffs has been met successfully. The rural sector has produced and mobilised an agricultural surplus for urban con-sumption without a pronounced shift in the sectoral terms of trade against urban areas. However, despite the general consensus on the macro-economic features of this performance, intense contro-versy surrounds the dynamics of agricultural expansion and its effects on agrarian structure and rural society.

This paper reviews the main points at issue in this debate and examines several conflicting interpretations of Northeastern rural development. The Marxist view is that recent output growth has consolidated the dominance of pre-capitalist modes of pro-duction. The agricultural surplus has been mobilised within the framework of the traditional latifúndio-minifúndio system. An alternative position is based on a *specialisation model* of rural change. This advances the hypothesis that the Northeastern rural economy is in transition towards capitalism and characterised by increasing social differentiation. In essence, greater commercial activity and the closer integration of regional markets have stimulated agricultural specialisation and the penetration of capitalist modes of production. Forman and Reigelhaupt present a further interpretation based on the analysis of peasant market places and regional marketing systems. Following Frank (1967), they argue that recent agrarian change must be seen in the context of a capitalist rural sector which is undergoing increasing commercialisation.

At a more general level, the paper is concerned with modes of production in peasant agriculture and articulation with an ex-panding capitalist industrial system. A subsidiary theme involves the interaction between backward peripheral regions and the centre of this system. These topics have attracted considerable attention

in the literature in recent years (Frank, 1967; Laclau, 1971) (2).
Articulation between industrial capitalism and non-capitalist
agrarian structures in peripheral areas also forms the cornerstone
of a recent Marxist analysis of Brazilian industrialisation
(de Oliveira, 1972). Certain macro-economic elements of this
framework, henceforth called the CEBRAP model, (3) are presented
in the introductory discussion of centre-periphery interaction in
Brazil. In the main, however, the focus is restricted more narrowly
to the characteristics of structural change in Northeastern agriculture.

1 THE CEBRAP MODEL AND CENTRE-PERIPHERY INTERACTION

The Northeast is an economically backward region of an expanding
national economy, which is dominated by a capitalist metropolitan
centre. This suggests that we approach regional under-development
by considering the region's integration and interaction with the
centre and the associated resource flows. In common with other
Marxist analyses, the CEBRAP model attributes regional backwardness to the spatially unbalanced nature of capitalist growth, which
involves the elaboration of exploitative relations between centre
and periphery. Articulation of these relations sustains under-
development, so determining the economic and social formations of
dependent, peripheral areas. These areas are closely integrated
with the capitalist centre; indeed, they are functional for its
expansion since their exploitation forms an integral element in
the process of capital accumulation. (4) On this view, Northeastern under-development thus must be analysed in terms of the
macro-dynamics of industrial capitalist expansion in Brazil. An
extended treatment of this topic exceeds the scope of the present
paper, but we can consider the CEBRAP analysis of interregional
migration and frontier settlement. This illustrates certain
relationships formulated in the CEBRAP model and also provides an
appropriate perspective for the subsequent discussion of agrarian
structure. (5)
    Migratory movements clearly are a major form of regional inter-
action in Brazil, as recent quantitative studies have amply shown
(Graham and Hollanda, 1971; Mata et al., 1973). The Northeast
has been a net contributor to these resource flows since the late
nineteenth century, playing an important part in the formation of
the labour supply in other regions. The position of the Northeast and several other states, notably Minas Gerais and Rio Grande
do Sul, as reservas populacionais for the dynamic Centre-South is
generally recognised in interpretations of urban-industrial growth
since 1930. However, there is no uniformity in the analytical
treatment of these population flows. Writers in the neo-classical
tradition represent migration as an equilibrating movement in
response to regional income differentials. Several studies have
examined the impact of migration on regional growth patterns and
whether convergent trends in income per head can be discerned
(Sahota, 1968; Graham, 1970; Graham and Hollanda, 1971; Mata et
al., 1973). This approach also is concerned that market imperfections, such as minimum wage legislation, will induce excessive

rural-urban migration, aggravating the dualistic structure of urban economies and the degree of under-employment in low productivity sectors. This dualistic model of urban labour markets is rejected in Marxist analyses, which stress the critical function of rural out-migration in the formation of the reserve army of urban labour. The existence of this labour pool, constantly replenished and augmented by further contingents of migrants, depresses the supply price of urban workers. Consequently, as industrial expansion and technological innovation proceed, real wage rates lag increasingly behind productivity gains, reducing labour's share in output and releasing resources to finance industrial capital accumulation (de Oliveira, 1972, p.20).

Despite their fundamental differences, both interpretations of urban labour markets assume that a labour surplus can be readily mobilised in rural areas. In the neo-classical model, migration arises from the response of rational maximising individuals to urban-rural income differences. The Marxist approach emphasises the disruptive effects of capitalist expansion in displacing labour engaged in relatively inefficient agricultural, industrial and handicraft activities (Brandão Lopes, 1973, pp.131-2).

Urbanisation and industrial growth also depend critically upon mobilising an agricultural surplus, comprising both real and financial flows, and the terms of this transfer (Byres, 1974, pp.221-9). The importance of the real or commodity surplus arises from the various roles assumed by food and raw materials as wage goods, industrial inputs and earners of foreign exchange. For example, rising real wages caused by increases in the relative price of food can retard industrialisation by reducing the rate of profit and internal sources of capital financing. If this occurs, urban interests will seek to provoke changes in the agrarian structure which ensure an adequate flow of marketed surplus and more favourable intersectoral terms of trade. In general, once urban-industrial groups achieve political and economic hegemony, as in Brazil from the 1930s onwards, the survival of agrarian structures will depend on their supply response to the requirements of the urban economy. Of course, these structures and the prevailing mode of production may present regional differences due to their location in relation to urban markets and conditions of land and labour supply. In other words, if the rate of release of resources from agriculture is satisfactory in the aggregate, there will be less pressure to transform the agrarian structure. Different modes of production then can coexist, each contributing to the process of capital accumulation in the metropolitan centre.

CEBRAP writers emphasise that this diversity characterises Brazilian agriculture. In peripheral regions such as the Northeast, the maintenance of non-capitalist relations of production is seen as being functional for the process of capitalist expansion at the centre. This is not advanced as a general proposition or intrinsic condition of capitalist growth but as a relation specific to the Brazilian case. (6) The distinctive features stressed in the CEBRAP model are the frontier and rapid rates of rural in-migration which furnish the manpower needed to extend the area of agricultural settlement. Land on the frontier initially is cultivated by families producing short-cycle subsistence crops, although

their surpluses typically will be appropriated by the landowner
where commercial distribution is possible. At the same time the
rural worker, whether squatter or employee (morador), also clears
the land, increasing its economic value and simplifying its subsequent preparation for permanent cash crops or conversion to
pasture. When this stage is reached, the subsistence holdings are
consolidated and the size of the resident labour force and tenurial
relations adjusted accordingly. The incorporation of frontier land
is founded on the exploitation of migratory labour seeking the
means of subsistence and proceeds via the reproduction of latifundia, so denying this labour permanent access to the land.

This pattern of frontier expansion, which Oliveira describes
as 'growth by the elaboration of peripheries', ensures the flexi-
bility of agricultural supply. Thus, 'the majority of the vege-
table food crops (such as rice, beans and corn) supplied to the
great urban markets come from zones of recent settlement'
(Oliveira, 1972, pp.16-17). Agricultural expansion involves
extensive methods, which require elastic supplies of land and
labour, and is consolidated by the formation of latifundia. The
existence of the frontier and rural in-migration create conditions
for the reproduction of pre-capitalist modes of production and the
extraction of the surplus by extra-economic means. This process,
it is argued, has characterised frontier occupation, at different
times, in Northern Parana, Western São Paulo, Mananhão and
Southern Goias and, more recently, South-West Parana, Northern
Goias, Para and Mato Grosso.

The CEBRAP interpretation also accords the frontier a pivotal
role in attenuating internal contradictions which might otherwise
have threatened the social stability of the system during the
recent industrialisation process. The potential for conflict
is inherent in the articulation of inter-sectoral relations between
industrial capitalism and agrarian structures inherited from the
colonial era. That is, how to reconcile the need to mobilise the
agricultural surplus, on terms which would ensure propitious conditions for industrial capital formation, with the retention of
extensive techniques and non-capitalist modes of production in
areas of early agricultural settlement. The CEBRAP view is that
frontier expansion, based on the exploitation of migratory labour,
has prevented any sustained trend in the internal terms of trade
against industry. Moreover, since food costs are a major factor
determining the reproduction cost of urban labour, these circumstances have combined with urban migratory flows to depress the
urban real wage rate and so facilitate rapid capital accumulation.
Overall, 'this model permitted the system to leave the basis of
agrarian production untouched, by-passing the problems of the distribution of land ownership which seemed critical at the end of
the 1950s' (de Oliveira, 1972, p.18). This schematic presentation
of the CEBRAP model clarifies the relationships between migratory
flows from the Northeast and other dependent regions of early
settlement and capital accumulation in the Centre-South. Labour
migration performs a dual function in this framework: as a source
for the urban reserve army and the population contingents extending
the agricultural frontier. In each case, these flows affect the
urban real wage and hence assume a central role in the expansion
of metropolitan industrial capitalism.

2   AGRARIAN STRUCTURE IN THE NORTHEAST

The model of agricultural expansion just outlined plainly incorporates hypotheses about agrarian structures in peripheral regions
of early settlement. Bluntly, the central thesis is that the
frontier not only re-creates conditions for the reproduction of
latifúndia but also permits the survival of this pre-capitalist
mode in long-settled regions, such as the Northeast. Oliveira
thus argues that the same system of exploitation characterises
the *external* and *internal* frontiers. Within long-established
latifúndia, the rotation of the land has the same function as
that performed by crop rotation in latifúndia on the *external*
frontier. 'The secular process that unfolds in the Northeast, for
example, is typical of this symbiosis. The morador, when planting
his "roça", also plants cotton, and the cost of reproduction of the
labour force is the variable that renders each of them saleable
as commodities' (de Oliveira, 1972, p.17).

Brandão Lopes presents a weaker, geographically differentiated
version of this thesis, implying that capitalist production and
free wage labour now prevail in the immediate rural hinterland of
the metropolitan centre. In these areas, such as Northern Parana,
Western São Paulo and Southern Goias, he stresses the importance
of rural migratory flows from the Northeast in the formation of the
rural proletariat. Nevertheless, 'in the greater part of the
country, the extensive growth, in new forms, of a primitive economy
of subsistence' continues. 'One can say that the style of development now underway continuously creates ... archaic forms of
agriculture' (Brandão Lopes, 1973, p.136). The following sections
describe the major hypotheses and research themes that emerge from
the CEBRAP approach and identify differences with alternative
interpretations.

Latifúndio and modes of production

The basic CEBRAP hypothesis is that analysis of rural society in
the Northeast should be formulated in terms of the social relations
associated with pre-capitalist modes of production. The latifúndia
is the dominant form of rural organisation in this model and its
pre-eminence has been reinforced, not eroded, by recent development
patterns. Both Brandão Lopes (1973) and Sá (1973) base their
interpretation of Northeastern agrarian change since the 1940s
on the vitality and resurgence of the binary latifúndio-minifúndio
system.

One immediate question is whether this model provides an
accurate empirical basis for generalisation about the dynamics of
Northeastern rural society during the past two to three decades.
Does agrarian structure, that is, 'the network of relations among
the various groups of persons who draw their livelihood from the
soil' (Thorner, 1956, p.2), exhibit the general characteristics
assumed in this model? Can we delineate the social relations of
production and the forces of production in agriculture in order to
identify the prevailing mode of production (Byres, 1974)? If, in
fact, there has been no substantive structural change, what factors

explain the consolidation of pre-capitalist modes during a period
of rapid urbanisation and increasing commercial activity in rural
areas?   The CEBRAP model, in short, emphasises the essential
stability of rural society in the Northeast.   These are major
issues to which future research on agrarian structure should be
addressed.

The agricultural surplus and urban growth

A crucial proposition of the CEBRAP model is that the latifúndio-
minifúndio sturcture has responded adequately to demands imposed
by rapid urban growth for increasing agricultural surpluses.
Furthermore, the successful mobilisation of the surplus explains
why a capitalist agriculture specialising in staple foodstuffs
has not emerged in the Northeast (Brandão Lopes, 1973, p.137).
The CEBRAP interpretation conflicts with several alternative views
of Northeastern agricultural development.   These include the
Ricardian pessimism of the 1959 GTDN report, with its stagnationist
prognosis, and more recent views that output growth reflects the
structural transformation of the rural economy.   The GTDN regarded
the inelastic supply of food to major urban areas as 'the most
fundamental obstacle to regional industrialisation'.   This alleged
inelasticity threatened to erode regional comparative advantage
based upon low-wage industrial labour.   As a result of the inefficient agrarian structure, rising urban food prices and increasing dependence on imports were steadily undermining the competitive position of regional industry.   Future industrial growth,
it was argued, would be inhibited by the failure to mobilise the
agricultural surplus.   Without prejudice to the question of
structural change, the performance of agriculture has invalidated
the GTDN diagnosis.   It is useful at this point to review the main
features of this expansion.

   Real output in the primary sector increased at an average
annual rate of 4.6 per cent in the period 1947-68, matching the
growth in net regional product at factor cost.   Arable crops
(lavouras) led this growth, and the output of staple food crops
for internal regional consumption, particularly rice, beans and
corn, increased more rapidly than that of industrial raw materials
and export crops, the so-called culturas nobres.

   There is scant evidence that output expansion has been achieved
by the diffusion of new inputs or improved techniques.   On the
contrary, the stability of average yields per hectare points to
continued reliance on the extension of existing low-productivity
techniques requiring higher inputs of land and labour.   As a recent
study concludes, 'the major, and almost only, source of growth for
the basic food crops in the 1948-69 period has been the increase
in area cultivated' (Patrick, 1972, p.84).   Indeed, the area in
arable crops rose from 4.5 million to 10.9 million hectares in
1950-68, increasing at virtually the same annual rate as real
output.   The availability of virgin land, notably in Maranhão,
Piauí and Bahia, is important in this pattern of extensive growth,
but it is striking that the acreage in crops on established farms
in long-settled areas has risen considerably.   During the years

1950-68, the land in crops increased by 102, 77 and 95 per cent in Paraíba, Pernambuco and Alagoas, respectively. Exploitation of this *internal frontier* presumably involves changes in crop rotation systems, and possibly the incorporation of marginal land, implying some recourse to modern inputs to maintain average yields.

Changes in the size distribution of agricultural establishments reveal further aspects of the way in which output growth was achieved (Table 2.1). (7)   The number of farm units under ten hectares more than doubled in the period 1940-60, although their share of the total area in farms only increased slightly.   In fact, 75 per cent of all new establishments created in these years were under ten hectares, and 65 per cent were below five hectares. Preliminary returns from the 1970 Agricultural Census indicate that the rapid numerical increase of minifúndia was sustained in the 1960s.   Establishments of less than ten hectares increased by 631 thousand, representing 78 per cent of all new farms.   Although these minifúndio units accounted for only 13 per cent of the rise in the total area in farms during the 1960s, their contribution toward extending the area devoted to arable crops has been remarkable.   Of the increase in arable acreage during the period 1940-60, fully one-third occurred on minifúndio properties and this proportion rose to 50 per cent in the 1960s.   If we assume that average yields are attained, the Census data suggest that minifúndio units accounted for an equivalent share of the increase in arable production. (8)   On this interpretation, incorporation of cultivable land by minifúndistas has played a decisive part in the expansion of Northeastern agriculture.

Of course, it does not follow that minifúndia have made an equally significant contribution to the net agricultural surplus in the post-war period.   This measures the flow of output released for non-agricultural use, which differs from gross output due to on-farm consumption and purchases or buy-back of agricultural produce by the rural sector (Byres, 1974).   Moreover, a regional sample survey undertaken in 1967 suggests that on-farm consumption varies inversely with farm size. (9)   An initial step, therefore, would be to determine the respective shares in the net marketed surplus of minifúndia, independent small and medium-size producers and latifúndia.   In the period 1940-60, for example, establishments of 20-500 hectares accounted for 50 per cent of the increased acreage in arable crops.   The assumption that average yields are attained can again be invoked to assess their participation in the expansion of gross crop output.   However, as these larger units are likely to be relatively more market-orientated, their share in net marketed surplus probably exceeds that in gross output by a substantial margin.   If we are concerned with rural-urban flows, and hence with the net agricultural surplus and its mobilisation, we must devote some attention to the mode of production adopted by this middle group of establishments.   Owners of farms in this size range are relatively wealthy, within the top two deciles of the rural income distribution, and may well constitute a modernising element, more responsive to commercial opportunities and prepared to adopt new techniques and capitalist labour practices. (10)   Research to clarify these points has an obvious bearing on the thesis that recent growth marks a transitional phase toward the capitalist transformation of Northeastern agriculture.

TABLE 2.1 The number and area of agricultural establishments according to size classes, 1940-70 (%)

Size class	1940		1950		1960		1970	
	No.	Area	No.	Area	No.	Area	No.	Area
Less than 10 hectares	50.0	3.4	53.2	2.8	61.7	4.3	68.3	5.5
10-20 hectares	14.9	3.6	13.0	2.6	10.9	3.3	9.9	4.1
20-50 hectares	16.1	8.7	14.7	6.7	12.7	8.7	10.5	9.7
50-100 hectares	8.1	9.7	7.8	7.9	6.3	9.6	5.1	10.5
100-500 hectares	8.8	31.6	8.9	27.0	6.6	29.8	5.1	30.5
500-1000 hectares	1.1	12.9	1.4	13.5	0.9	13.6	0.6	12.9
1000 or more hectares	0.7	30.1	1.0	39.5	0.5	30.7	0.4	26.8
TOTALS (1)	737,604	42,888	844,510	58,341	1,409,740	63,571	2,199,538	73,813

Note: (1) The total area of agricultural establishments is given in 1000 hectares.

Source: Agricultural Census data.

The marked concentration of new farms in the minifúndio category also has been interpreted as prima facie evidence of rural
population pressure. Certainly the long-term trend towards greater
fragmentation was not arrested in the 1960s, although new minifúndia occupied an additional area of 1.3 million hectares. A
secular morcellement process is suggested by the decline in the
average size of minifúndio establishments from 3.95 hectares in
1940 to 2.72 hectares in 1970. In the ecological and present
technical conditions of Northeastern agriculture, farms of this
size give inadequate support for a family, even where the operator
retains full entrepreneurial control. It is likely that minifúndistas thus enter the labour market to earn supplementary income,
joining the mass of truly landless labour. If this is the case,
morcellement is contributing to the formation of a dependent rural
labour force (Scandizzo, 1974). This trend can be reconciled
both with the CEBRAP hypothesis and the alternative view of increasing capitalist penetration.

Finally, with the exception of drought years, the implicit price
index for arable crops has remained reasonably stable in the period
1947-68 (Patrick, 1972). This suggests that the agricultural
surplus has been mobilised without any pronounced deterioration
in the sectoral terms of trade against industry. (11) Despite
the virtual stagnation of crop yields, agriculture has responded
adequately in macro-economic terms and not constrained regional
growth as the GTDN envisaged. This general outline also reveals
the extensive nature of agricultural expansion and the key role
of labour supply and uncultivated land on both the *external* and
internal frontiers of the Northeast. This reading of the Census
data is quite consistent with the CEBRAP approach, particularly
the evidence suggesting the reproduction of minifúndia within
latifúndia. However, recent trends in the agricultural sector
have been interpreted in radically different terms.

The *specialisation model*

Several writers interpret agricultural output growth as the result
of a widespread response by producers to income opportunities
generated by rising urban demand. This response was facilitated
by the spread of the road network, which brought greater integration of regional markets and stimilated commercial production.
This *specialisation model* is advanced by Castro (1971), who
stresses the importance of small merchants and lorry drivers as
outlets for 'the surplus generated by small producers' dispersed
throughout the region's semi-arid interior. These entrepreneurs
and middlemen 'not only offered secure outlets ... but also broke
down the relative commercial monopoly exercised by the great
landowner-merchants' (Castro, 1971, pp.204-5). Castro argues that
increased commercial activity stimulated previously-isolated
interior areas to specialise in the production of staple food
crops for urban markets. On this view, the 1950s witnessed a
fundamental structural change as agriculture became increasingly
commercialised and market-orientated. The role of better communications and the activities of urban-based merchants and

truckers in transforming the rural economy of the interior also
has been stressed by Vilaça (1969), Patrick (1972), Forman and
Riegelhaupt (1970a, 1970b) and Goodman and Cavalcanti (1974).

This model implies that various rural classes, including small
owner-operators, tenants and sharecroppers, respond to market
incentives and base their production decisions on relative profit
opportunities. Furthermore, these producers market their surpluses
directly to local merchants, middlemen and wholesalers or assume
retail functions themselves. The essential point is that producers exercise entrepreneurial functions and can choose from a
range of possible marketing alternatives. This ensures that price
fluctuations, in some measure, are communicated to the producer,
who can then adapt and specialise accordingly. Commercialisation
and expanding profit opportunities in turn create conditions for
increasing socio-economic differentiation in the rural economy,
heralding the disintegration of pre-capitalist modes of production.

This *orthodox* interpretation of Northeastern agricultural growth
is in conflict with the CEBRAP approach on many points. One extremely vital issue turns on the transmission of market incentives.
That is, how deeply has commercialisation penetrated into the
agrarian structure? On the CEBRAP view, the large landowner still
exercises monopolistic power and has not ceded his position as
commerciante to a new generation of highly specialised middlemen
and merchants. Retention of this function permits the landowner
to extract surpluses by maintaining pre-capitalist relationships
with his sharecroppers and tenant farmers. The surplus, extracted
mainly in the form of rent but also as interest payments, is then
transferred by the landowner to urban markets, typically by direct
and regular transactions with large-scale wholesalers. Since
rising urban food prices do not permeate down to the farmer and
affect his real income, the monopolistic landowner continues to
appropriate the surplus value generated by this disparity. That
is, the landowner is under little pressure to revise land use
patterns on his property and cultivate his land directly as a
capitalist producer. Under these conditions, it is argued, large
landowners respond to the profit opportunities offered by rising
food prices by increasing the number of sharecroppers and tenant
farmers on their property. Urban expansion and, more recently,
industrialisation, have not initiated a process of structural
change in agriculture characterised by increasing specialisation,
widespread real income gains and greater differentiation. Rather,
conditions in the Northeast still support and reproduce archaic
forms of agrarian organisation.

Since there is obviously a profound source of disagreement here,
it is useful to have an explicit statement of the CEBRAP position
on the extraction and transfer of the agricultural surplus. This
has been put in the following terms:

As the urban food supply is composed, basically, of innumerable
small surpluses from subsistence minifúndia, oligopsonistic
buyers prevent rising urban food prices from being transmitted
as higher prices (in real terms) to small producers. In fact,
food production expands independently of market behaviour or
trends, rising as the population engaged in subsistence crops
and on the land increases. Since prices to the producer are

maintained at a low level, there are no incentives to attract large-scale agriculture to the sector producing foodstuffs and this preserves its non-capitalist character. The explanation of the increase in food supply to the urban sector thus depends on understanding the extensive growth of a subsistence peasant economy (Brandão Lopes, 1973, p.137).
The author emphasises specifically that the *oligopsonistic buyers* in question are the landowners, who thus commercialise their tenants' surpluses. (12) Sá (1973) also identifies exchange relations between producer and landlord-middleman as the source of exploitation. Similarly, he underlines the multi-faceted function of the landowner in providing the link between the external capitalist system and agricultural units in which non-capitalist production relations prevail (Sá, 1973, pp.142-3).

The CEBRAP and orthodox views clearly diverge sharply in analysing the adaptations forced upon the agrarian structure by the increased urban demand for food surpluses. To recapitulate briefly, the orthodox position is that various classes of producers have been able to participate in the real income gains generated by higher urban food prices and the increased specialisation which access to wider markets permits. Moreover, individual peasant producers articulate direct relations with buyers operating in a complex, diversified marketing system (Forman and Reigelhaupt, 1970a, 1970b; Castro, 1971). Increased commercialisation thus creates widespread profit opportunities, leading to differentiation of the peasant economy and its gradual penetration by capitalist modes of production. These propositions are a far cry indeed from the CEBRAP model of surplus mobilisation. More detailed empirical research into the process of surplus extraction and transfer is needed to clarify these issues.

This disagreement about peasant economic integration is hardly surprising in view of the more fundamental divergence over modes of production. Although this dispute cannot be resolved by evidence on exchange relations alone, articulation between the rural sector and the wider regional economy deserves some attention. As the CEBRAP and specialisation models offer conflicting formulations of this articulation, it is interesting to examine the structural characteristics of regional marketing systems. A convenient starting point is the Forman-Reigelhaupt interpretation of Northeastern agricultural development, since its empirical foundation is derived from studies of economic brokerage systems. This analysis also stands as a distinctive contribution to the debate under discussion. Subsequently we review empirical surveys of rural marketing processes in the Northeast.

3 PEASANT ECONOMIC INTEGRATION AND AGRICULTURAL COMMERCIALISATION

The Forman and Reigelhaupt (F-R) analysis is presented in two papers on regional marketing systems, (1970a, 1970b). Fundamental changes in land tenure and land use again are attributed to pressures generated by the mobilisation of the agricultural surplus. However, F-R argue that peasant agriculture has not responded adequately to this challenge and now is in process of extinction. Their basic empirical proposition is stated in the following terms: 'What we are seeing today is the increasing commercialisation of agriculture, which alters the role of the peasantry - from small-scale producers to rural proletariat' (F-R, 1970b, p.115). Although F-R describe the Northeast as a 'transitional agrarian society', the theoretical foundations of this characterisation are not elaborated. The authors apparently are not referring to the lack of dominance by one mode of production. (13) 'The peasant in Northeast Brazil operates within a capitalist society where land, labour and product all have a market' (F-R, 1970a, p.189). The transition in question thus must involve rationalisation within a capitalist agriculture. Furthermore, this adjustment process in production systems is determined by exogenous commercial demands emanating from the expanding urban centres. 'Modernisation in the distributive sector of the rural economy is reflected in pressures upon the system of production, leading to the displacement of the peasantry' (1970b, p.114).

F-R, rejecting the Marxist position, repeatedly assert the causal pre-eminence of exchange relations and neglect to analyse the social relations of production: 'peasant economies are best understood through an analysis of exchange networks' (F-R, 1970b, p.100). Or, again, 'since Colonial times, the most important single element in the transformation of rural Brazilian society has been, and continues to be the commercialisation of the agricultural sector' (F-R, 1970b, p.101). (14) Their general thesis, formulated with reference to Northeastern experience, is that 'the marketing system will lead to a restructuring of the production system when the latter is unable to meet consumer demands' (F-R, 1970a, p.210). Although essentially a variant of the specialisation model, the F-R analysis is distinctive for the emphasis that agricultural growth and change occur within a capitalist rural economy. There is no suggestion here of pre-capitalist modes, vestiges of feudal social formations nor transition to the capitalist mode.

F-R state that their general purpose is to clarify 'the nature of articulation between the peasant sector and the national society' by investigating rural marketing systems. The role and economic integration of the peasantry in 'a dynamic national economy' is revealed by 'analysis of the peasant Market Place within the rationalising marketing system' (F-R, 1970a, p.189). In the specific case of the Northeast, F-R concentrate on the marketing systems for food staples and elaborate a typology of market places. They look first at the traditional peasant marketing system and describe the participants and organisation of the periodic peasant market place or feira. This focus reflects a basic premise that peasants with entrepreneurial control over their own produce constitute a major source of urban food supplies. Indeed, 'the peasant has always been the principal producer of food staples' (F-R, 1970a, p.207). In sharp contrast to CEBRAP, it is suggested that many independent producers, including medium-sized and small peasant farmers, are in a position to profit from the rising urban demand for food. This hypothesis, and the differential effects of output expansion on various rural classes, is central to Forman's interpretation of rural discontent and the emergence of the peasant leagues in the 1950s and 1960s (Forman, 1971). F-R's review of the peasant Market Place network also reveals the range of selling options open to small peasant producers. At this level, they imply that competitive, or at least non-collusive, arrangements characterise the retail and wholesale trade in food staples.

F-R then argue that the Northeast presents 'the phenomenon of an on-going, increasingly viable system of peasant Market Places which are, at the same time as their peasant participants, well on their way to extinction in a modern world' (F-R, 1970a, p.193). This eclipse of the peasant marketing system is attributed to its inefficiency in channelling food supplies to the growing urban centres. F-R contend that the peasant market place network is being superseded due to the activities of urban wholesalers, 'who are rapidly coming to dominate the marketing system in Northeast Brazil' (F-R, 1970a, p.200). The urban wholesaler, the key figure in the F-R analysis, emerges with the increasing commercialisation of agriculture and 'is the centre of a rationalised marketing system' (F-R, 1970a, p.201).

> Traditionally, the peasant producer entered the system through the local Market Place, which was the starting point in the upward flow of primary produce. Now, food staples have begun to follow the model of commercial export crops in the funnel-like movement from producer to consumer through large warehouses. Wholesalers go to the farm to buy produce in bulk. In this way, crops by-pass the traditional peasant Market Place, which comes to serve primarily as a mechanism for the horizontal movement of foodstuffs (F-R, 1970a, p.202).

These changes are due to urban commercial elites 'attracted to the marketing system by high middleman profits' (F-R, 1970a, p.206). The crucial hypothesis here is that the urban wholesaler initially obtains supplies in the rural market place but eventually resorts to direct on-farm purchases from peasant producers. As this practice develops, the peasant middleman loses his traditional role in the movement of foodstuffs to the major urban centres. The modernisation of wholesale distribution activities thus reduces the importance of small local-assemblers and the multiplicity of middlemen who operate in the traditional marketing system. F-R cite a study of the Recife marketing system to support the trend towards large-scale wholesale operations and a lower number of intermediaries in the rural-urban flow of food staples (LAMP, 1969). This study and other fragmentary evidence on regional marketing systems is reviewed below.

F-R advance the further hypothesis that the entry into the marketing system of urban commercial elites 'reaches into the very heart of the system of land tenure and land usage' (F-R, 1970a, p.205). First, it is argued that 'atomistic peasant producers and middlemen' alone are unable to satisfy the food requirements of the expanding urban centres. Second, as the rationalisation of marketing systems involves investment in more capital-intensive facilities which afford scale economies in bulk handling, wholesalers increasingly will prefer to engage in direct transactions with large-scale producers. (15) 'In effect, food crops become commercial crops and those producers who can provide bulk shipments

are placed in a favoured economic position' (F-R, 1970a, pp.205-6).
This advantage to larger production units, which is conferred by
modern marketing systems 'will result in further concentration of
land-holdings and the increased proletarianisation of the rural
masses' (F-R, 1970a, p.206). F-R thus offer a dismal perspective
for the peasant producer 'in a highly competitive rural economy'.
They conclude that

> The data from Northeast Brazil suggest that there is a point
> at which capitalisation in the distributive sector of a rural
> economy requires like commitments of capital in the production
> sector, leading to the displacement or transformation of a
> peasantry (F-R, 1970a, p.207).

The F-R analysis and their prognosis of structural change in
Northeastern agriculture is diametrically opposed to the CEBRAP
position. For example, the CEBRAP model represents the urban food
supply as the accumulation of 'innumerable small surpluses from
subsistence minifundia' (Brandão Lopes, 1973, p.137). This system,
moreover, has been equal to the task of mobilising the agricultural
surplus, and non-capitalist modes of production retain their
vitality. F-R, on the other hand, following Frank (1967), start
from the basic premise of a capitalist rural economy. Within this
economy, commercial pressures on agricultural production systems
have intensified with the recent acceleration of urbanisation,
forcing adjustments in land tenure and land use. This process,
particularly the modernisation of marketing systems, has created
competitive advantages for large production units rather than
small peasant producers, hitherto the main source of urban food
supplies. While CEBRAP writers refer to the prevailing non-
capitalist mode as isolating minifúndia producers from market
forces, F-R already are lamenting the passing of an independent,
profit-orientated peasantry. 'Peasant farms are viable and competitive as commodity producers given the Market Place network as
a means of distributing minimal euantities of goods' (F-R, 1970a,
p.206). However, this traditional system has failed to adjust to
the increased scale of urban food requirements and modern marketing
practices. The consequent metamorphosis of the capitalist mode,
according to F-R, is displacing peasant producers and accelerating
rural proletarianisation. It is difficult to imagine two more
contrasing interpretations of rural society and the nature of
peasant economic integration.

4 REGIONAL MARKETING SYSTEMS AND ENTREPRENEURIAL CONTROL:
   SOME PARTIAL EVIDENCE

Evidence on regional marketing systems has obvious relevance to
two crucial interrelated questions in this debate: the control
producers retain over production and sales decisions and the
transmission of price incentives. The CEBRAP view is quite un-
equivocal:

> Oligopsonistic buyers prevent rising urban food prices from
> being transmitted as higher prices (in real terms) to small
> producers. In fact, food production expands independently of
> market behaviour or trends, rising as the population engaged

in subsistence crops and the land increases (Brandão Lopes,
1973, p.137).
It is argued that as comerciante functions typically are exercised
by landlords, tenants are forced to sell them their output. This
domination permits the extraction of the surplus by extra-economic
coercion and so accounts for the continued reproduction of pre-
capitalist forms of organisation.

Despite their strong hypotheses, F-R present remarkably little
impirical evidence on marketing systems. Their generalisations
for this huge region are based on first-hand observation of a
limited number of Market Places. (16) The LAMP (1969) study of
the Recife marketing system is a second major source of information. Methodological affinities also are apparent in the
typology of intermediaries and Market Places presented in these
two studies. The LAMP (1969) survey does furnish some examples
of wholesale activities which by-pass peasant Market Places.
However, the statement that is 'amply documents this trend' (F-R,
1970a, p.204) is completely unwarranted. In this respect, F-R
at times fail to indicate where the demarcation line between
analysis and prognosis is drawn. This may well reflect the lack
of a clearly formulated analysis of the articulation between the
'traditional market network' and the 'developing marketing system'.
Are small local assemblers and middlemen really marginal in the
present system, as F-R contend? Similarly, the reference to the
dichotomy between marketing systems is misleading. F-R themselves
acknowledge various points of overlap and interaction between
urban-based wholesalers and peasant middlemen. The LAMP survey
and other studies suggest that it is more accurate to speak of
new elements and agents being inserted and absorbed into the
traditional marketing system. Moreover, if the introduction of
new trading practices means that the internal marketing system no
longer is fully specified by the classic hierarchical model, it
is even more vital to clarify interrelationships between marketing
networks. Given the limited field information available, the
conclusion that these are dichotomous or closed systems appears
both hasty and unnecessarily dogmatic.

Five major commodities are examined in the LAMP study of the
Recife marketing system during the years 1966-7: beans, rice,
manioc, cotton and milk. The survey is a partial one, both in
terms of geographical coverage and agricultural commodities, and
its results are not representative of the entire region. In
addition, attention is drawn to possible sources of bias and
sampling error. First, farmers are identified as property-owners
and not farm operators, which excludes a wide range of tenure
relations. (17) The farm sample also 'tends to have a disproportionate number of middle-sized landowners' (LAMP, 1969, p.9-83).
The authors also refer explicitly to the difficulties encountered
in sampling the population of small intermediaries and assemblers,
particularly itinerant truckers. (LAMP, 1969, pp.9-13 and A-9-14).

Bean marketing systems are investigated in two major supply
zones, Irecê in Bahia and an area on the frontier between the
states of Algoas and Pernambuco (AL-PE). The Irecê system is the
more modern, with markedly fewer intermediaries and larger transactions size, due mainly to the activities of itinerant middlemen.

Rural gatherers, carters, muleteers and many small assemblers have disappeared from the Irecê system but still survive in the AL-PE channel. However, these structural differences are primarily a reflection of the primitive rural road network in AL-PE area. Conversely, the characteristics of the Irecê channel, on which the F-R prognosis is founded, are determined by the greater year-round accessibility of farms, which encourages the entry of itinerant truckers. The importance of these assemblers as a modernising force in commodity markets is stressed repeatedly in the LAMP study. In general, however, 'A variety of assembler types exist in both areas' and 'the basic market structure is one of many firms, characterised by large variations in size within and between categories' (LAMP, 1969, pp.9-4-7). Both small and large producers evidently face competitive buyers and choose between several sales options.

Many of these structural features, particularly the variety of intermediaries, also characterise the marketing systems for manioc flour, rice and cotton, although each has distinctive aspects. For example, local millers are the focus of rural assembly channels for rice. The rural feira remains the main assembly point for manioc flour and attracts virtually all types of intermediary. The quality of rural feeder roads again appears as a major influence on the diversity of brokerage activities. This point supports the F-R thesis, but the *trend* towards the modernisation of the rural distributive sector is only incipient as yet. In fact, the LAMP survey confirms the continued vitality of many traditional elements in food marketing systems. The competitive nature of these systems, the variety of intermediaries and the ready access of farmers to buyers and market information also emerge strongly. In these respects, the LAMP study is consistent with the specialisation model.

Further evidence on food supply systems is furnished by the series of studies undertaken by the BNB and SUDENE in the early 1960s. (18) Curiously, this source is overlooked by F-R. A summary statement of the Salvador system emphasises the rising relative importance of two types of middleman at the expense of commission agents: traders located in the production zones and itinerant truckers. Direct sales by producers to Salvador wholesalers are of minor importance. The role of the truck again is stressed as the novel element modifying traditional distribution channels. (19) The São Luis (Maranhão) system is complicated by the importance of rice, which attracts large-scale specialised intermediaries supplying regional and national markets. For other food staples, however, this system closely resembles that of Salvador (BNB-SUDENE, 1965a, 1965b).

A wider study based on a random sample of 2,300 establishments in 38 selected municipalities offers additional evidence on the question of entrepreneurial control (SUDENE-UFPE, 1969). This survey, undertaken in 1966, reports that only 4 per cent of owner-operators face restrictions on their freedom to sell their output, whereas the proportion rises to 23 per cent for resident workers (moradores), 28 per cent for tenants (arrendatários) and 34 per cent for sharecroppers (parceiros). These results 'must be used with care'. 'They only permit one to affirm that the predominant

systems of land tenure in the Northeast do not limit directly, to
any significant degree, the right to sell output' (Figueroa,
1973, p.42). Information of this kind obscures the complexity
of the situation and it is dangerous to generalise these aggregative findings. 'In certain areas, and for some crops - particularly cotton - the morador still is obliged to sell his entire
share of the output to the landowner' (Figueroa, 1973, p.42). In
his view, the structure of rural distribution systems imposes
strong sales limitations on producers by virtue of their endemic
and acute indebtedness to intermediaries. The LAMP study of the
Recife cotton marketing system reinforces this position in the
case of small producers and sharecroppers. (20)

A more complex picture is given by Sampaio (1974), who presents
a typology of sharecropping (parceria) and identifies several
associated channels of commercialisation. He confirms that sharecroppers usually sell their share of the main cash crop to the
landlord but suggests that this rarely is true of subsistence
crops. These products, which are interplanted with the principal
export or cash crop, generally are marketed by the sharecropper,
although in some cases the cash proceeds are divided subsequently
with the landowner.

A different, though related, contribution to this discussion
is made by Carvalho (1973), who argues that the imperfection of
rural markets causes excessively high intermediary margins. As
a result, rising urban food prices are poorly reflected in those
paid to producers. Distributive margins are extensively documented
in recent SUDENE surveys of the distribution of horticultural
products and cereals in seven state capitals of the Northeast
(SUDENE, 1974). Carvalho (1973) also suggests that 'vertical
integration is still virtually absent' from food marketing systems,
although itinerant truckers and urban supermarket chains 'may
constitute powerful forces in the rationalisation of these circuits
in the near future' (p.130).

The studies of regional marketing systems generally run counter
to the CEBRAP proposition that non-capitalist modes prevail in
the production of food staples. These sources represent the
structure of these systems as atomistic and imply that peasant
producers have considerable entrepreneurial freedom to respond to
market incentives. These conclusions are open to question on
several counts, notably the partial and fragmentary nature of the
underlying evidence. In particular, the studies cited patently
fail to draw adequate distinction between the behaviour of
farmers operating under different tenancy arrangements. The
major source of difficulty is that surveys generally are based on
property or ownership units and samples are taken from land title
registers. (21) This procedure thus omits many production units.
The LAMP survey, for example, explicitly excludes sharecropping
and other forms of economic dependence (moradoria). The BNB-
SUDENE studies generally ignore farm unit decisions and focus
on rural assembly practices and urban wholesale structures. (22)
We also lack any reasonable basis for estimating the relative
contribution of different rural classes to the flows of food
staples which enter regional marketing systems. In these circumstances, it would be rash to attempt a general categorisation of
farm marketing behaviour in the Northeast.

5 LABOUR SUPPLY, TENURE STRUCTURE AND PROLETARIANISATION

This review of the F-R analysis and regional marketing studies illustrates the great diversity of opinion in the current debate. These sources also delineate relationships between local rural economies and the capitalist urban sector, albeit in broad, incomplete terms. Analysis of the mechanisms by which the agricultural surplus is mobilised and channelled to urban areas clearly is a promising and relevant field for further detailed research (Long, 1975). However, the characteristics of exchange relations and brokerage networks can afford only secondary evidence on the central question under discussion. That is, has recent agricultural growth consolidated pre-capitalist modes or been accompanied by the increasing penetration of capitalist relations of production? The present essay makes no pretence to offer a definitive answer to this question. On the contrary, the available empirical base, whether detailed field studies or official sources, is completely inadequate for this purpose. The data are seriously deficient for analysing the dynamics of agrarian structure at the regional level, and different sources support conflicting views of the cross-sectional position. In the following discussion, we consider some interpretative difficulties raised by the data on labour supply, tenure structure and employment practices which have a direct bearing on points at issue in the current debate.

Rural labour supply

The CEBRAP model identifies increasing population pressure in rural areas as the principal reason for the continued reproduction of minifundia in the Northeast. This pressure emanates from several sources and is related to changes in patterns of migration. The volume of net migration from the Northeast declined from 1.8 million in the 1950s to 1.2 million in the 1960s (Graham and Hollanda, 1971, p.98). It is argued that intra-regional migratory flows also changed following the extension of labour legislation to rural areas, particularly the sugar plantations of the zona da mata. This change accelerated the expulsion of resident field workers (moradores) from the plantations, creating a reserve of rural wage labour. As a result, opportunities for seasonal employment on the plantations previously open to migratory labour drawn from the small farms and minifúndia in the agreste were curtailed. With the loss of this source of supplementary income, these agreste contingents have been forced to enter into tenancy arrangements on latifúndio properties. A different process has brought a similar outcome on the former pioneer frontier lands of Maranhão, which had attracted large numbers of migrants during the 1950s. These migrants, who often settled as squatters on uncultivated land, either have been expelled or absorbed as dependent workers and tenants on latifúndia as road construction and greater commercial activity have raised land values. 'For all these reasons, the pressure on the land exerted by peasant minifúndiarios seems to have encountered its principal *safety*

valve in the renting of miniscule tracts of land within latifúndios' (Brandão Lopes, 1973, p.139).

Attempts to test these hypotheses, even in the most preliminary
way, are inhibited by statistical difficulties. Nevertheless,
the relation postulated in the CEBRAP model between rural population growth and minifundia expansion is open to question. The
slow and declining growth rate of the rural labour force presents
major difficulties for this interpretation. Demographic Census
estimates yield an average annual rate of 1.1 per cent in the years
1950-70 and 0.4 per cent during the 1960s. In absolute terms, the
agricultural labour force increased by 814 thousand in the 1950s
and 211 thousand in the following decade. Urban population
growth easily outstripped that of total population, averaging 4.7
per cent between 1950 and 1970 and 4.5 per cent in the 1960s. (23)
Rule-of-thumb estimates indicate that rural out-migration to
urban areas in the Northeast reached 1.8 million in the 1950s and
2.1 million in the 1960s. On this evidence, rural-urban migration
within the region still constitutes a very important *safety valve*
for rural population pressure.

However, the whole issue is clouded by the alternative estimates
of the rural labour force presented in the Agricultural Census.
Due to a variety of basic conceptual differences, including the
unit of enumeration and the treatment of unpaid family workers,
these estimates exceed the Demographic Census figures by a wide
margin. This discrepancy amounts to 1.6 million in 1960 and 2.6
million in 1970. If the Agricultural Census is used, rural labour
force growth is 3.0 per cent for the period 1950-70, averaging
4.4 per cent in the 1950s and 1.6 per cent in the 1960s. The
causes of this precipitous decline, which significantly weakens
the CEBRAP case, are not readily apparent. Unfortunately, re-
conciliation of these alternative sources requires sweeping conceptual adjustments and the arbitrary manipulation of occupational
categories. (24) The source of the population pressure allegedly
underlying minifúndio growth thus must remain an enigma. (25)

Land tenure and occupational structure

At a very general level, it is relatively easy to characterize
the socio-economic classes of Northeastern rural society. Three
broad strata can be identified: a landlord class of large and
medium landowners; landless wage labourers; and the peasantry,
comprising small owner-operators, principally minifúndistas and
producers subject to various tenancy and sharecropping arrangements. A recent study based on farm survey data for the semi-arid
interior region distinguishes three sub-groups within the class
of large landowners (IBRD, 1975). *Traditional* landlords have
under-utilised estates, rely almost entirely on dependent labour,
particularly resident workers (moradores) and sharecroppers, and
retain strong personalistic ties with their work force. (26)
Transitional landlords are more commercially-orientated and
utilise both dependent and free wage labour, but pre-capitalist
forms of exploitation, notably sharecropping, still are more
important. The third group of *commercial* landlords mainly use

free wage labour, although they still find advantage in maintaining pre-capitalist production relations. This typology gives
a cross-sectional categorisation of landlords and suggests that
different modes overlap and co-exist. However, despite the linear
progression implicit in the terminology employed, no analysis is
offered to indicate the dynamics of transition and articulation
between these modes. (27)

The lack of consistent, unambiguous data is felt acutely when
analysing trends and characteristics of differentiation within
the peasantry. The size distribution of operational farm establishments can be used for this purpose, but more subtle measures
are needed to capture changes within social strata (Table 2.1).
Thus, although the inference appears reasonable at this aggregative
level, it is misleading without further criteria to delineate
operators of holdings in the 10 to 50 hectare size-range as *middle*
or *rich* peasants. These operators certainly are differentiated
from the minifúndistas, however, as they stand in the 85-95 per
cent decile of the rural income distribution (IBRD, 1975). We
have already noted the marked concentration of land ownership and
increasing fragmentation of small farms under 10 hectares. Within
this poor minifúndio category, this process has become acute on
establishments of less than two hectares. Such units increased
by 407 thousand in the 1960s, accounting for 50.5 per cent of all
new farms but only 3.2 per cent of new farm land. Farms under
two hectares represented 34 per cent of total farm establishments
but cultivated 1 per cent of the total area in farms in 1970 (Table
2.2). Furthermore, the 1970 Agricultural Census figures indicate
that these farms absorbed 24 per cent of the rural labour-force.
(28)

TABLE 2.2   Minifúndio establishments of under ten hectares, 1960
and 1970

Size of Establishment	Percent of total farm establishments		Percent of total area in establishments		Percent of total labour-force	
	1960	1970	1960	1970	1960	1970
Less than 1 hectare	8.1	15.8	0.1	0.3	4.3	10.3
1 but less than 2 hectares	16.4	18.3	0.5	0.7	10.3	13.9
2 but less than 5 hectares	25.0	22.4	1.7	2.1	19.3	19.8
5 but less than 10 hectares	12.5	11.8	2.0	2.4	11.4	11.7
Total under 10 hectares	61.7	68.3	4.3	5.3	45.3	55.7

Source: Agricultural Census data

Operating units under two hectares, although enumerated by
the Census as independently managed farms, are too small for
family subsistence. Holders of these units, whether owner-
occupiers, sharecroppers or tenants, thus must sell their labour
for payment in money or kind. In a priori terms, this substantial
contingent of independent farm operators arguably is functional
for both pre-capitalist and capitalist modes of production in
meeting temporary or seasonal peak labour requirements. Indeed,
the functional interdependence between peasant minifúndio agriculture and large farms, based on pre-capitalist or capitalist
modes, has frequently been observed (Laclau, 1971; Long, 1975).
The intricate web of interaction between socio-economic groups
and their involvement in different production relations also is
exemplified by the substantial resort to hired wage labourers
(assalariados) by poor farmers operating minifúndia. In 1950,
19 per cent of landless wage labour was utilised on establishments
under ten hectares, and this proportion rose to 23 per cent in
1960 (SUDENE, 1969).

Rural occupational structure and tenancy forms also suggest
the co-existence of different modes, but these data are notoriously
complex. Thus, a recent analysis of farm survey data observes
that 'Owner-operators of very small farms often are sharecroppers
or moradores on other farms' and 'the differentiation of sharecroppers and moradores (also) is often difficult: a sharecropper
may administer part of the farm other than his sharecropped plot,
and moradores often *share* in the output of the farm as part of
the remuneration' (Kutcher and Scandizzo, 1974b, p.3). The considerable overlap between occupational and tenancy groups and
frequent changes in their Census enumeration militate against
empirical analysis of the social relations of production in agriculture. Present empirical sources do not enable us to distinguish dominance by one mode of production or transitional
social formations (Balibar, 1970).

These difficulties can be illustrated by the treatment of pre-
capitalist tenure forms, like sharecropping, in alternative
sources. Sharecropping is the most widespread tenancy arrangement, according to one recent investigation, absorbing one-fifth
of. the rural labour force (IBRD, 1975). This estimate is obtained
by applying occupational weights drawn from farm survey data to
the active population given in the 1970 Agricultural Census. The
same source also suggests that pre-capitalist tenure forms control
the larger share of the area in farms (Table 2.3). However, a
radically different tenure and occupational structure emerges
from the 1970 Census, which enumerates farm establishments under
separate management. Owner-operator units constitute 56.8 per
cent of all establishments (29) and control 89.3 per cent of the
total area in farms (Table 2.3). The size of occupational groups
can be estimated indirectly by assuming that each establishment
is controlled by a single family with two workers. (30) The rural
labour force can then be distributed as follows: landless labourers
and unpaid family workers (43.3%), owner-operators (32.2%),
squatters (12.0%), renters (9.7%) and sharecroppers (2.8%). It
is difficult to know where to begin in order to reconcile such
glaring differences (Table 2.3).

TABLE 2.3 Distribution of the agricultural labour force and area in farms in 1970 by major tenure and occupational groups (%)

Tenure and occupational groups	Agricultural labour-force		Area controlled by major tenure groups	
	IBRD	Agricultural Census	IBRD	Agricultural Census
Owner-operators	16.1	32.2	38.3	89.3
Sharecroppers	21.5	2.8	25.3	1.6
Moradores	14.9	-	)	-
Squatters	6.3	12.0	)36.4	6.1
Renters	4.8	9.7	)	3.0
Wage labour	36.4	)		
Unpaid family workers	-	)43.3		

Source: IBRD (1975) and estimates derived from establishment data in the 1970 Agricultural Census.

Analysis of intercensal changes in tenure structure confronts similar problems. In the 1940 Agricultural Census, for example, sharecroppers are not enumerated separately but combined with tenters (arrendatários) on the ground that they lack autonomous control over their establishments. As a recent survey comments, (In many cases such autonomy is practically non-existent, rendering them similar to wage labourers' (SUDENE, 1969, p.25). Subsequent Agricultural Census estimates indicate that sharecropping has declined sharply as a major tenure form, notably during the 1960s (Table 2.4). Conversely, renters have increased in both absolute and relative terms. The distinction between these categories can be a fine one, however, particularly since rental contracts may permit payment in kind (Patrick, 1972). In practice, the criterion appears to be that renters pay a fixed amount, whereas the payment made by sharecroppers fluctuates with the level of production (S Sund, 1965; SUDENE, 1969). Variations in the importance of money payments, labour service and exchanges in kind also may distort the enumeration of other occupational categories, such as share-croppers, resident workers (moradores) and wage labourers (Sá, 1973).

The decline in sharecropping revealed by the Census is analysed in more specific terms by Sá (1973). Traditionally, the most common form of sharecropping in the Northeast was that of meacão. Under this arrangement, the sharecropper (meeiro) is required to cultivate and harvest a major cash crop on land previously cleared by day labourers, retaining a half share of the output. Sá suggests that the meeiro customarily was free to dispose of the staple food crops he interplanted (em consorcio) with the prin-cipal cash crop. The sharecropper under this system thus stood to reap considerable benefit from the post-war growth of urban demand for food staples. However, Sá argues that real income gains have been restricted severely by the way landowners have responded

to these market opportunities. This response has taken several
forms but the central two-fold purpose is clear. That is, to
reduce the share of labour remuneration in output, and to
eliminate tenure arrangements and employment practices which en-
croach on landowners' freedom to determine land use. One such
reaction involves the adoption of capitalist labour relations,
substituting temporary, hired wage labour for both sharecroppers
and resident workers (moradores). In each case, labour's cus-
tomary rights of access to the land are severed, along with the
network of layalties and obligations between landlord and worker.
An intermediate change occurs where moradores are deprived of
their subsistence plots or sítios but remain as resident wage
labourers. In areas where meacão has survived, contracts typically
have been revised in order to extend the share provisions covering
the main cash crop to food staples.

TABLE 2.4 Distribution of the agricultural labour force by tenure
and occupational groups, 1950-70

Tenure and occupational groups	Absolute numbers ('000)			Percentages		
	1950	1960	1970	1950	1960	1970
Owner-operators and administrators	664.2	959.8	1,256.7	15.3	14.6	16.1
(a) Owner-operators	609.8	884.5	-	14.1	13.5	-
(b) Admini-strators	54.4	75.3	-	1.2	1.1	-
Renters (arrendatarios)	84.3	272.5	377.9	1.9	4.2	4.8
Squatters (ocupantes)	96.2	175.7	467.5	2.2	2.7	6.0
Sharecroppers (parceiros)	326.6	388.8	110.3	7.5	5.9	1.4
Unpaid family workers	1,615.9	2,820.7	)	37.3	43.0	)
Wage labour (assalariados)	1,547.6	1,950.4	)	35.7	29.7	)
(a) Permanent workers	375.0	378.5	) 5,602.3	8.6	5.8	) 71.7
(b) Temporary workers	1,172.6	1,571.9	)	27.1	23.9	)
Total labour force	4,334.8	6,567.9	7,814.7	100.0	100.0	100.0

Source: 1950 and 1960: SUDENE (1969) based on Agricultural Census
                       data.
       1970:   Agricultural Census (Sinopse Preliminar).

Nevertheless, Sá regards the sub-letting of large and medium
size properties as the most significant change in post-war
tenancy patterns. As a result, renters have increased in relative
importance at the expense of other tenure groups, especially

sharecroppers. 'Today, sharecropping is still found in a
generalised way only in the states of Ceará and Rio Grande do
Norte' (Sá, 1973, p.135). (31) Sá lacks data on different types
of rental contract and so is unable to distinguish empirically
between modern tenant farming and *regressive* forms requiring
payment in kind or labour service. The latter type of rental
arrangement evidently is increasingly common on properties
devoted to mixed farming in the agreste of Pernambuco. In conjunction with these tenancy changes, many landowners have assumed
intermediary functions in both commodity and credit markets.
These various adjustments have enabled landowners to appropriate
a greater share of the surplus in a period of rising commercial
activity.

The absolute and relative increase in the number of renters
during the 1950s is readily confirmed by the Census data (Table
2.4). In fact, the number of arrendatários more than doubled.
Yet by far the greatest absolute increase occurred in the owner-
operator category and this alone exceeded the total number of
arrendatários in 1960. The apparent shift towards arrendamento
also may reflect the more rigorous enumeration of this category
in the 1960 Census (Patrick, 1972, p.118). More significantly,
this trend has weakened perceptibly during the 1960s and no longer
threatens the pre-eminence of the owner-operator category. Sá
also contends that the growth of arrendamento is the mechanism
setting 'Northeastern agriculture on the road towards the re-
storation of the latifundio-minifundio complex (Sá, 1973, p.142).
(32) The palpable decline in arrendatário growth observed in the
1960s suggests that large latifúndio properties may well be pur-
suing several alternative survival routes, including resort to
capitalist relations with the labour force presently concentrated
on owner-operator minifúndia.

Proletarianisation

One strength of Sá's interpretation is the explicit consideration
of spatial variations in social relations of production. He recognises that the process of commercial penetration does not proceed
along a simple continuum but responds to differences in special
locational factors, such as accessibility, labour supply, crop mix
and natural conditions. For these reasons inter alia, the incorporation of rural areas in the larger market system is specific
and the response to the *incorporative drive* varied (Pearse, 1968).
As this process unfolds, the agrarian structure is unlikely to
present uniform features and Sá carefully avoids the trap of
dogmatic categorisation. His analysis demonstrates the resilience
of pre-capitalist production relations, such as sharecropping in
areas producing tree cotton, as well as archaic forms of production.
Thus, he notes the tenacity of the latifúndio, although the landowner increasingly moves towards rentier status, sub-letting to
small tenants and exploiting his position as monopsonistic buyer
and usurer. Equally, Sá observes incipient signs of rural proletarianisation in the relative growth of tenancy and occupational
groups whose ties with the soil are tenuous and ill-defined. This

process is most obvious where moradores and sharecroppers are being superseded by temporary wage labourers or diaristas, who live away from the farm in nearby towns and villages.

Although Sá notes the employment of wage labour in commercial agriculture (agricultura de mercado), his attention is concentrated on arrendamento expansion, which he regards as powerful evidence that pre-capitalist relations are being reproduced in the rural Northeast. This conviction may explain why he does not dwell on the question of proletarianisation, that is, the creation of an independent, free wage labour force. However, the scant, dismissive treatment of this issue seriously impairs Sá's analysis. The superficial discussion of the shift from resident farm workers to temporary wage labour is illustrative. Sá simply offers the bald, ambiguous conclusion that this denotes 'the evolution of the economy towards more purely capitalist forms of employment' (Sá, 1973, p.136). The circumstances and extent of this transition and interaction between these *forms* and pre-capitalist production systems are largely ignored.

This omission is complemented by the general dearth of empirical evidence and research on wage employment in the rural Northeast. Few estimates are available even at the aggregate level and the labour force engaged in full-time wage employment is not presented in the preliminary tabulations of the 1970 Agricultural Census (Tables 2.3 and 2.4). The IBRD (1975) survey suggests that 36 per cent of the rural labour force is in wage employment, with 26 per cent as full-time hired workers living away from the farm. Of course, the existence of landless labourers and wage employment does not provide incontrovertible evidence that capitalist relations prevail in rural labour markets. These markets encompass a variety of employment relationships, including those involving monetary remuneration which are still essentially of a pre-capitalist kind. Occupational groups such as resident workers or moradores although increasingly paid cash wages, nevertheless remain dependent on the landowner in many ways. The polyvalent activities of rural workers noted in the discussion of tenurial arrangements introduce further difficulties. Small owner-operators who employ wage labour during certain periods of the crop cycle may reverse this role at other times and seek wage employment. Rural labour markets thus exhibit a complex spectrum of free and dependent relationships between employer and worker.

This juxtaposition of labour market roles and relationships warns that aggregative data on wage employment are unlikely to provide reliable measures of rural proletarianisation. (33) This point is decisive for the present debate since the emergence of a free labour market, with labour power transformed into a commodity, forms the basis of capitalist production. It is necessary to determine whether the wage employment shown in Agricultural Census returns does in fact signify the existence of capitalist relations of production, particularly in the staple food crop sector. The lack of research specifically addressed to this issue is a conspicuous and lamentable gap in the study of rural economy and society in the Northeast. (34)

CONCLUSION

Although the CEBRAP and F-R interpretations bring certain major
features into sharper focus, both ultimately fail to offer a convincing analysis of Northeastern agrarian structure. This short-
coming can be traced to one outstanding characteristic they have
in common: each asserts a priori that the social formation in
question results from a single mode of production. Northeastern
rural society is labelled *capitalist* and *pre-capitalist* but neither
model convincingly demonstrates the validity of its respective
characterisation via rigorous analysis of the forces of production
and the social relations of production. Both models apply the
concept of mode of production mechanistically to the socio-
economic framework, and so the central issue, the processes shaping
the agrarian structure, is not brought under detailed analytical
scrutiny. The prevailing mode of production is identified by
prior assumption, not by theoretical and empirical analysis. The
same premise also excludes from consideration the possible arti-
culations of different modes, dominant and subordinate, and the
influence these combinations exert on the social formation under
observation. (35) As a result, CEBRAP and F-R not only give incomplete specifications of the agrarian structure but also posit
a false dilemma between capitalist and non-capitalist modes.
    CEBRAP insists, rightly so, on the persistence of pre-capitalist
relations of production, but the owner-operator and wage employment
sectors are only superficially explored. Indeed, the CEBRAP
analysis concentrates mainly on minor tenurial categories and
neglects the interdependence between different modes of production.
The F-R analysis is marred by an uncritical acceptance of the
Frankian scheme and its consequent failure to consider the
articulation of production systems and the specificity of the
Northeastern economic structure. This is not to doubt the importance of exchange or market relations but to ask whether these
have penetrated the sphere of production and constitute the basis
of the relations of production (Laclau, 1975). This question is
ignored by F-R by virtue of their basic premise that the Northeast
has a capitalist agriculture.
    This review, in contrast, has emphasised the co-existence and
interaction of different production relations in the rural Northeast. This heterogeneity means that the social formation is the
product of the articulation of several modes of production. Future
research must consequently undertake the arduous task of identifying these modes and their combinations as it is these characteristics which determine the social formation and define its
specificity. With this perspective, unimpaired by simplistic
prior assumptions, progress can be made towards a more comprehensive analysis of agrarian structure.

NOTES

1 We adopt the administrative definition of the Northeast used
   by SUDENE, the regional development agency, which includes
   the states of Maranhão, Piauí, Ceará, Rio Grande do Norte,
   Paraíba, Pernambuco, Alagoas, Sergipe and Bahia.

2   Several recent contributions to this debate, as well as reviews of the current position, can be found in Oxaal (1975).

3   This term is adopted for convenience and is not meant to suggest that writers associated with CEBRAP (Centro Brasileiro de Análise e Planejamento) conform rigidly and slavishly to any single interpretation of Brazilian society.

4   The CEBRAP approach thus emphasises the interdependence between centre and periphery, rejecting the orthodox dualistic model of regional under-development with its focus on obstacles to modernisation.

5   This exposition is based mainly on de Oliveira (1972), but see also Malan and Pereira (1973).

6   In several respects, there is a close resemblance between de Oliveira's model of industrial capitalist expansion in Brazil after 1930 and the Marxist perspective proposed by Laclau (1971) to analyse metropolitan-periphery relations in the growing nineteenth century world economic system.

7   The Agricultural Census defines an establishment as a production unit under one administration. A size distribution based on ownership or property units probably would reveal a higher degree of concentration.

8   This seems a reasonable working assumption as the aggregative Census data show that increases in crop output and area cultivated are roughly proportional. In addition, small units tend to be cultivated more intensively.

9   Of the farm units examined in the survey, 8 per cent had retained their output of rice, and higher retention ratios occurred in the cases of manioc (17 per cent), dry beans (45 per cent) and corn (58 per cent). Virtually all the farms that failed to market these crops were small establishments in the minifúndio category. See SUDENE-UFPE (1969).

10 This view is canvassed in IBRD (1975).

11 A necessary caveat here is that we cannot construct sectoral terms of trade series for the Northeast due to the absence of regionally-based price indices. The implicit price index for arable crops mentioned in the text is derived from indices of current product value and real output, both measured at constant prices.

12 Brandão Lopes reiterates this point in an unpublished paper Aspects of Agrarian Structure in Brazil (1975). A preliminary version of this paper was read to the Brazil Seminar at the Institute of Latin American Studies, London, in April 1975.

13 For a theoretical discussion of the transition between modes of production, see Balibar (1970).

14 F-R follow Frank (1967) in this emphasis on exchange relations rather than production relations in defining capitalism. For a recent review of Frank's writings and the critiques of his position, see Booth (1975).

15 F-R recognise that preference for direct bulk transactions reinforces sharecropping arrangements since the landowner typically controls the marketing of output. However, F-R imply that this tenure form is more important in the production of export products and major cash crops than food staples.

16 F-R's field results are based on the investigation of two

market places distributing four food staples - corn, beans, rice and manioc flour - in the county of Guaiamu in the state of Alagoas. Subsequently, ten market places in a three-state area were surveyed to embrace the ecological zones of the agreste and the sertão.

17 The marketing of output produced under sharecropping arrangements is specifically excluded from the LAMP (1969) study.

18 The following comments are based on only two volumes in this series, now out of print, which investigate the food supply systems of Salvador (Bahia) and São Luis (Maranhão). The volumes for Recife, Campina Grande and Fortaleza were unobtainable at the time of writing. See BNB-SUDENE (1965a, and 1965b).

19 The Salvador study refers to the rising importance of trucking in opening up oroduction zones hitherto inaccessible to the main consuming centres. The Irecê area of the Chapada Diamantina included in the LAMP (1969) survey is one of the zones cited in this context.

20 For an analysis of economic dependence based on more recent survey data for Rio Grande do Norte, a major cotton-producing state, see Kutcher and Scandizzo (1974b).

21 The large-scale farm survey recently undertaken by SUDENE and the IBRD follows this practice by using the 1972 INCRA *Cadastro*. Kutcher and Scandizzo (1974a) discuss methods adopted to attenuate the problems posed by the difference between ownership and entrepreneurial units.

22 Concern with the urban segments of distribution channels is even more pronounced in the series of food supply studies published by SUDENE-UFPE (1974).

23 Demographic Census data give annual average growth rates for the total population in the Northeast of 2.2 per cent and 2.5 per cent in the 1950s and 1960s, respectively.

24 For further details, see CIDA (1966), Costa (1968, 1969), Patrick (1972) and Sund (1965).

25 This puzzle is all the more difficult since the preliminary 1970 Agricultural Census returns show a greater absolute increase in the labour force employed on holdings of under ten hectares than in the total rural labour force.

26 Johnson (1971) gives a detailed analysis of socio-economic relations on a large fazenda in the semi-arid backland of Ceará.

27 The IBRD (1975) study of the semi-arid interior region distributes the area in farms controlled by these landlord-types as follows: *traditional* (48 per cent), *transitional* (38 per cent) and *commercial* (14 per cent).

28 The problem referred to in note 25 above should be borne in mind.

29 Approximately 50 per cent of owner-operator establishments have less than ten hectares.

30 The preliminary results of the 1970 Agricultural Census do not distinguish full-time wage labourers and unpaid family workers separately.

31 Sund (1965) also notes the lack of uniformity in the spatial distribution of the major tenure groups.

32 As Sá fully recognises, this view rests on the critical
assumption that the expansion of arrendamento is concentrated
within large and medium properties. However, sub-letting may
equally form one aspect of the fragmentation process observed
on minifúndia holdings. At present, there is no way to clarify
these questions empirically.

33 Redclift (1975) gives a recent assessment of the literature
on proletarianisation in Latin America.

34 There is some field research which bears on this question,
notably that undertaken by CIDA (1966) and Nicholls and Paiva
(1966-67), but it is not the primary concern. Some fragmentary
evidence on employment practices is reported by Nicholls (1974)
for selected farm establishments in Caruaru (Pernambuco),
Crato (Ceará) and Caxias (Maranhão). This paper is particularly interesting as changes which have occurred in areas
and farm establishments covered by the earlier Nicholls-Paiva
survey are analysed. Unfortunately, it is impossible to
generalise these trends to the entire Northeastern region.

35 Recent contributions to the literature on the articulation
of modes of production are reviewed by Taylor (1972) and Long
(1975).

REFERENCES

BALIBAR, E. (1970), Elements for a theory of transition, in
ALTHUSSER, L. and BALIBAR, E., Reading Capital (London, New Left
Books).
BNB-SUDENE: (1965b), Abastecimento de Gêneros Alimentícios da
Cidade de São Luís (Fortaleza, Ceará).
BOOTH, D. (1975), André Gunder Frank: an introduction and
appreciation, in Oxaal, I. et al (eds), Beyond the Sociology of
Development (London, Routledge & Kegan Paul).
BRANDÃO LOPES, J.R. (1973), Desenvolvimento e Migrações: Uma
Abordagem Histórico-Estrutural, Estudos Cebrap 6, pp.127-42.
BYRES, T.J. (1974), Land Reform, Industrialization and the
Marketed Surplus in India: An Essay on the Power of Rural Bias,
in LEHMANN, D. (ed.), Agrarian Reform and Agrarian Reformism
(London, Faber & Faber).
CARVALHO, O. DE, et al. (1973), Plano Integrado para o Combate
Preventivo aos Efeitos das Secas no Nordeste (Brasilia, MINTER).
CASTRO, A.B. DE (1971), Sete Ensaios sobre a Economia Brasileira,
vol.2 (Rio de Janeiro, Editora Forense).
CIDA: Comitê Interamericano de Desenvolvimento Agrícola (1966),
Posse e Uso da Terra e Desenvolvimento Sócio-Econômico do Setor
Agrícola - Brasil (Washington, D.C., Pan-American Union).
COSTA, M.A. (1968), Aspectos Demográficos da População Econo-
micamente Ativa (Rio de Janeiro, IPEA-MINIPLAN, mimeo.).
COSTA, M.A. (1969), Aspectos Econômicos e Demográficos da Mão-
de-Obra no Brasil, 1940/60 (Rio de Janeiro, IPEA-MINIPLAN, mimeo.).
DE OLIVEIRA, F. (1972), A Economia Brasileira: Crítica à Razão
Dualista, Estudos CEBRAP 2, October, pp.3-82.
FIGUEROA, M. (1973), Cuestiones de Política Agrícola Regional -
NE del Brasil (Recife (?), SUDENE-MINTER).

FORMAN, S. (1971), Disunity and Discontent: A Study of Peasant
Political Movements in Brazil, *Journal of Latin American Studies*,
3 (1), pp.3-24.
FORMAN, S. and REIGELHAUPT, J.F. (1970a), Market Place and
Marketing System: Toward a Theory of Peasant Economic Integration,
Comparative Studies in Society and History, 12 (12, pp.188-212).
FORMAN, S. and REIGELHAUPT, J.F. (1970b), Bodo was never Brazilian:
Economic Integration and Rural Development among a Contemporary
Peasantry, *Journal of Economic History*, 30 (1), pp.100-16.
FRANK, A.G. (1967), *Capitalism and Under-development in Latin
America* (New York, Monthly Review Press).
GOODMAN, D.E. and CAVALCANTI, R. (1974), *Incentivos a Indus-
trialização e Desenvolvimento do Nordeste* (Rio de Janeiro, IPEA-
INPES, Relatório de Pesquisa No. 20).
GRAHAM, D.H. (1970), Divergent and Convergent Regional Economic
Growth and Internal Migration in Brazil, 1940-1960, *Economic
Development and Cultural Change*, 18(3), April, pp.362-82.
GRAHAM, D.H. and HOLLANDA, S.B. DE (1971), *Regional and Urban
Growth and Development in Brazil: A Selective Analysis of the
Historical Record, 1872-1970*, col. 1 (São Paulo, Instituto de
Pesquisas Econômicas - USP).
GTDN: Grupo de Trabalho para o Desenvolvimento do Nordeste
(1959), *Uma Política de Desenvolvimento Econômico para o Nordeste*
(Rio de Janeiro, Presidência da República).
IBRD: International Bank for Reconstruction and Development (1975),
Rural Development Issues and Options in Northeast Brazil
(Washington, D.C., mimeo.).
JOHNSON, A.W. (1971), *Sharecroppers of the Sertão: Economics and
Dependence on a Brazilian Plantation* (Stanford, Stanford Uni-
versity Press).
KUTCHER, G.P. and SCANDIZZO, P.L. (1974a), *Northeast Brazil
Regional Studies Project: Sampling Procedures* (Washington, D.C.,
IBRD-DRC - Development Planning Division, Working Paper No. RPO
273/XII/1).
KUTCHER, G.P. and SCANDIZZO, P.L. (1974b), *Land Tenure, Employment
and Farm Performance in Rio Grande do Norte* (Washington, D.C.,
IBRD-DRC - Development Planning Division, Working Paper No. RPO
273/XVII/1).
LACLAU, E. (9171), Feudalism and Capitalism in Latin America,
New Left Review, No. 67, May-June, pp.19-38.
LACLAU, E. (1975), The Specificity of the Political: The
Poulantzas-Miliband Debate, *Economy and Society*, 4 (1), February,
pp.87-110.
LAMP: Latin American Market Planning Center (1969), *Market
Processes in the Recife Area of Northeast Brazil* (East Lansing,
Latin American Studies Center, Michigan State University, Research
Report No. 2).
LONG, N. (1975), Structural Dependency, Modes of Production and
Economic Brokerage in Rural Peru, in Oxaal, I. et al. (eds),
Beyond the Sociology of Development (London, Routledge & Kegan
Paul).
MALAN, P. and PEREIRA, J.E. DE C. (1973), A propósito de uma
Reinterpretação do Desenvolvimento Brasileiro desde os Anos 30,
Dados, No. 10, pp.126-45.

MATA, M. DA, CARVALHO, E.W. and CASTRO E SILVA, M.T. (1973), *Migrações Internas no Brasil* (Rio de Janeiro, INPES-IPEA, Relatório de Pesquisa No. 19).

NICHOLLS, W.H. (1974), Changes in the Agricultural Economy of the Brazilian Northeast, 1963-73, unpublished paper presented to the Conference on the Brazilian Northeast, Racine, Wisconsin.

NICHOLLS, W.H. and PAIVA, R.M. (1966-67), *Ninety-nine Fazendas: The Structure and Productivity of Brazilian Agriculture, 1963* (Nashville, Center for Latin American Studies, Vanderbilt University).

OXAAL, I. et al. (eds) (1975), *Beyond the Sociology of Development* (London, Routledge & Kegan Paul).

PATRICK, G.F. (1972), *Desenvolvimento Agrícola do Nordeste* (Rio de Janeiro, INPES-IPEA, Relatório de Pesquisa No. 11).

PEARSE, A. (1968), Metropolis and Peasant: The Expansion of the Urban-Industrial Complex and the Changing Rural Structure, in SHANIN, T. (ed.) (1971), *Peasants and Peasant Societies* (Harmondsworth, Penguin).

REDCLIFT, M.R. (1975), The 'Proletarianisation' of the Latin American Peasantry: A Theory in Search of the Facts, unpublished paper.

SÁ JR., F. (1973), O Desenvolvimento da Agricultura Nordestina e a Função das Atividades de Subsistência, *Estudos CEBRAP 3*, January, pp.87-147.

SAHOTA, G.S. (1968), An Economic Analysis of Internal Migration in Brazil, *Journal of Political Economy*, 76 (2), pp.218-45.

SAMPAIO, Y. (1974), Modelos de Parceria em Agricultura de Consorciação no Nordeste do Brasil, paper presented to the Conference of the National Association of Post-Graduate Centres in Economics, Belo Horizonte, Minas Gerais.

SCANDIZZO, P.L. (1974), Resistance to Innovation and Economic Dependence in Northeastern Brazil (Washington, D.C., IBRD-DRC - Development Planning Division, Working Paper No. RPO 273/XIV/1).

SUDENE (1969), Estudos Preliminares do Setor Agrícola do Nordeste, *Boletim Econômico da SUDENE*, V (1), pp.7-96.

SUDENE (1974), Aspectos da Comercialização de Produtos Horti-Fruti-Granjeiros e Cereais (recife (?), several volumes).

SUDENE-UFPE: Universidade Federal de Pernambuco (1969), *Pesquisa sobre o Setor Agrícola no Nordeste* (Recife, several volumes, mimeo.).

SUDENE-UFPE (1974), *Abastecimento Alimentar no Nordeste Urbano* (Recife, Convênio SUDENE-UFPE, Série Pesquisas 1 - 5).

SUND, M. (1965), Land Tenure and Economic Performance of Agricultural establishments in Northeast Brazil (Madison, Land Tenure Centre, University of Wisconsin, Research Report No. 17).

TAYLOR, J. (1972), Marxism and Anthropology, *Economy and Society*, 1 (3), March, pp.339-50.

THORNER, D. (1956), *The Agrarian Prospect in India* (Delhi University Press).

VILAÇA, M.V. (1969), *Em Torno da Sociologia do Caminhão* (Rio de Janeiro, Tempo Brasileiro).

Chapter 3

HUNGER IN THE NORTHEAST: SOME HISTORICAL ASPECTS
Jaime Reis

I

Over the past two decades, the Northeast of Brazil has become
internationally accepted as a region of acute poverty where hunger
and malnutrition are present on a vast scale. A good deal of
attention has been devoted by social and other scientists to
these problems, but little is known or has been written about
its historical dimensions. Apart from the pioneering efforts
by Gilberto Freyre and Comara Cascudo on the history of food and
the diet in Brazil, there is a great void with respect to this
subject. (1)
 One of the consequences of this state of affairs is that we do
not know, for example, when malnutrition became endemic in the
region. Nor do we know how much deterioration there has been
since, whether this has been a continuous process, or occurred
only at certain times, and what circumstances determined this
evolution. Equally important is our ignorance of the kinds of
malnutrition present and what they meant in terms of the everyday
existence of the rural working class. Nevertheless, the belief
has arisen from time to time that standards of nutrition in the
Northeast were declining as a result of certain changes in the
region's social and economic conditions. Already in the 1930s
the view was expressed by several authors that, in this respect,
matters had been getting worse since the decline of the traditional
sugar plantation and its replacement by the larger, impersonal
central sugar mill. They were referring therefore to a discernable
change over the past generation or so. (2) The same preoccupation
is to be found more recently, in the late 1950s and early 1960s,
when the region was felt to be on the verge of a revolution. Part
of the Northeast's becoming an explosive area was the fact that
hunger was stalking the land, with the consequent harm to health,
increased mortality, reduced economic efficiency of the population,
and general misery, which drove people to desperation and a
search for extreme political solutions. (3)
 The aim of this article is to provide a historical background
into which to fit these views. We shall present, therefore, an
account of how the nutritional status of the mass of the population

has evolved over the past hundred years, and follow this with some
comments on its possible implications for the health and pattern
of life of the people in question. (4) The problem presents
itself in two ways. One is the catastrophic crisis, the famine
induced by drought, crop failure and cattle decimation in the
arid uplands of the region (sertão), and usually leading to vast
migrations to the cities or down to the humid coast lands. The
other is the unspectacular, more or less continual, grinding lack
of sufficient food endured possibly for generations, and which
Josué de Castro has called 'endemic hunger' in contrast to the 'epi-
demic hunger' of the first case. (5) It is with the second that we
are concerned here, and we shall be examining it as regards only
the more densely populated and economically more significant forest
zone (zona da mata) of Pernambuco, one of the principal Northeastern
states. This is a coastal strip, some fifty miles wide, where the
land has been traditionally taken up by sugar plantations and the
economy entirely geared to the export of their single product.

II

If we go back to the late nineteenth century, contemporary observation suggests that as far as the mass of the population was
concerned, the golden age of plenty, if ever it had existed, had
long passed by. In 1888, for instance, the provincial president
described the diet of the poor classes as 'frugal', while in 1913
the British consul in Recife commented: 'It is a marvel how many
of these unfortunate people manage to keep body and soul together'.
(6) During a visit in 1889, Silva Jardim, the Republican propa-
gandist from the South, remarked on the dire penury he encountered
everywhere he went in the sugar zone. (7) These impressions are
confirmed by the physical appearance of most rural dwellers at
the time. Plantation labourers were invariably portrayed as weak,
apathetic and stunted individuals. In the words of a local writer,
they reminded outsiders of 'a population of convalescent, limping,
miserable people'. (8) In the early 1900s Octavio de Freitas, a
doctor at the Pedro II hospital in Recife, found that 70 per cent
of his patients who hailed from the countryside were anaemic, in
addition to the complaint that brought them there in the first
place. (9) Somewhat later, a survey of 1600 sugar workers carried
out in 1936 established that 77 per cent of all males were less
than 5 feet 5 inches in height, and that 79 per cent of all adult
females were under 5 feet 3 inches. (10)
   Despite the lack of information on the everyday life of the
common people, it is possible to put together a reasonably accurate
picture of what their daily fare included. This was principally
black beans, manioc meal, jerked beef and to a lesser extent dried
salted cod (becalhau); and in addition, sugar, sugar cane and
molasses, depending on the will of the landowner and/or the stealth
of the consumer. To drink, there was an occasional cup of thin
coffee, a rather more frequent and stimulating dose of cane spirit
(cachaça), and water. From time to time, there might be some game
or fish, although the progressive deforestation of Pernambuco and
the pollution of its rivers by the usinas (central mills) made

these items increasingly rare. Domestically raised chicken or
pork were another possibility which again depended on the will of
the landowner - in Escada, in 1922, a government report noted that
this was forbidden by sugar planters. (11) On the other hand, such
luxuries as bread, milk, eggs, butter and cheese were 'mythological
entities, possibly only observed on the tables of white people'.
(12)

It was the typically monotonous diet of the poor agriculturist
the whole world over, yet it was undoubtedly better than many of
its kind. Instead of a single carbohydrate staple food, as in
most tropical countries, it was based on two which complemented
each other nutritionally, namely beans and manioc. (13) In this
respect, it constituted an intelligent adaptation to local conditions of the traditional Portuguese diet, which at the time of
the colonisation of Brazil was based on a combination of beans and
cereals. (14)

From another point of view, however, it represented a degen-
eration. Fruit and vegetables played an important part in the diet
of medieval Portugal, yet they were absent from the catalogue of
foodstuffs consumed in Pernambuco. It has been claimed by modern
authors that they were, in fact, an integral part of the diet of
both slaves and free labourers in the late nineteenth century,
while they were despised by the well-to-do. (15) In support of
this it is pointed out how easy it was to grow vegetables on any
patch of land and to gather fruit in any nearby wood. This impression is certainly corroborated by the German naturalist Konrad
Guenther, who lived in the area during the late 1920s and described the typical squatter's hut as surrounded by vegetables and
fruit trees. (16) On the other hand, it is striking that the
contemporary accounts consulted failed to mention the consumption
of these items, whether dealing with slaves or free men. (17)
The omission might simply reflect the belief a hundred years ago
that they were not nutritionally of value although people ate
them. It is significant, however, that Vascomcellos Torres reported in 1945 a strong prejudice among workers in the Northeast
against eating green vegetables. (18) On present evidence the
matter cannot be settled, which is unfortunate because it has
serious nutritional implications. In the meantime, we shall bend
to the weight of our sources and assume that fruit and vegetables
had little or no part in the diet of the sugar zone. (19)

The next step, which takes us from the qualitative to the
quantitative aspects of this analysis, is a difficult one. The
period considered was not one in which the literate segments of
Brazilian society concerned themselves much with the condition of
the labouring population, and least of all, bothered with scruti-
nising and quantifying their diet. Concern with the *social
question*, which is the impetus to social enquiries, and more particularly to family budget studies, was not developed enough in
Pernambuco until the third decade of this century. In any case,
it would have been difficult to find out the total food consumption of each family. The majority of the population enjoyed
the use of subsistence plots allowed them by the plantations and
were probably self-sufficient with respect to such staples as
beans and manioc, and this would render satisfactory measurement

extremely arduous if not impossible. As it is, the few estimates that have come down to us are those recorded for certain special categories (e.g., the inmates of the Recife jail) and none for the rural labourer and his family.

To surmount this problem we have to consider separately the two sets of foodstuffs into which the diet could be divided: those acquired by purchase, thanks to the income derived from working on the plantations; and those which were the result of the squatter's cultivation of his plot. The per capita cash income of plantation labourers for different years has been calculated elsewhere, and this makes it relatively easy to ascertain the quantity of purchased food they would have consumed on average. (20) As one would expect under conditions of acute poverty, most of the money earned on plantations - 80 or 90 per cent (21) - was spent on food. There was usually no rent to be paid and the only other necessities which had to be bought were kerosene for lighting, tools, household implements and clothing. How little went at least on the last of these can be judged from the ragged and bare-footed appearance characteristic of most of the rural population. (22) Using Recife prices inflated by 20 per cent to allow for handling and transport, we can arrive at an estimate for the daily average daily per capita consumption of jerked beef (to simplify matters, we have assumed that only jerked beef and no bacalhau was consumed) and then convert this into adult-equivalent figures, as shown in Table 3.1.

TABLE 3.1   Cash income per capita and jerked beef consumption, 1870-1920

	Income	Jerked beef (grams per day)
1870*	14$038	88
1900	15$344	47
1920	26$662	27

* Does not include slave population

Obviously, this exercise cannot be duplicated in the case of the second category of foodstuffs. Instead we have considered the allowances of beans and manioc made by the provincial autho-rities in 1878 to the drought-sticken retirantes they employed to do relief work on sugar estates as typical in this region of the amounts normally consumed by working adults. These amounts (125 grams of beans and 400 grams of manioc meal a day) are similar to the fares issued to two other groups of similar social rank: the inmates of the Recife jail and the European peasants sent to settle a government colonia in Mucuri. (23) For lack of data, we have further assumed them to have remained constant during the next fifty years, which does not seem unreasonable. There is no evidence of restrictions being placed by landlords on how much beans and manioc were produced for subsistence providing squatters did not market their surplus, in which case a rental was exacted.

Nor would the production of the beans and manioc necessary for

feeding the population at these rates of consumption have placed
an undue strain on available land resources. In 1920, for example,
of the approximately one million hectares which formed the forest
zone, 90,000 were in use for sugar cane cultivation and a maximum
of 60,000 hectares would have been needed for subsistence crops.
(24) The reckoning is completed with two more locally produced
items. One of these is a figure of 30 kilograms of sugar per year.
The other is cane spirit, the output of which was consumed almost
entirely in the region and, we have assumed perhaps somewhat rashly,
exclusively by an adult population devoid of teetotallers. This
would give an annual capitation of 28.6 litres, which is also
supposed constant during the period. (25)

III

The nutritional value of the diet thus put together can be calculated from a suitable table of food values. (26) The results are
given in Table 3.2 for the three different dates on which we have
all of the required data. This involved a regrettable restriction
to the scope of our analysis, but we have tried to maximise the
significance of these results by using averages for the five-year
periods which straddle these benchmark years, whenever this has
been possible, e.g., sugar output.
   The first point to emerge from the examination of this table is
the worsening of the nutritional status of the forest zone's population during the half century in question. For some nutrients
(protein, iron, riboflavin, niacin) the trend is more marked than
for others, and in certain cases (vitamins A and C and carbohydrates) there was no change at all. Such a decline raises a
second question, which is whether adequate nourishment was available in these diets, or to what extent they departed from the
levels recommended by nutritionists for a normal, healthy existence.
The latter are set out in column 4 of the same table, for comparison with the intakes corresponding to 1870, 1900 and 1920,
respectively. (27)

TABLE 3.2 Nutritional content of diets, 1870-1964

	1 1870	2 1900	3 1920	4 FAO	5 1945-III	6 1963	7 1964
Calories	2186*	2069*	2012*	2686	1805*	2172*	2744
Protein (gm)	86	62*	51*	80	60*	75*	92
Carbohydrates (gm)	422*	422*	422*	500	355*	447*	617
Calcium (mg)	928	894	877	500	731	583	907
Iron (mg)	39	35	33	10	19	34	39
Vitamin A (mg)	5.4*	5.4*	5.4*	750	2.2*	340*	22.4*
Vitamin C (mg)	1.4*	1.4*	1.4*	10	0.7*	34*	3.8*
Thiamine (mg)	0.96*	0.96*	0.96*	1.2	0.82*	0.81*	0.81*
Riboflavin (mg)	0.73*	0.64*	0.59*	1.8	1.34*	0.62*	0.76*
Niacin (mg)	21.2	15.7*	13.7*	19.8	15.6*	13.2*	23.3

* Indicates deficiency.

From a nutritional point of view the situation was neither brilliant nor uniformly bad. In 1870 the diet implied deficiencies in terms of calories, carbohydrates, vitamins A and C, thiamine and riboflavin. By 1900 the level of protein had fallen well below the acceptable limit and the same is true, though to a lesser degree, of niacin. By 1920 the list of deficiencies had not lengthened, but several of them had continued to become more severe: riboflavin, niacin, protein and calories. Thus both in terms of quantity and quality, the picture of malnutrition was turning increasingly sombre during this time. It should be stressed, on the other hand, that none of the deficiencies regis-tered could be termed acute and that some of them were probably quite mild, given that nutritionists always include in their recommendations a *safety factor* which renders their standards somewhat higher than strictly necessary.

Any inference based on these findings and regarding the physical condition of the population which lived on Permanbuco's sugar plantations calls for the greatest caution. From the point of view of the nutrition scientist several reservations have to be made. The first is that deficiencies such as emerge from the use of nutrition tables do not lead inevitably to pathological con-ditions, and if they do, their clinical features are variable. In sub-acute cases they may not even manifest themselves in a dis-cernable manner. (28) Moreover, it is impossible to tell the level of deficiency beyond which nutritional diseases set in. This varies from individual to individual, and from group to group, and the matter is further complicated by the adaptability of the human body to a certain measure of chronic deprivation, which enables it to function quite efficiently. (29)

From the point of view of the method of our analysis itself, there are shortcomings too. One of them is the omission in the tables of nutrition of the results of the hunting and gathering activities of the moradores of the forest zone. A more serious one lies in the inequalities which undoubtedly existed between individuals regarding food acquisition and consumption and which our averaging obliges us to ignore. Some of this would arise from variations from family to family in income, health and family size and composition. An illustration of this is offered by a study of living conditions among sugar workers in 1945, some of the results of which are summarised in Table 3.3. (30) The three types repre-sented are the bachelor cane-cutter (I), the supervisor with two children (II), and the unskilled labourer with a family of eight (III), and the contrast between their respective nutritional statuses could not be more eloquent.

But within the family, too, the allocation of food may not have been *fair*, i.e. according to need. It is not unlikely that the head and principal breadwinner of the family should have taken the lion's share of its scarce resources, leaving the children with proportionately less and the wife the most sacrificed member of the group. Such was the pattern among working-class families in England at the end of the nineteenth century, and, given the pattern of familial authority in the Northeast, it is easy to believe that the situation there was no different. (31) All in all, and to be fair to the available evidence, we can go no further than to say that there would have been a high incidence in this population of the clinical features associated with a certain deficiency when the average intake of the relevant nutrient fell noticeably below the recommended level.

TABLE 3.3 Nutritional content of sugar workers' diet, 1945

	I	II	III
Calories	4869	4397	1805
Protein (gm)	116	154	60
Carbohydrates (gm)	995	891	355
Calcium (mg)	1939	1660	731
Iron (mg)	75	76	19
Vitamin A (mg)	7.1	3.6	2.2
Vitamin C (mg)	1.9	2.8	0.7
Thiamine (mg)	1.11	1.25	0.82
Riboflavin (mg)	1.46	1.49	1.34
Niacin (mg)	35.08	44.09	15.6

Sub-nutrition in the form of a lack of calories was a worsening feature of these years. By 1900, it was compounded by a lack of protein which was probably greater than the figures suggest, given that caloric deficiencies cause the body to burn protein for additional energy and divert it from its proper function. Under these conditions many people would be emaciated, they would be apathetic; given the role of protein in the growth of tissues, they would tend to be small in stature. The chronic protein deficiency might also be the cause of hormonal and enzyme failures leading to intermittent bouts of diarrhoea, delayed puberty and menstrual irregularity. It is interesting that two São Paulo doctors who visited the region in the early twentieth century remarked that 'it is unusual to find a woman in the Northeast who does not suffer from some trouble in the ovaries, menstrual irregularity and the like, for which the picturesque expression locally is to be "dismantled". (32) At the same time, it should be noted that the levels of protein-energy malnutrition considered here are hardly crippling and can only be spoken of after 1900. A loss of 25 per cent in body weight relative to the norm is thought by nutritionists to be more or less harmless and it has been found that survival is possible on as little as 48 grams of protein a day, although a question mark hangs over the long-term effects of such a regime. (33)

The *niacin gap* recorded in Table 3.2 from 1900 on seems not to have been large enough to produce dramatic results either. The corresponding disease is pellagra, but it is questionable whether this eas present in the Northeast at that time in a serious form. (34) Its mild manifestations, which are the more likely to have occurred, are nothing more than physical weakness, sometimes

tremors in the body, mental depression and irritability. (35)
The shortage of thiamine was similarly not great and we should
consider as more likely the lesser effects of this, which are
again physical apathy, an ill-defined malaise causing a mild incapacity for manual labour, rather than wet or dry beriberi.
With the riboflavin deficiency there is more of a case to expect
the full symptoms which, although uncomfortable, do not impair
the normal performance of the patient to any degree. (36) They
are skin irritation, chapped lips and sores in the corner of the
mouth, which undoubtedly contributed to the frequently recorded
unprepossessing appearance of the poorer residents of the forest
zone, just as the other clinical features noted above must have
done to their equally noted indolence and lack of interest in
personal improvement.

The staggering inadequacy of the diet with respect to vitamins
A and C is less easily reconciled with the qualitative evidence
at hand. The principal effect of the former is, at best, night
blindness and at worst, permanent blindness, caused by the destruction of the cornea. Yet neither of these conditions has been
referred to as present in the forest zone of Pernambuco. Xerophthalmia was found in the nineteenth century among the slaves in
the coffee-growing areas of Rio de Janeiro, but Figueira de Mello,
in his treatise on Pernambuco published in 1852, while describing
in some detail the most common complaints of all classes of society,
said nothing about blindness. (37) Nor did the national census
of 1872, which listed the infirmities of the Brazilian population,
register any unusual number of blind people in the area. (38)
The normal effect of a deficiency of vitamin C is scurvy, but
again there is no indication in the literature of the time of its
prevalence, or even of its existence.

Both these puzzles raise once more the question of the presence
of fresh fruit and vegetables in the diet of the poor in the zona
da mata, since they are the main sources for either vitamin.
While it is hard to believe that the regular consumption of green
vegetables may have been overlooked by contemporary observers, it
is not implausible that small amounts of fruit should have been
regularly eaten but not considered worthy of mention. In the case
of scurvy this would resolve our difficulty, since it would only
take the daily equivalent of half an orange or 18 grams of the
locally abundant cashew fruit to make good the vitamin C deficiency. (39) As regards night blindness, it is credible that
it was so common that it went by unnoticed, since the amounts of
fruit which would have had to be eaten daily exceed the bounds of
the probable 630 grams of cashew fruit or 1.5 kilograms of bananas.
False blindness, as it is sometimes called in Brazil, has been
recorded in endemic form in the Northeast as early as the seventeenth century through the observations of Wilhelm Piso; and a
recent survey of the Cariri region showed that 85 per cent of its
population suffered from different kinds of blindness associated
with vitamin A deficiency. (40)

The inadequate nourishment received by the labouring population
of the sugar belt could have had other, indirect ill-effects on
health. It would have aggravated the states of anaemia caused by
the parasitic infections common to the tropics, and which in this

region reached enormous dimensions. Ankylostomiasis, for example, was estimated to afflict from 70 to 80 per cent of the population. (41) While there is no evidence that protein-energy malnutrition increases the susceptibility to infection, it seems clear that it renders more difficult the recovery of patients from infectious diseases, and one may speculate that considerable harm was done in this way too. (42) The sugar plantation belt was swept almost yearly by epidemics - apparently originating in Recife - of small-pox, cholera, yellow fever or bubonic plague, which left behind a wide swathe of deaths and probably many more whose health was impaired. Contemporary accounts confirm that it was the poorest and presumably the worst fed who suffered the most, the so-called indigent population, and it is not hard to deduce that the viru-lence of these attacks had something to do with the generally low level of nutrition. (43)

The diet in Pernambuco was clearly inadequate for a fully healthy and active existence, but it was not the sole cause of the ill health, apathy and poor appearance noted and inferred for a large part of the population. Most of the symptoms described above could have been caused by non-nutritional factors, though often stemming from the same state of poverty that was at the root of malnutrition. The lack of hygiene, the parasitic infections or the climate might just as easily account for diarrhoea, eye complaints and dematitis. Although it is impossible, therefore, to pin down accurately anything on the poor nutritional status, there can be no doubt that it contributed to the health problems so prevalent everywhere.

The picture thus far presented possibly understates the gravity of the consequences of malnutrition because it is confined to the adult world. A protein-energy deficiency that can be more or less weathered by a mature body, for example, has severe impli-cations for that of a child. The consequences are not only physical and mental retardation in the child's development, but far more acute clinical features of malnutrition diseases generally than would be found in adults. (44) Unfortunately, we can only speculate about these matters, owing to our already noted ignorance as to how food was distributed within the family. Infant mortality rates would have shed some light on this, but in rural Pernambuco they were not recorded at this time. The closest one can get is the statistics for Recife; if they are an indication, then the problem was a grave one. Between 1923 and 1927 children between 0 and 1 year of age accounted for 25 per cent of all deaths. (45)

IV

Were the workers of Pernambuco's sugar zone worse off during the supposedly hungry 1960s than their forefathers early this century? Before answering this question, it is useful to sketch briefly the social and economic background to it. It should be noted first of all that the low standard of living of the popu-lation between 1870 and 1920 has to be ascribed to the plantation system, which grossly under-utilised human and natural resources and ensured a highly uneven distribution of income and wealth.

The great estates monopolised the land, offered relatively paid employment and left little economic opportunity for escape from grinding poverty to those who did not leave; yet it permitted them to survive, thanks to the squatting arrangement available to most. The decline in nutritional status between 1870 and 1920 was caused primarily by the expansion in the supply of labour out of all proportion with the demand for it by the sugar sector. By 1890, the output of sugar, a good index of employment in the area, had reached the level at which it would remain for the next thirty years, a period during which the population grew by 50 per cent. Not only real wages fell - 60 per cent in 1870-90 and 30 per cent in 1890-1920 - but un- or under-employment increased substantially. (46) The rigours of this state of affairs were mitigated, however, by the continuing flow of the income from subsistence agriculture. As long as the supply of agricultural land remained far in excess of the needs of the sugar mills planters could truthfully say to their workers: 'On the plantations we give a house, firewood, land for raising cereals without having to share any produce, the help of the landowner in times of difficulty, and the right to raise small animals'. (47)

The social and economic history of sugar since the First World War is less well known, but its main features are not hard to discern. By the mid-1960s, the output of sugar had expanded considerably to about five times its 1920 size. Cane land had also expanded enormously, and well over half the total area of the forest zone was under commercial cultivation. (48) The population had only tripled in the meantime; and since the labour input per ton of sugar had barely changed, it is safe to say that the demand for labour had grown more than its supply. Paradoxically, employers seemed to improve their bargaining position in that they were increasingly able to use hitherto unknown methods for compressing labour costs. Rents for their houses began to be deducted from the wages of moradores, a practice unheard of before 1914. Whenever subsistence plots were allowed they had to be requited with a number of days of unpaid or under-paid labour, an arrangement that seems to have emerged during the 1930s and was certainly prevalent two decades later. (49)

Behind this lay the gradual disappearance of the traditional superabundance of unused land. Although the planter needed the worker more now, in another way the worker needed the planter even more, because there was little to fall back on beyond plantation work or migration to the swollen city. The planter no longer needed to offer subsistence plots to secure a cheap and stable labour force, but it may also be that he was not in a position to do so either. Population pressure was such in the early 1960s that the region's food output averaged only 1,921 calories and 36.3 grams of protein per person per day, not to mention the fact that export crops drained away 37 per cent of the calories produced. (50) The progressive erosion of subsistence agriculture obliged the squatter to become a plantation wage labourer, and this meant that he had to rely on his cash income primarily for the acquisition of the necessities of life. (51)

The unfavourable evolution in their social and economic position was not reproduced in the matter of the living standard of the rural working class. Thanks to technological advances, by the 1960s a few of them were able to enjoy radios, wristwatches and sewing machines, which they obviously would not have had before. (52) But in a region of such poverty and where so much of the family's budget went on food the crucial test must be the nutritional status. Two surveys of family food consumption taken in 1963 and 1964 respectively are used here as the term of comparison (see Table 3.2, columns 6 and 7). (53) In most respects the 1960s on this reading were no worse than 1920 or 1900, and there is roughly an equivalence with conditions in 1870. The exceptions are the intakes of calcium and thiamine. If the 1964 figures are used instead of those for 1963, then conditions recently appear far better, and the caloric consumption emerges as larger than anything previously experienced for at least a hundred years. On the whole, the differences are not great, however, and the list of nutritional deficiencies does not vary much from the earlier to the later dates. Protein consumption departs from this in that it had recovered to an acceptable level by the 1960s, whereas it had been steadily in decline between 1870 and 1920. The case of niacin is unclear because of the difference between the 1963 and 1964 figures.

It would have been useful at this point to have at least one intermediary benchmark date between 1920 and 1963. Unfortunately, the value of the 1945 figures in the present context is limited (see Table 3.3) as they are derived from evidence concerning single though supposedly typical families, rather than from a broader data basis as with the other ones. Column III probably comes closest to the model family, although with so many dependants it may not be entirely representative. If we were to use it, nevertheless, what would emerge would be a pronounced decline from 1920 to 1945, followed by an improvement to 1964. This corresponds reasonably well to our knowledge of the economic difficulties of the zona da mata during the 1930s and the period of the Second World War; and to the improvement in their conditions achieved by plantation workers at least from the late 1950s. All the same, the gaps in our knowledge of the period yawn widely, and clearly much research is needed to fill them.

Despite the contraction of the subsistence sector during the twentieth century, the labouring population was able to nourish itself not worse than when it had enjoyed land privileges because its cash income in real terms grew till it more or less made up for the difference. In this sense it was not worse off, but in snother it was. In order to achieve this position in 1964 the labouring population had to work several times harder than it would have had to in 1870 or 1920, and had lost much of the freedom that characterises the existence of squatters. According to one of the surveys we have been following here, in 1964 95.5 per cent of all workers were employed on plantations at least 200 days in the year. (54) Although the average length of the working day was shorter than in 1920 or before, this is still four or five times as much as the average worked by adults in a year during the earlier period. (55) When we consider the physical state in which these people found themselves owing to malnutrition and other problems, this increased burden should not weigh lightly in the felicific calculus we are attempting here.

The undernourishment of generations of Northeasterners undoubtedly has had an influence on many aspects of their lives,
such as mortality and fertility, labour productivity, and patterns of social behaviour. It was not the only factor affecting
them and for this reason it would be unwise to discuss these
variables purely in terms of nutrition. The strong similarity of
nutritional status encountered at different points along the past
century encourages, however, the scrutiny of two such aspects for
which evidence is available. One of them is stature, which is of
interest, given the likelihood of an influence of the protein
intake on it. In the 1936 survey mentioned earlier, it was found
that the average adult male height was 161.7 cm, and for females
it was 152.0 cm. Thirty years later, the results of another survey
were almost the same: 160.6 cm for men and 150.4 for women. (56)
Clearly, the diet did not change sufficiently for this to make
an impression on the pattern of physical development.

The second aspect is labour productivity in cane cultivation,
which has improved slightly since a hundred years ago. It took
3.6 man-days on average to produce a tone of cane in the mid-
1960s, with roughly the same technique as it did to produce the
same ton with approximately the same labour input between 1870
and 1920. Since the working day had meanwhile become shorter and
the soil on the whole had become poorer through constant cultivation, one has to infer that the effort put into the task by cane
workers in the 1960s was greater. The increase might be of the
order of 20 per cent, and could be simply the result of higher work
norms exacted by employers who were in a position to demand them.
It is tempting to suppose that nutrition may have played some part
in this too, and that the slightly better fed worker of the 1960s
was also in a better position to respond to this exaction.

V

This study has attempted to show that the population of Pernambuco's
sugar zone suffered a decline in the value of its diet between
1870 and 1920. From then until the 1960s, a time of controversy
over living standards in the region, the evolution is not clear,
but at the later date the nutritional level was higher than it was
early in the century. At its worst, malnutrition was never so
acute as to cause widespread and severe states of ill-health, but
it undoubtedly contributed to some of this population's most unfavourable physical conditions. To reach these conclusions,
certain strong assumptions had to be made. This is not only un-
avoidable in the present state of knowledge, but will probably
remain so in any conceivable future one, owing to the nature of
the evidence and of the subject of the study. It is suggested,
therefore, that although our findings are tentative, this is as
firmly as they can probably be made.

With this example of Northeast Brazil, we have also tried to
illustrate an approach to the historical analysis of the standard
of living of a population on which there has been too little
emphasis and which we regard as important. Much that has been
done in this field, usually concerning Northern Europe, has been

to determine the variations in and the pattern of distribution of real income. In areas of deprivation (and few places in the past would escape this designation) where most of the income goes on food and that food is insufficient, this is not enough. The discussion must be pursued to its logical conclusion, in terms of nutrients, of standards of adequate nutrition, and of the implications of malnutrition for individuals and the groups they constitute. Without such a step any standard of living controversy is only half the story. (58)

REFERENCES

1 LUIS DA CAMARA CASCUDO, *Historia da alimentação no Brasil* (2 vols, São Paulo, Editora Nacional, 1967). Most of the works of Gilberto Freyre contain some reference to food and its historical aspects. See also LUIS LISANTI, Sur la Nourriture des *Paulistes* entre le XVIIIe et XIXe siècles, *Annales E.S.C.*, XVIII (1963), pp.531-40. Although mainly concerned with the present and the future, two other works take useful glances at the past: JOSUÉ DE CASTRO, *Geografia da Fome (O Dilema Brasileiro: Pão ou Aço)* (10th edition, São Paulo: Brasiliense, 1967); F. POMPEO DO AMARAL, *O Problema da Alimentação: Aspectos Médico-Higiénico-Sociais* (2 vols, Rio de Janeiro, Olympio, 1963).

2 GILBERTO FREYRE, *Nordeste* (Rio de Janeiro, Olympio, 1937); PUBLIO DIAS, Condições Higiénicas de Trabalhadores dos Engenhos de Pernambuco, *Fronteiras* V, n.20, 1936; JOSUÉ DE CASTRO, *As Condições de Vida das Classes Operárias no Recife: Estudo Económico da sua Alimentação* (Rio de Janeiro, pub. unknown, 1935). During the 1930s Gilberto Freyre and a local doctor attempted a survey of the living conditions of cane workers but were thwarted by suspicious landowners. Such a survey is mentioned, however, in VASCONCELLOS TORRES, *Condições de Vida do Trabalhador na Agro-Indústria do Açucar* (Rio de Janeiro, pub. unknown, 1945, p.224).

3 For recent social and economic conditions, see MANUEL CORREIA DE ANDRADE, *A Terra e o Homem no Nordeste* (2nd edition, São Paulo, 1964); DE CASTRO, *Geografia da Fome* op.cit. There are numerous accounts of the political tensions of the 1960s. See, for example, RIORDAN ROETT, *The Politics of Foreign Aid in the Brazilian Northeast* (Nashville; Vanderbilt University Press, 1972); JOSEPH A. PAGE, *The Revolution that Never Was: Northeast Brazil 1955-1964* (New York: Grossman, 1972).

4 In this we follow Fernand Braudel's suggestion for a *regressive method* in history. See his Vie Matérielle et Comportements Biologiques, *Annales E.S.C.* (1961), pp.548-9.

5 DE CASTRO, *Geografia da Fome* op.cit., p.39.

6 Great Britain, *House of Commons Accounts and Papers* (HCAP), 1913, vol. 71, p.136.

7 ANTÓNIO DA SILVA JARDIM, *Memórias e Viagens: Campanha de um Propagandista, 1887-1890* (Lisbon, Nacional Editora, 1891), p.372.

8 A. CARNEIRO LEÃO, *Oliveira Lima: Conferência* (Recife, 1914), p.9.

9   As Moléstias dos Trabalhadores do Campo, *Boletim da União dos Syndicatos Agrícolas de Pernambuco*, October 1913, p.587.
10 DIAS, Condições Higiénicas, op.cit., p.427.
11 BRASIL MINISTÉRIO DA AGRICULTURA, INDÚSTRIA E COMMERCIO, *Estudo dos Factores de Producção nos Municípios Brasileiros e as Condições Económicas de cada um. No.2. do Estado de Pernambuco - Municipio de Escada* (Rio de Janeiro: Imprensa Nacional, 1922), p.20.
12 JOSÉ MARIA BELLO, *Memórias* (Rio de Janeiro, Olympio, 1958), p.16.
13 HEBE WELBOURN, *Nutrition in Tropical Countries* (London, Oxford University Press, 1963), p.43.
14 A.H. DE OLIVEIRA MARQUES, *Daily Life in Portugal in the Middle Ages*, trans. S.S. WYATT (London and Madison, University of Wisconsin Press, 1971), pp.16-35. See also STANLEY STEIN, *Vassouras, a Brazilian Coffee County, 1850-1900* (Cambridge, Harvard University Press, 1957), pp.173-4.
15 MANUEL DIEGUES JR., População e Açúcar no Nordeste do Brasil (Rio de Janeiro, Comissão Nacional de Alimentação, 1952), p.198; GILBERTO FREYRE, *Sobrados e Mucambos: Decadência do Patriarcado Rural e Desenvolvimento do Urbano* (3rd edition, Rio de Janeiro; Editora Nacional, 1961), p.283.
16 KONRAD GUENTHER, *A Naturalist in Brazil: The Record of a Year's Observation of her Flora, her Fauna and her People*, trans. Bernard Miall (Boston and New York, pub. unknown, 1931), p.150. This view is supported by Andrade, Terra e o Homen, op.cit., p.89.
17 The only exception found to date is Doyle to Earl Granville, Report on the Industrial Classes, Pernambuco, 12 March 1872, Foreign Office Papers, FO 83/379, Public Record Office.
18 TORRES, *Condições de Vida*, op.cit., p.158.
19 This involves rejecting De Castro's interesting but still to be demonstrated view that these foodstuffs were abundant once and were widely consumed, but that the habit for them has been gradually lost (*Geografia da Fome*, op.cit., p.135).
20 For a fuller discussion, see JAIME REIS, From Bangue to Usina: Social Aspects of the Growth and Modernisation of the Sugar Industry of Pernambuco, 1850-1920, in IAN RUTLEDGE and KENNETH DUNCAN (eds), *Land and Labour in Latin America: Essays in the Development of Agrarian Capitalism in the Nineteenth and Twentieth Centuries* (forthcoming, Cambridge University Press). The income figures have been corrected to allow for an assumed migrant labour component of one fourth at harvest time and for 30 per cent of the total labour input to be taken by the harvest. See PETER L. EISENBERG, *The Sugar Industry of Pernambuco, 1840-1910: Modernisation Without Change* (Berkeley, University of California Press, 1974), p.183; AGRICULTURA, *Diário de Pernambuco*, 26 May 1897.
21 HENRIQUE MILET, A Trégoe, *Revista Agrícola e Commercial*, 20 December 1876.
22 See for example, OLIVEIRA LIMA, Letter, *Diário de Pernambuco*, 3 March 1918.
23 RELATÓRIO, Commissão das Seccas, p.6. in *Falla com que o Excellentissimo Senhor Dr. Adolpho de Barros Cavalcanti de*

Lacerda abrio a Assembleia Provincial Legislativa em 19 de Dezembro de 1878 (Recife, Faria, 1879); *Falla ... Dezembargador Joaquim José de Oliveira Andrade ... em 15 de Setembro de 1888* (Recife, Faria, 1889), annexo B, p.23; ROBERT AVE-LALLEMANT, *Viagem pelo Norte do Brasil no Anno de 1859* (2 vols, Rio de Janeiro, Instituto Nacional do Livro, 1961), vol. 1, p.181.

24 For average yields of beans and manioc, see BRASIL MINISTÉRIO DA AGRICULTURA, INDÚSTRIA E COMMÉRCIO, *Aspectos da Economia Rural Brasileira*, (Rio de Janeiro, Villas Boas, 1922) table facing p.338. For cane land area, see BRASIL MINISTÉRIO DA AGRICULTURA, INDÚSTRIA E COMMÉRCIO, *Recenseamento do Brasil realizado em 1 de Setembro de 1920* (5 vols, Rio de Janeiro).

25 For sugar consumption, see HENRIQUE MILET, *A Lavoura da Canna de Assucar*, (Recife, Journal do Recife, 1881), p.3; and GASPAR PERES and APOLLONIO PERES, *A Industria Assucareira em Pernambuco*, (Recife, Imprensa Industrial, 1915), p.120. On spirit, see Quadro Estatístico, *Boletim da União dos Syndicatos*, May 1907, pp.306-7. The 1936 survey by Publio Dias found that only 39.7 per cent of adults admitted to drinking cane spirit, but the figure is hardly reliable given the notorious deceitfulness elicited by questions on the subject.

26 Northeast Brazil Nutrition Survey (Washington, D.C., Interdepartmental Committee on Nutrition for National Development, 1965), pp.282-7. The figures have been deflated by 10 per cent to take into account food wastage.

27 *Handbook on Human Nutritional Requirements* (Rome; Food and Agriculture Organisation, 1974).

28 This is repeatedly made clear throughout STANLEY DAVIDSON et al., *Human Nutrition and Dietetics* (5th edition, Edinburgh and London, Churchill Livingstone, 1972).

29 MIRIAM E. LOWENBERG et al., *Food and Man* (2nd edition, New York, John Wiley, 1974), p.281.

30 TORRES, *Condições de Vida*, op.cit., pp.210-20.

31 JOHN BURNETT, *Plenty and Want: A Social History of Diet in England from 1815 to the Present Day* (Harmondsworth: Penguin, 1968), p.161; D.J. ODDY, Working Class Diets in Late Nineteenth Century Britain, *Economic History Review*, 23 (1970), pp.314-23.

32 ARTHUR NEIVA E BELISÁRIO PENA, *Viagem Científica pelo Norte da Bahia, Sudoeste de Pernambuco, Sul do Piauhi e do Norte ao Sul de Goiaz* (Rio de Janeiro Inspectoria de Obras contra as Secas, 1916), p.139.

33 DAVIDSON et al., *Human Nutrition*, op.cit., p.59.

34 It has been found that subject on a diet of 4.7gm a day got it after fifty days. See RICHARD H. FOLLIS JR., *Deficiency Disease: Functional and Structural Changes in Mammalia Which Result from Exogenous or Endogenous Lack of One or More Essential Nutrients* (Springfield, Ill., Charles C. Thomas, 1958), p.220.

35 DAVIDSON et al., *Human Nutrition*, op.cit., p.295.

36 FOLLIS found that on a diet similar to this one the full clinical features of riboflavin deficiency materialised. See *Deficiency Disease*, op.cit., p.217.

37 RUY COUTINHO, Alimentação e Estado Nutricional do Escravo no Brasil, *Estudos Afro-Brasileiros: Trabalhos Apresentados ao 1º Congresso Afro-Brasileiro Reunido no Recife em 1934* (Rio de Janeiro, Ariel Editora, 1935), pp.199-213; JERONYMO MARTINIANO FIGUEIRA DE MELLO, *Ensaio sobre a Statistica Civil e Politica de Provincia de Pernambuco* ... (Recife, 1852), p.7.

38 *Recenseamento da População do Império do Brasil a que se procedeo no Dia 1º de Agosto de 1872: Quadros Estatísticos* (Rio de Janeiro, Directoria Geral de Estatistica, 1873-1876), vol. 13.

39 These figures are estimated from the already mentioned nutrition tables, but see also DE CASTRO, *Geografia da Fome*, op.cit., p.143.

40 AMARAL, *Problema da Alimentação*, op.cit., vol. 1, pp.27-9. Xerophthalmia was common in Northeast Brazil in 1963 too. See *Northeast Nutrition Survey*, op.cit., p.197.

41 ARMANDO GAYOSO, A Ancilostomose, *Diário de Pernambuco*, 11 March 1917. This may have included schistosomiasis which was not identified in the Northeast until the 1920s. See FLÁVIO MARAJÓ, Frequência da Schistosomose na Parahyba, *Arquivos de Medicina de Pernambuco*, January 1925, pp.151-4.

42 For a detailed discussion of this topic, see N.S. SCRIMSHAW et al., *Interactions of Nutrition and Infection* (Geneva, World Health Organisation, 1968).

43 See for example, Juiz de Direito do Presidente, Itambé, 2 May 1884, *Juizes de Direito*, JD/78, in Arquivo Publico Estadual de Pernambuco.

44 DAVIDSON, *Human Nutrition*, op.cit., pp.59-60.

45 *Annuario Estatístico de Pernambuco - 1927* (Recife, 1928), pp.122-3.

46 REIS, From Bangue to Usina, op.cit. In one sense, this was the problem of population pressure which has recently received attention as possibly the most serious one affecting the Northeast economy at present.

47 Centro dos Fornecedores de Cana, *Diário de Pernambuco*, 22 August 1919.

48 *Pernambuco: Problematica de suas Ativadades Economicas: Agro Industria Açucareira* (mimeo., 1970), p.49.

49 DIAS, Condições Higiénicas, op.cit., p.334; FRANCISCO JULIÃO, *Cambão - The Yoke: The Hidden Face of Brazil* (Harmondsworth, Penguin, 1972).

50 *Northeast Nutrition Survey*, op.cit., p.37. For an even blacker picture at the end of the decade, see DUARTE, Nutrição e o Problema Populacional, op.cit., p.21.

51 J.M. DA ROSA E SILVA NETO, *Contribuição ao Estudo da Zona da Mata em Pernambuco (Aspectos Estruturais e Econômicos da Área de Influêcia das Usinas de Açucar)*, (Recife, Instituto Joaquim Nabuco de Pesquisas Sociais, 1966), p.116.

52 FERNANDO ANTÓNIO GONÇALVES, *Condições de Vida do Trabalhador Rural de Zona da Mata do Estado de Pernambuco* (Recife, Instituto Joaquim Nabuco de Pesquisas Sociais, 1966), p.153.

53   The first was based on 142 families containing 956 persons
     and is in *Northeast Nutrition Survey*, op.cit., p.95. The
     second is in GONÇALVES, *Condições de Vida*, op.cit., pp.139-141
     and is based on 477 families with 2573 persons. By the time
     of the second, conditions for cane workers were probably better
     following a spate of labour legislation and wage rises caused
     by pressure on employers by recently founded unions. See
     CYNTHIA N. HEWITT, Brazil: The Peasant Movement of Pernambuco,
     1961-1964, in HENRY A. LANDSBERGER, *Latin American Peasant
     Movement* (Ithaca and London, Cornell University Press, 1969),
     p.397.
54   CONÇALVES, *Condições de Vida*, op.cit., p.147.
55   REIS, From Bangue to Usina, op.cit. Working days of ten to
     twelve hours used to be the norm, according to HENRIQUE MILET,
     Cultura da Canna, *Revista Agrícola e Commercial*, 20 August
     1876. In 1964, 62 per cent of the workers surveyed did seven
     to eight hours a day and only 28.6 per cent did more than this.
56   DIAS, Condições Higiénicas, op.cit., *Northeast Nutrition
     Survey*, op.cit., p.210.
57   Compare, for example, CORREIA DE BRITO, Conferencia, *Diário
     de Pernambuco*, 11 September 1909 with *Agro Industria
     Açucareira*, p.112.
58   For Britain, where the standard of living controversy has
     raged for two decades, there are only two studies concerned
     with nutritional aspects: ODDY, Working Class Diets, op.cit.,
     and J.C. McKENZIE, The Composition and Nutritional Value of
     Diets in Manchester and Dunkinfield in 1841, *Transactions of
     the Lancashire and Cheshire Antiquarian Society*, 72 (1962).
     The signs from France are more encouraging, however. A
     recent collection of articles on *L'histoire de la consommation*
     contained several which analysed the nutritional implications
     of their findings. See Dossier: Histoire de la Consommation,
     Annales E.S.C., 30 (1975), pp.402-632.

Chapter 4

THE HUNGRY IMAGINATION: SOCIAL FORMATION, POPULAR CULTURE AND IDEOLOGY IN BAHIA
Colin Henfrey

Food is good, my people,
Food is good to share.

(Song of the divinity Omulú in the cult-house of Catarina, Liberdade, Salvador, Bahia).

We must go among all classes of the population.

(V.I. Lenin, What Is To Be Done?, Selected Works. Progress Publishers, Moscow, 1977, Vol. I., p.155).

1 THE DIALECTICS OF IMAGERY: THE TRANSFORMATIONS OF OMULÚ

The first image of Brazilian popular culture which generally comes to mind is either carnival in Rio or the famous candomblés of Bahia. (1) The latter are voodoo-like cult houses in whose best known rituals initiates become possessed by orixás. These divinities came to Brazil with the slave population which continued to arrive from West Africa until well into the nineteenth century. Possession by them takes the form of trances, with distinctive costumes, songs and dances which dramatise their different characters and the relationships between them. (2) Perhaps the best known orixá is Omulú, the doctor figure. He has a vivid, particularly African presence. Like many orixás he is old and moves unsteadily, but his costume lends a unique effect. His whole figure is covered with strands of sisal. They rustle as he moves, cascading to the floor, and are attached to his head with a band of small white cowry shells, another very African trait. He seems, as most anthropologists insist, like an incarnation of the persistence of an 'Afro-Brazilian' sub-culture, especially in the urban Northeast. If you visited Bahia and its cult houses, encouraged and guided typically by the official tourist department, this deeply conservative pluralism is the image, not just of Omulú, but of Bahian popular culture and society in general, which you would take away with you.
    Yet there is another variety of Omulú, which suggests that this

culture is less exotic and more contemporary. He is often
simply called 'o médico'; or 'o médico dos pobres' (the doctor
or poor people's doctor). As this suggests, his healing activities
are his most outstanding feature. His other traits are rather
modest by orixás' standards, especially his willingness to mix
with caboclos, a quite different set of candomblé divinities.
This term caboclo has several overlapping meanings, ranging from
the semi-affectionate, semi-perjorative 'country bumpkin' to a
primarily ethnic connotation, especially in literary sources, of
'person of mixed Portuguese and Amerindian descent'. The candomblé
caboclos have something of these qualities, albeit in a more
positive way, since they represent the archetypes of Brazilian
peasant society: cowherds, fishermen, and so on. Most of their
performances are unpredictable and even unruly, and whilst they
are shared by other divinities (mainly Indians, who are often
thought of as caboclos), the dignified orixás avoid them, keeping
to their own ceremonies. Caboclos are unsuitable company for
these Afro-Brazilian ancestors, on ritual grounds with distinctly
social and almost moral overtones. Exceptions like the Omulús who
cross this boundary are disapproved of in other cult houses and
even thought to become caboclos. In short, behind the traditional
dramas, fixed characters and stable facade of the tourist department's 'popular culture', there are ambiguities and conflicts.
How extensive are they? What lies behind them? Why are they
not more widely acknowledged?

Far from answering these questions, the anthropologists concerned with this culture and principally with candomblé have hardly
acknowledged their existence. They, too, have stressed its orixá
and under-played its caboclo dimension and the relationship
between them, presenting the former as an authentic, Afro-
Brazilian tradition, and the latter as little more than a random,
degenerate departure from it. (3) There is in effect a consistent
exclusion of the right-hand pole of the opposition in figure 4.1,
and thus of the opposition itself, and its implications for the left
hand column which is the conventional object of study.

orixá	:	caboclo
(Omulú as orixá	:	Omulú as or with caboclos)

FIGURE 4.1

So what? One might reasonably ask. This paper will answer as
follows. First, that such issues are symptomatic of a generally
restricted focus applied not only by social science, but also by
society, to the whole of Brazilian popular culture. And second,
that this reflects this culture's most essential feature, namely
its ideological place in the socio-economic relations of its main
participants - the poor of all the major Northeastern cities.
Thus the issues involved in details like the transformations of
Omulú are not just anthropological quibbles, far removed from the
modern Brazil of miraculous economic growth. They include some
basic questions about methodology and culture, and also about the
class identity and consciousness of the sub-proletariat or

'marginal sector'. Moreover, they have implications not only for Northeastern culture, but for the general ideology of peripheral capitalist formations.

The implication of this perspective (which is not adopted a priori, but emerged from an essentially empirical approach to the subject) is that culture must be seen as related first and foremost to production: specifically to the reproduction of the social relations of production in a particular social formation. However, within this theoretical framework I have tried to retain what is traditionally a feature of non-Marxist anthropology, its attention to the empirical data which any theory should seek to account for - in Marxist terms, the *lived relations* which are all too often treated as secondary. It is something of a lonely task to maintain to non-Marxists on the one hand that culture can be understood only in the light of relations of production, and to Marxists on the other hand that phenomena as distinctly lived as candomblé are integral to these relations. However, I make no further apology to non-Marxists for this premise; nor to Marxists for using not empiricism, but the empirical observation through which the relations between symbols can be seen as the shadows of social relations in which their meanings lie concealed. Not only are these symbols an object of interest in their own right, within a materialist perspective on the creative and the cultural. They also afford a new vantage point for looking at a sphere of relations (those of the sub-proletariat) traditionally neglected by Marxists, in theory and practice.

More generally, it is also important to show quite simply that Marxist theory is still concerned and able to deal with the evident content of social experience, in any context. The divinities of the urban poor, with all their elaborate variations, should be no exception. Indeed Marxist theory, with its claims to account for flux and contradictions, should be well able to discern a structure in the variations neglected by more normative authors, and hence to unravel their social meaning. First, then, to describe them briefly.

I first encountered Omulú as a caboclo, or at least consorting with them, in a tiny, flea-bitten cult house in the heart of Liberdade (Freedom), Bahia's biggest low-income bairro (residential neighbourhood). It was a tatty affair compared to the often lavish cult houses of the Afro-Brazilian orixás. One drum instead of the ritual three. An earth dance floor in a one-room adobe house, perhaps thirty feet square. No electricity, not even tapped. No audience except for some children, but even they tended either to sleep or else join in the singing and dancing. The twenty or so participants, of whom several were possessed by caboclos, were obviously badly off, even by Liberdade's standards. They had no ritual costumes, not even the Omulú among them. The woman possessed by him was Catarina, head of the cult house or mãe de santo (mother in sainthood). (As there are also fathers in sainthood, the term 'cult head' will be used from now onwards.) She was about forty, squat and black, with the typically commanding presence of almost every cult head, unruffled by my sudden appearance, unlikely though it was in this setting. In keeping with the other divinities, her Omulú sang in a sotaque de caboclo (caboclo accent,

a seemingly garbled Portuguese full of rustic inversions and
indigenous Amerindian phrases, in contrast to the African dia-
lects of the orthodox orixás. The refrain of his main song was
as follows:

Comida é bôa, mi'a gente, bôa p'ra dividír

(Food is good, my people, good for sharing out.)

As Omulú sang this, he distributed popcorn to all those
present - provided, as I later discovered, by a participant who
was in work, 'thanks to Catarina's Omulú'. To anticipate slightly,
this ritual had several layers of meaning. Popcorn represents
the scars of smallpox, and thus the healing powers which earn Omulú
his 'doctor' title and popular following and personality. This
originally African symbol seems to live on where others have faded
(in Catarina's cult house, for instance) because of its practical
connotations. Smallpox epidemics are vividly recalled by older
people in Bahia, while healing in general is a major concern in
the relative absence of socialised medicine in low-income bairros
like Liberdade. Yet perhaps the most immediate meaning of this
sharing ritual was simpler. The popcorn was food. Many of those
present were probably hungry, and certainly they were often dependent on the cult house community for their subsistence. Thus
the most basic of material conditions, health and food, were interwoven with this one item of popular culture, just as the sum of
these conditions in fact underlies the totality of its forms and
meanings and their dynamics.
I later attended Catarina's cult house for well over a year.
Living close by it, I also got to know its participants outside
this context. Most were local members of the marginal sector, or
sub-proletariat: domestics, street-sellers, artisans, and occasionally unskilled factory workers, usually on a short-term basis; they
were of all ages, the majority but not all of them women. Occu-
pationally and in their social conditions they were typical of
roughly a third of Bahia's one million population, and of two-
thirds of Liberdade's. Typical also, in one form or another, was
their involvement with cult houses of much the same kind as
Catarina's, small, poorly endowed and with a marked bias toward
the caboclos. Existing on almost every street in Liberdade and
similar bairros, they are usually unregistered with the authorities
and also under threat of closure due to their unorthodoxy, in
contrast to the fewer but bigger, more Afro-Brazilian cult houses
where Omulú can afford his full costume as an unambiguous orixá.
This predominance of unorthodox culture in Liberdade was no coincidence. All that occurred in these cult houses was intimately
interwoven with their members' everyday social existence. This
proved to be the case in every field of popular culture, from
candomblé and carnival groups to language and concepts of local
history. Their overlapping imagery was rooted in the same set of
social relations.
This is not to suggest that this or any other culture is a
static or inert reflection of socio-economic conditions. Rather
the imagination, both individual and collective, is acting

creatively on conditions such as those of Liberdade, to produce
the only tangible form of this culture's existence, its actual
expression. Hence its only way of existing is by definition one
of movement, a constant becoming of image and meaning, like some
ever-changing tapestry which by virtue of being interwoven with
socio-economic conditions is always being not just woven, but un-
ravelled and rewoven; and this in response not just to changes in
these conditions but also to the wider society's intervention in
these responses. The analysis of culture as ideology consists
largely in identifying the structure of this image movement and
its continuous interplay with socio-economic structure, including
its changes and contradictions.

The denial of this movement of culture by so many anthropologists is therefore complementary to their neglect of its
social context. Nor is this just a matter of alternative ways of
looking at culture. The extrapolation of imagery and construction
of orthodox cultural systems, though a priori a negation of this
culture's essence, its constant movement, nevertheless becomes a
part of it and the social relationships behind it. The idealisation
of Afro-Brazilian sub-culture becomes an internalised variant of
Bahian sub-proletarian culture, with particular ideological and
thus social effects. Just how this happens will soon be detailed.
The point at this stage is simply that images like Omulú have no
fixed or wholly autonomous existence of the kind conventionally
attributed to them by so much cultural anthropology, not to
mention tourist departments. If Omulú *exists* at all, it is as
the sum of his transformations from one cult house to another,
and between the implicitly contending orixá and caboclo dimensions,
with his meaning lying in neither of them, but in the dialectic
between them. In so far as this dialectic is one between symbols
with definite social values in terms of relations of production,
the meaning becomes determinate: their variations and gyrations,
contradictions and ambiguities, have an ideological coherence which
is the object of this study.

So too with the whole of this popular culture. Each of its
infinite image-moments is one in a series of moving refractions,
or rather belongs, as these movements are linked, to a mobile in
a hall of mirrors. The angles and curves of such settings bemuse,
but they do so systematically. Identified and analysed, their
refractions or forms of appearance acquire a basically logical
structure, in this case an ideological one, in which the angles
and curves involved are those of a definite social formation and
the section of it which carries this culture: the Bahian sub-
proletariat. We must therefore begin by determining its class
dimensions. Only then can we follow the movement of these image-
moments out of the shadow of cultural expression into the light
of the social relations to which they ultimately allude, as a
condition of their existence and symptom of their contradictions.

2   THE REDEFINITION OF MARGINALITY AS RELATIONS OF PRODUCTION:
    THE MATERIAL CONTEXT OF POPULAR CULTURE

The tendency is for the urban poor to be most closely observed

by those inclined to attribute their poverty to their apparent
culture and values, which Marxists take to be secondary. Hence
the latter have neglected a field of Latin-American social relations which others commonly reify with descriptive concepts like
clientelism and pluralism, as elements of a general theory explaining poverty in terms of a lack of capacity or inclination
for integration with the wider society. Of course such concepts
are not irrelevant. Indeed they are accurate reflections of how
such relations are lived and thought by those involved at every
level, the exploited as well as the exploiting classes. Marxists
should no more neglect them than other theorists should reify them
by treating them as explanatory concepts, instead of collective
representations: as the essence rather than the forms, at once
real and ideological, of relations involving the urban poor, which
therefore require an explanation at a more objective level.

The core of such reification is the dualist perspective underlying most sociology of under-development, including the evo-
lutionary Marxist theory. (4) This perspective takes at face
value the gulf between the so-called 'backward' (originally the
rural) sector and the 'modern' (urban or national) one. The occur-
rence of backwardness within cities merely replicates this dualism,
being characterised as 'marginality'. Yesterday's stagnant folk
communities become the shantytowns of today, its folk the urban
marginals of Lima or Rio de Janeiro. Their poverty is associated
with their apparent isolation from the city's institutions and
ethos, in place of which they live in a world of their own sub-
culture and typically clientelistic relations. Beginning as an
image of poverty, this grows into its sociological and ideological
explanation, so that poverty's cultural forms of appearance
become a deliberate court of appeal against the relations which
underlie them. In the words of a Brazilian ambassador explaining
the discrepancies in his country's income distribution, in carefully chosen contrast to Sweden's, 'Sweden is a fairly homogeneous
country in terms of race, culture and physical space, and not the
melting pot, the cultural mosaic ... of Brazil'. (5)

The ambassador to the Court of St James can call on an eminent
array of sociological witnesses to this attribution of economic
to cultural disparities and their concomitant sub-system of
clientelistic social relations. For instance, Wagley's *Introduction
to Brazil* describes the 'urban lower class' as having an 'essentially rural sub-culture', entailing social disorientation in the
absence of its traditional landed patrons, whom it endeavours to
recreate in the church and state. Though weakened, such relations
remain the sub-culturally determined horizon which keeps these
'traditional Brazilians ... mild and passive', and by the same token,
'illiterate, hungry and sick'. (6) Applications of this dualism to
the Brazilian lower orders, citing both their sub-culture as such
and their clientelism as its social dimension, and treating both
as independent rather than dependent variables, could be illustrated
ad infinitum. The writings of Lambert (7) and Hutchinson (8) are
two of the most predictable examples, echoed by other commentaries
on Latin America in general which are more specifically developmental
and also urban-orientated. As Eisenstadt has it, for example,
Latin-American societies are in 'the second stage of modernisation',

with their further advance inhibited by cultural and psycho-
logical dualism. Thus he finds outside the modern sphere a
'disengaged traditional sector and a semi-urbanised and un-
integrated modern one', of which slums are a specific feature.
The 'lower groups' in both these sectors display 'a great extent
of rigidity in their concept of society in general and of their
own place in it in particular ... with a minimum development of
any aspirations beyond the traditional scope of occupations'.
Hence, too, 'traditional types of relationships, i.e. of pater-
nalist arrangements' persist even in cities. (9) One can't help
wondering, as one reads this wisdom, if its victims will be able,
some day, to reply with their own account of the sub-culture of
development sociologists. More exclusively on urban poverty,
the politically influential DESAL school attributes an almost
bizarre importance to ethno-cultural pluralism. Much of its
argument consists of country-by-country correlations between
marginality and 'its ultimate basis in a cultural disposition,
correlated with skin colour (sic), reflecting quite distinct value
systems'. Poverty and illiteracy, it explains, are 'attributes
of an ethnically different world'. (10) And so on.

There is little to gain by illustrating these arguments further;
as they accumulate, they tend to regress instead of advancing.
Their essential feature is their opaqueness, their interpretation
by purely descriptive generalisation rather than any sort of
analysis. The distinction is perhaps worth repeating. That
clientelism and pluralism exist among the urban poor of any Latin-
American country, as the very real form and content of their
social relations, is beyond dispute. So too is their part in reproducing social inequality, as opposed to explaining, let alone
causing it. Indeed it will be argued that these two traits of
clientelism and pluralism are major conditions of poverty in the
urban Northeast, and as such two consistently central themes of
popular culture in Bahia. The issue is not their reality but
their status, their widely implied autonomy as the motor of the
marginality with which they are associated. Is this really rooted
in the dualists' gulf between 'lower groups' and the rest of society, or rather in exploitative relations, of which clientelism and
pluralism and their institutionalised reproduction are not so much
autonomous as ideologically sustained conditions?

Whilst the concept of internal colonialism occasionally hovers
close to these questions, it says much less about their class than
about their cultural dimensions. The problem is: How do the two
relate? And this can be answered only from a theoretically clear
position as to the class relations involved, the material basis
of marginality - in short, the fundamental questions: Who are the
urban poor in class terms, and how do these account for their
culture? Specifically, in what relations of production are such
people involved? Are these in fact as involuted and self-contained
as they appear, or rather more articulated with the Brazilian
economy and particularly with its current model of capital accumulation? What are the specifically social aspects of these relations of production? How are they reproduced, and what is the
place in this process of popular or marginal, or better still,
sub-proletarian culture?

The class analysis of these relations is much less advanced
than one might expect in view of the current radicalization of
Latin-American social science. Hampered by the frequent vagueness
and rhetoric of the dependency concept, Marxist-influenced
approaches have dealt mainly with the ruling classes. Discussion
of the relations in which the urban or rural poor are involved
has only recently moved beyond the establishment of a basic premise:
their partly non-capitalist nature, within and somehow relating
to a predominantly capitalist mode of production. (11) In the
context of urban poverty, the progress of this analysis is best
measured by the growing obsolescence of the dualists' marginality
concept. In practice this resulted from asking how the labour
of the poor is organised, and how its surplus is transferred from
whatever relations of production to the dominant pole of accumulation in the capitalist sector. Only within the framework of
some answers to these basic questions can one gauge the role of
low income culture in the ideological reproduction of what would
then be reasonably specific relations of production.

The first step in this direction was Nun's, with his identi-
fication of what he called the 'marginal mass' as an effect of the
form of growth in the modern sector, whose capital-intensive nature
excluded this mass from the labour market. Hence, rather than
even being exploited as an industrial reserve army, it was an
historically specific and effectively 'afunctional' form of the
relative surplus population which Marx had depicted as resulting
from the more gradual concentration of capital in the nineteenth
century. (12) However, Nun neglected to ask what relations of
production do occur among this marginal mass, and whether these
might somehow contribute to capital accumulation, despite their
apparent marginality. Indeed, his notion of marginal afunction-
ality precluded any such connection. It seems to have been Quijano
who first posed some such articulation, in seeing the 'marginal'
labour force as the industrial reserve army at least of the more
traditional and labour-intensive enterprises below the dominant
monopoly level. Moreover, since much of their profit is invested
at the dominant level, the marginal labour underlying it does contribute indirectly to the economy's dynamism. More significantly,
though less emphatically, Quijano also pointed out that this same
labour provides certain inputs for the monopoly enterprises - significantly, because this would increase their rate of profit by
lowering their outlay of constant (circulating) capital. (13)

Suggestive as this model is, its application is limited by the
fact that even the reserve army at Quijano's 'intermediate level'
of labour-intensive enterprises is only a relatively minor proportion of the total urban poor. Are those beyond it, who virtually
never sell their labour power in the capitalist sector - street-
sellers, odd-jobbers (biscateiros) and so on - wholly unconnected
with it? Inevitably it was soon pointed out, and principally by
de Oliveira, that whilst such activities entail non-capitalist
and semi-capitalist relations (self-employment, family labour,
outwork, apprenticeship, and so on), they do in fact produce
indirectly for the capitalist sector, especially in providing
cheap wage goods and services for workers in it. The result is
a lower cost of the reproduction of these workers' labour power,

and hence an increased rate of relative surplus value and
thus of profit.

Indeed, in de Oliveira's view this was so extensive that it
amounted to the keystone of the rate of profit in the Brazilian
miracle of recent economic growth, alongside a basically similar
articulation of peasant production. (14) Statistically and structurally, this degree of strictly economic importance for the
marginal sector now seems unlikely: for one thing, capitalist
production is expanding steadily to compete with and reduce the
role of marginal inputs. However, the existence if not the growth
of this articulation is undeniable; so too is its intensification,
mainly by increased family labour, precisely in response to the
growing competition from capitalist production. Even if Brazilian
capitalism can dispense with the labour of the poor, it clearly
entails their existence and allows few strategies for their survival, except by articulation with it, the effect of which must
logically be a cheaper reproduction of labour-power, for marginal
inputs to be competitive. Moreover, in addition to wage goods,
marginal labour offers services (slum housing, retailing, repairs,
and even makeshift private schooling) which lower the cost of the
social wage and thus release state capital for productive investment at the dominant level or in its infrastructural interests.

Abstract as all this may seem, it does relate quite concretely
to the conditions of existence and livelihood of people like
those in cult houses like Catarina's: the woman and her children
who have spent all day at a factory gate selling foodstuffs prepared since dawn at home; the carpenter who makes a living from
odd jobs in Liberdade; and so on. The range of such articulated
activities is almost endless. Even candomblé itself is one, since
its caboclo rituals act as a virtual marginal health service.
Cheap and effective medical treatment, herbal and ritual or psycho-
somatic, is afforded daily by most caboclo cult houses to many
wage-earners, among others. Not only does this compensate for
the low rates and employers' avoidance (as a condition of employment) of social security contributions, a significant saving on
the cost of cheap, intensive labour. It also allows such capital
as accumulates from these contributions, including those of
workers, to be invested not in health, but in the National Housing
Bank, whose mortgages are heavily funded by capital from the
national health service, INPS, and help to sustain the middle
and luxury housing sectors. Whilst it may be that de Oliveira
overestimates the contribution of marginal articulation to Brazilian
capital accumulation, the range of this articulation and its penetration of the overtly insulated world of the poor can hardly be
exaggerated.

Whilst this picture of the mechanisms of the transfer of surplus
from the marginal to the capitalist sector is fundamentally convincing, it is almost exclusively economic. One still has to ask,
from a structural viewpoint, what relations of production are
entailed in this demonstrable articulation of the labour of the
self-employed with the process of capital accumulation. The most
informative concept for these relations is petty commodity production: market-orientated enterprises on anything from a one
person to a family or workshop scale, whose owners also work as

producers. (15) Since we are referring to typically small and
usually family undertakings, it would perhaps be more accurate to
talk of restricted petty commodity production; this also brings
out their incapacity for achieving a level of internal accumulation
which would enable them to develop into capitalist enterprises,
instead of just reproducing themselves as petty commodity production. Together with the forms of involvement in the industrial
reserve army outlined by Quijano, this concept completes the
essential outline of the relations of production underlying urban
poverty as a feature of Brazilian growth.

Yet even this says very little about these relationships' social
dimensions. If there are two such sets of relations, are marginal
people a class in themselves, and if so, what are their social
relations of production? The fact is that whilst petty commodity
production and engagement in the reserve army are conceptually
and structurally distinct, they are empirically interwoven among
the urban poor in Bahia, and no doubt elsewhere. Since each is
inherently unstable, people tend to move between them, as is also
the case with analogous positions in the peasant sector. For
example, in Liberdade most seamstresses and market vendors of home-
made wares, both petty commodity producers, have worked for a spell
in one of the labour-intensive factories which have ringed the
bairro since its inception, producing foodstuffs and textiles with
a deliberately rapid turnover of young and mainly female workers.
Simultaneous combinations of the two types of relations occur in
very many low-income families, whose average number of workers
rose sharply in the last decade. One person may even combine a
low-paid job with some self-employment - sixteen hours is not an
exceptional working day for the 'under-employed' in Liberdade.
This, on the one hand, has interesting implications for a closer
class relationship between marginals and the proletariat than is
usually suggested; on the other, it does point to the formers'
empirical unity as a sub-proletariat and class in itself, since
its theoretically diverse relations of production are not just
similarly impoverishing, but also in practice overlapping.
'Reserve army' and 'petty commodity' producers are both abstract
categories rather than fixed social groups; in reality their
occupants combine and also move between them, as well as living
together and sharing the same social conditions, uncertainties and
evident interests arising from them.

To some extent at least, this determines the unity of the poor
as a class, and a class not simply by default of proletarian
characteristics, as 'sub-proletariat' might seem to imply, but
with an identity of its own. What then of its social relations
of production, which may not simply be given by its relations to
the means of production, but will provide the links between its
material conditions of existence and its popular culture, as
ideology reproducing its social relations? To answer this question
and trace these links, we have to return to Liberdade.

3   PATRONAGE AND PLURALISM: THE SOCIAL RELATIONS OF PRODUCTION,
THEIR IDEOLOGICAL EXPRESSIONS AND THEIR CONTEMPORARY TRANS-
FORMATIONS AMONG THE BAHIAN SUB-PROLETARIAT

It is precisely the combination of myriad forms of petty commodity
production and irregular wage labour in the industrial reserve
army which provides the hard-won livelihoods of some 100,000 people
in Liberdade's steep baixadas, narrow valleys each side of a
winding escarpment increasingly densely occupied by a generation
of land invasions. By most prevailing criteria - land titles,
amenities, housing standards and especially its dubious reputation
among gente bôa (respectable persons) - much of the bairro is
still a favela (shantytown), though many of its occupants have
won some security and comfort. In general its material and social
conditions are fairly typical of low-income urban areas in Northeastern Brazil and even beyond it. However, its particular history
is symptomatic of important changes in both the occupational
patterns and world-views of Bahia's sub-proletariat.
    Older low-income housing areas, established by emancipated and
mainly former domestic slaves from the mid-nineteenth century onwards, are closer to the city centre, in smaller valleys overlooked originally by baroque mansions, and now by luxury apartments.
Being small and close to the upper class whose wealth derived from
the sugar plantations, these older areas afforded an intimacy with
its members - material and ideological, as employers, customers
and general patrons - which supports the image of Northeastern
society purveyed by a succession of authors: one of patriarchal
symbiosis and ethno-cultural pluralism, only faintly acknowledged
as cushioning the social inequality and masking the economic gap
between the descendants of masters and slaves. (16)
    The birth of Liberdade was a major break with this social ecology
in ways almost unremarked by such authors. (17) The bairro bur-
geoned roughly a generation ago, as demographic pressure on the
older residential areas and the crumbling inner-city tenements of
the port and red-light districts led to overcrowding and rising
rents. This pressure was increased by immigrants from a largely
stagnant rural economy, as in most Northeastern cities. The
collective invasion of semi-abandoned private estates and public
land became the city's main form of growth, establishing much bigger
and homogeneously low-income bairros in a northerly direction,
where there was room for such expansion. Liberdade was the first
such bairro: it remains the largest and most densely populated,
and is generally recognised as the frontier of a now vast low-
income area. Its inhabitants value its distinctive history and
social identity and regard themselves as essentially urban. Many
were born in Liberdade and most in the city, as were their parents
and even grandparents in many cases.
    Occupationally they are subject to much the same structural
constraints as the rest of the low-income population: the scarcity
of stable wage employment and the insecurity and obstacles to the
expansion of self-employed activities, including petty commodity
production. Yet Liberdade's specific conditions are distinctly
conducive in either case to the less dependent, but generally more
arduous, intensive and productive forms of labour which cut across

these two categories. In contrast to the older bairros, most
wage-earners in Liberdade have all the basic attributes of the
industrial reserve army. They move on a typically short-term
basis between the large old local factories and employment in
services quite closely linked to production or productive workers,
in transport, retailing, and so on. Strictly personal service
employment is scarce, and whilst there is a variety of small
capitalist enterprises and workshops conducive to personal dependence on a patron/employer, these are less esteemed, because
of their insecurity, intensive labour and low pay, than the many
outlets which the bairro offers for self-employment, including
petty commodity production, whether individual or with equal
partners or family labour. On the other hand, in the older,
socially mixed areas most low wage-earners are in the inherently
clientelistic personal service occupations, as janitors, maids
and waiters and so on, depending often on tips and leftovers as
much as wages. So too with autonomous activities. Seamstresses
in these older areas usually count on the jealously guarded custom
of a handful of wealthy individuals, rather than outwork for larger
producers and/or retailers: yet in Liberdade the latter is typical,
alongside a wider and lower income, less profitable direct market
of near social equals. As well as making for a relatively independent, patron-free situation, this means that Liberdade's seamstresses have a necessarily higher output, and are correspondingly
subject to a high rate of self-exploitation. (Since their products
are less profitable, they must be produced on a larger scale in
order to secure their producers' subsistence, or the reproduction
of their own, effectively cheapened labour power.)
  There are corresponding differences attaching to most occupations, whether typically autonomous or wage-earning, for
mechanics, artisans, laundresses, street-vendors and so on. An
autonomous joiner or construction worker in Liberdade will be
moving mainly and of necessity rapidly between small jobs, since
these are poorly paid by his neighbours, the reproduction of whose
labour power for the capitalist sector is cheapened by this underpayment brought about by acute competition. On the other hand,
in the older areas he might work, and no doubt less arduously,
for one wealthy customer for weeks, and aspire to base his livelihood on three or four such reliable patrons, as they are invariably called by this marginal labour aristocracy. Similarly,
with regard to wage labour for the construction industry, it is
to bairros like Liberdade that the large enterprises look for the
reserve army typically subject to unpaid overtime, poor and
hazardous working conditions, withholding of wages, the dodging
of redundancy and social security payments, and so on. Again,
by contrast, a builder or joiner resident in the older areas,
even when working for a wage, will typically be doing so for a
personal employer, in circumstances whose effects are quite
similar to those of self-employment in such areas, with much the
same individual benefits to offset a lack of collective agreements.
  In all, what emerges is a distinction governed not by wage or
self-employment, the direct or indirect sale of labour power, so
much as by the different social relations which cut across these
categories, yet still have important material correlations. The

less personalised sale of labour power in the newer areas tends
also to be much more intensive and productive in a number of senses:
the production of commodities rather than services; the production
of either for productive rather than unproductive workers; and
finally, production for other units of production rather than
individual consumers. All these are only tendencies, but strong
ones; and whilst quantitatively they signify a greater intensity
of labour, qualitatively they also entail an increasing degree of
articulation with the capitalist sector, which is also an increasing involvement with the production of surplus value, directly
in the reserve army and indirectly through petty commodity production. Since both of these are confined to the employment
situations typical of Liberdade, there are strong grounds for
suggesting a different class division within the poor, between
those who are articulated either way with the capitalist sector,
and thus a sub-proletariat, and those who are not, and might therefore be classified as the 'traditional urban poor' - an unusually
large, though relatively diminishing group in Bahia, because of
its particular social history. Whether one sees this as a distinction between two classes or fractions of a single class depends
on the relative weight one gives, within a materialist perspective,
to economic and other factors in the determination of class in
cases like this, where the former are fluid; and this must surely
hang on which option throws more light on the social process. In
this respect it will be suggested that in fact all sections of the
urban poor are socially articulated predominantly through ideology,
and that in this sphere, unlike that of production, its traditional
and newer sections are dialectically related; on these grounds
they are seen as *old* and *new* fractions of the sub-proletariat,
rather than strictly separate classes. First, though, their contrasting social relations of production, which give rise to this
dialectic in ideology and popular culture, need some further
illustration.

In effect this social contrast hinges on the comparative degree
of personalised dependence through direct inter-class relations,
which is relatively low in situations typical of Liberdade. For
instance, an out-of-work family in the older, socially mixed
bairros would look typically for domestic employment with nearby
wealthy potential patrons. In Liberdade and beyond, the obvious
strategy for survival would be rubbish-picking or the collection
of industrial waste for use as slum building material or sale to
a recycling business. The correspondence with the contrasting
economic and social factors distinguishing the *old* and *new* fractions
of the sub-proletariat is easily apparent. Or take what is probably
its largest occupational group, the thousands of food producers
and vendors. Most of those living in Liberdade sell outside the
bairro to relatively anonymous customers in the centre of the lower
city around the docks and offices, at factory gates, or in the
huge Agua de Meninos market serving the northern, low-income end
of Bahia. Where their relations with customers are regular and
personal, they are relatively intra-class and often established
through neighbours working in such settings. A typical instance
is that of the women who have spent much of their lives selling
foodstuffs on the waterfront to dockers waiting for their shifts,

who sheltered them from the protection rackets operated by the
police. Both tend to have come from Liberdade, and it is no
coincidence that in days gone by political journals like *O Momento*
(the Communist Party's) were sold alongside their Bahian sweet-
meats.

In the older areas the social content of such relations between
vendor and customer is radically different. Here success depends
not so much on the volume of production and cheap sales, as on
competition for a well-placed corner where the same wealthy customers pass each day and pay twice the Agua de Meninos price in
return for a respectful personal greeting. Again we find the
same correlations between relatively articulated, productive and
intensive labour and interaction with social equals, in contrast
to their linked opposites, economic and social, in the older areas.
In the event of the vendors' failure and the search for employment
in the wage sector, the contrasts would tend to be sustained:
Liberdade's vendor is most likely to work in a cheap local res-
taurant, and her counterpart from the older area in domestic
service, quite possibly with a former customer. And so on, with
mobility tending to occur within as opposed to between these two
basic fractions.

The fact that the distinction between them is also historical
and dynamic suggests an obvious social tension. The spatial expansion of Liberdade and beyond expresses not just a quantitative
growth of the sub-proletariat, but a concomitant qualitative transformation of its labour into the more articulated, productive
channels characterising the new fraction. At the same time the
direct inter-class relations and accompanying clientelistic values
with their ethno-cultural underpinning, which cushioned inequality
traditionally, are clearly weakening. What replaced them as a
source of the sub-proletariat's view of its position in society?
The obvious answer in Brazil is populism, the state's assumption
of the symbiotic paternalism traditionally vested in class relations and operative at the economic, political and ideological
levels. However, populism's impact on the new sub-proletariat is
structurally restricted by its members' lack of incorporation
into the stable working class and the institutions to which this
is subject, particularly the trades unions controlled by the
Ministry of Labour. With regard to the urban poor, its economic
and political levels must operate not through productive relations
so much as those of distribution - through the clientelistic
politics of all aspects of the social wage, from schooling to
drainage and health facilities. Such issues, playing off one
neighbourhood against another in the competition for scarce resources, are the stuff of the clientelistic politics of Liberdade
and similar bairros. Yet even within this restricted sphere of
the economic and political there has obviously been a severe contraction: whilst the sub-proletariat has been growing, the model
of accumulation has reduced the proportion of GNP expended on such
social items. (18) For these structural reasons having to do with
the nature of the sub-proletariat and the model of accumulation,
ideology must have an increasing role in this class's social articulation, unless one takes the simplistic view that this is achieved
by sheer repression. The question then is: what ideology and how

does it work, above all how effectively, in the face of these transformations and tensions?

There are rather few guidelines for any such empirical analysis of ideology, and virtually none for this social context. Perhaps the best known is Althusser's notion of ideological state apparatuses, a rather mysterious term quite simply for ideological institutions, with the added implication that those which are formally of civil society are in fact increasingly state-directed. (19) (An obvious example would be the British trades unions in the context of the social contract of the 1970s.) This tendency for the state to assume the direction of ideology is in fact occurring in Bahia, and will soon be illustrated. But what of the 'apparatuses'? Those Althusser cites - trades unions, the church, education, the media and so on - are clearly metropolitan-centred. The Bahian sub-proletariat has relatively little access to them, by reason of its class position, both in terms of production (e.g., the trades unions) and distribution (its limited contact with most of the media, and the relatively scant provision of education and even churches). In fact, the institutional contexts in which the poor tend to aggregate are governed, like their social relations, by largely residential factors. Although there are associations of the self-employed (for instance, street vendors) their scope is restricted; neighbourhood associations are typically much more of the politics of redistributive populism with which they were mainly associated. The types of institution which are congruent, above all others, with the class and the times are the possession cults and samba schools and less institutionalised phenomena like language and concepts of social history: in short, all aspects of popular culture.

There is a deeper question about this simple way of looking at ideology through institutions. It is plainly not the way of Marx in *Capital*, where it is not institutions but the themes whereby actors are defined as subjects which are the stuff of ideology: (20) what Althusser calls the 'interpellations' (the 'hailing mechanisms' or in-built idioms of social relations), a concept which Laclau has used effectively to analyse both fascism and Latin-American populism. (21) In such mainstream contexts the idioms involved - the national question, or that of popular democracy - are relatively universal. Those amongst the sub-proletariat of peripheral capitalist formations are likely to be less apparent, and obviously very different from those imputed to capitalist relations, which run like veins through *Capital* - the tendency for relations between persons to appear as relations between things (a fair day's wage for a fair day's work) established by contractual equals (i.e. capital and labour). On the contrary, the social relations of the poor in Bahia are traditionally highly personalised, as the patron-client literature, however theoretically weak, bears accurate empirical witness. (22) Moreover, rather than being ideologically equated, the parties involved are actively differentiated by the implication that their different traditions - the modern culture and the sub-culture of the poor, in this case the Afro-Brazilian one so emphasised in the literature - explain their different situations: in short, through the notion of

pluralism. It is therefore the double interpellation of dependence
and cultural ethnicity, as the building blocks of the social
relations of patronage and pluralism, which has been the ideological basis of the whole historical gamut of Brazil's non-
capitalist relations, from slavery to modern marginality.

However much weakening there may now be of the social contexts
which nourish these themes, they certainly form the raw material
of how the poor have traditionally lived their wider relations.
They have clearly had to construct their world on a largely clientelistic basis, not, as conventionally implied, because this is
the inherent way that 'lower-class' Brazilians think, within an
'essentially rural sub-culture' (Wagley); but because their material
constraints and persistently limited opportunities have made such
relations a way of survival which fostered patterns of thought and
expression contributing to their reproduction. Similarly, ethno-
cultural pluralism is a reality in Brazil, to the extent that the
labour market has always been somewhat ethnically structured,
particularly in the coastal Northeast and at the margins of
capitalism - traditionally among slaves and peasants and more
recently in the low-income urban sector. Quite simply, ethnic
identity and poverty still coincide sufficiently for this correlation to enter from 'lived' into 'thought' relations, ideology
and culture. If Brazilian whites are by no means exempt from
poverty, non-whites are near assured of it, a situation germinated
by Portuguese colonialism and black slave labour, sustained by
Brazil's South/North correlation of development/under-development
with a largely white/non-white population, and reinforced increasingly by discrimination over employment. (23) Add to this the persistence of ethnic sub-cultures (for historical reasons discussed
below), and ethno-cultural pluralism interweaves with traditionally
personalised dependence as the living core of social relations, not
merely a descriptive cliché or ideological fabrication. Indeed,
their ideological effectiveness hinges on their correspondence to
the real, if subjective forms of the structural relations which
they obscure, the client's yielding of surplus (seen as his dependence on favours) and the Afro-Brazilian's articulation in terms
of relations of production (seen as sub-cultural non-integration).
Through these forms of appearance the sub-proletariat still lives
its contradictions with capital as the interdependence of individuals distinguished by their respective sub-cultures; and in
some degree such forms remain real to all parties to them,
exploiters as well as the exploited. Ideology builds on substance,
not fancy: on its victims' own reproduction of it, through a
process of selective perception, and not on inventive manipulation.

Obviously this paradigm of ethno-cultural dependence is built
on factors originally common to most colonial situations: the
concentration of economic, social and political power along substantially ethnic lines and resting on largely non-capitalist
relations. (24) Why then has it had such special prominence in
Brazilian social history, to the extent that the tensions within
it are still the core of popular culture? Brazil's rural patriarchalism has plainly furnished the precedents for the sub-proletariat's social dependence, though this continuity is not so much
at the cultural level as at the level of material conditions whose

renewal in cities reproduces originally rural forms of relations and associated ways of thinking. Job scarcity and restricted markets for the self-employed in the urban Northeast are fore-shadowed by the concentration of land and merchant capital which has always obliged the agrarian poor to serve as the basis of coronelismo, the politics of the rural bosses, historically rooted in their remoteness from a weak colonial and post-colonial state apparatus, which devolved so much of its power to them. (25) Both economically and politically the objective roots of these patterns persist and have arguably become even stronger in a contemporary urban context. Economically, in that both employment and self-employment depend so often on building submissive personal ties with the relatively powerful - employers, foremen, customers, the police who control street-vendors, and so on - in competition with others engaged in the same struggle for survival, and typically by sacrificing their few collective social gains like the right to social security payments. Politically, in that the military regime has reconcentrated local power in the hands of the tra-ditional few, so that they and their agents still control the poor's scant outlets, like education, to a remarkable degree, and on an essentially patronage basis. In such circumstances, escape from dependent patterns of thought is as much of a break with material constraints as were peasant migrations or social banditry within traditional rural structures.

Why, though, should this dependence have the ethno-cultural dimension which is equally central in popular culture? To some extent the two themes are even contradictory, since personal dependence cuts across and fragments class identity, whilst, as already pointed out, ethnicity runs parallel to it. The effect of this is not so much to reinforce class as translate it into other terms, enabling dependence to expand into a wider relation-ship between culturally distinguished groups, in addition to one between individuals. Moreover, when the ethnicity is further differentiated into its own sub-categories, such as tribal ones (the 'nations' within the Afro-Brazilian), this compounds the frag-menting effect of personal dependence. (26) However complex in the abstract, this structuring of the perception of social re-lations runs quite smoothly within an institutional framework such as that of candomblé, much as a complex piece of machinery needs only a switch to set it in motion. What is it, though, in Brazilian history which makes this ethnicity so central?

Its sheer components are obviously a relatively contingent matter of the multi-racial origins of the Brazilian population, reinforced by such facts as the high mortality among slaves, necessitating the constant import of replacements from Africa until well into the nineteenth century. (27) However, none of this explains the social role which ethnicity played, as opposed to the potential for it. For this one has to look back again at the weakness of its state apparatus within the political economy of Luso-Brazilian colonialism. The latter could simply never afford to develop a strongly coercive state, with what little it retained of a surplus which accumulated mainly in Britain, as the dominant metropolitan economy. Whilst this meant that power was devolved to landowners, it also left them dependent on their

own quite limited resources for the complex task of social control
in what was the first colonial economy based directly on production,
as opposed to trade or plunder. Thus even in Brazilian slavery,
co-optive and divisive as opposed to coercive mechanisms were im-
perative: cultural ethnicity simply provided a ready raw material
for them. Hence, instead of suppressing ethnic distinctions among
African slaves, as did the much stronger colonial British, the
Portuguese and Brazilian masters tended to manipulate them. For
instance field slaves, imported mainly from Angola, were of predominantly Bantu descent, while groups selected apparently for their
more cohesive socio-political and cultural backgrounds, notably
the Yoruba, were drawn into the more privileged and fragmented
spheres of domestic slavery, crafts and overseeing, etc. (28) It
was such status, with its prospects of emancipation, which involved
some slaves in the symbiosis with the planter's big house (casa
grande), idealised by Gilberto Freyre. Here, it seems, they quite
often informed on discontent among the field hands and served as
models of deference and its rewards. (29)

The history of the quilombos, communities of runaway slaves
which were a constant colonial nightmare, illustrates this ethnic
mechanism and also confirms its material basis. Suppression of
them was an economic as much as a military problem: it often took
years to raise troops for the purpose. Moreover, the quilombos'
make-up was clearly predominantly Bantu. Finally the troops,
once raised, were of deliberately Indian rather than black composition, not so much for knowledge of the terrain (since they
were mainly supplied from São Paulo), but explicitly to avert the
danger of any sense of identity between the troops and quilombeiros.
To this day the folk drama depicting the end of the most famous
quilombo, Palmares, assumes the form of a ritual conflict between
an Indian and Ganga-Zumba, its black leader, a living symbol of
the ethno-cultural divide and rule of Luso-Brazilian colonialism.
(30) Correspondingly, when this collapsed and black and Indian
and caboclo (in both the ethnic and social senses) united in the
rural revolts which swept Pará and Maranhão in the nineteenth
century, the colonial power structure crumbled - not least because
of the local planters' contravention of pluralism, in having used
unique combinations of black slave and Indian forced labour. (31)

It is much the same dialectic between ethno-cultural and social
identity which has filtered through time and into the cities to
shape the spectrum of popular culture mirrored in Omulú's transformations from orixá into caboclo. Though distinctive Afro-
Brazilian sub-cultures have by now almost withered at the roots,
they were still an overt consideration in urban social policy in
both Bahia and Recife in the emancipation period and on into the
twentieth century. We find a governor of Bahia deciding to
tolerate candomblé explicitly as a source of division between the
various African 'nations' (sub-cultures like Yoruba and so on) with
which the traditional candomblés are to this day associated. They
were, he wrote, a crucial defence against the cohesion and consequent dangers of social unrest among the black urban population.
(32) In Recife craft guilds were organised on the basis of nations
and pitted one against the other, at this same juncture of the
transition from slave relations of production to the incipient

formation of a free urban labour market. (33) So, too, in
Liberdade, older people still recall how festivals of the Kings
of the Congo, a Bantu grouping, were patronised by local landowners right up to the time of its invasion and occupation as a
low-income bairro, scarcely a generation ago.

No doubt this cultivation of such complex forms of pluralism
was accentuated in Bahia, as the first city to pose the problem
of a growing, newly emancipated low income urban population.
Ethnicity also played a perceptible ideological role in the
formation and expansion of a national labour market. When in the
1930s the Northeast became the labour pool, in effect the regional
reserve army of an industrialising South, the symbiotic antithesis
of the (Euro-) Brazilian and Afro-Brazilian, as a form of appearance of social relations between labour and capital, moved South
with the Bahian migrants into a national ideology. The genius of
this transformation was, of course, Gilberto Freyre, whose theme
of 'the Negro's contribution to Brazilian society' (34) helped to
mediate the contradiction between this new influx of mainly black
labour and the South's traditional racism (the philosophy of
branqueamento, or the 'whitening' of the population through European
immigration). However much Freyre's writing was about Northeastern
social history, its institutionalisation belonged to the ideological management of a new set of social relations emerging in
a national context, and evident in other ways at the level of
popular consumption: for instance, in a 1937 regulation of the Rio
de Janeiro tourist department that each of the carnival samba
schools from the new worker-migrant bairros should have a section
of Bahianas, women in the Afro-Brazilian dress of Bahia's traditional sweetmeat sellers, (35) an ethno-cultural insertion into
a new sub-proletarian culture.

At this structural-historical boundary between pre-capitalist
relations, an industrial reserve army and a new working class in
the making, a tension appears in the operation of this ethno-
cultural ideology, which is also apparent in Freyre's work. On
the one hand it is playing the new role of indigenismo and
negritude in other peripheral capitalist societies, as the integrative interpellation of an expanding capitalism, with a message
of national identity in place of class antagonisms: hence Freyre's
integrative theme of 'The Negro's contribution to Brazilian society',
or rather, society's adoption of it. On the other hand, its
effective object (the black low-income population) remains very
much of a reserve army and marginal mass whose apartness demands
an ethno-cultural form of appearance. The ideological 'Negro' must
remain just that, and wear the mask of the Afro-Brazilian exposition of his position in society. Hence the tension in both
Freyre's work and the ideological apparatus, between the theme
of *racial democracy* on the one hand, with social mobility for
blacks and a unified Brazilian culture, and *racial harmony* on
the other, with an Afro-Brazilian sub-culture as the mask of social
inequality and an element of the reproduction of partly non-
capitalist relations.

There is no such tension in the capitalist sphere's appropriation
of the dependent interpellation, as the key to the populist reproduction of a generation of capitalist relations. Collective

dependence on the state apparatus involves no logical opposition
to dependence on traditional, personal patrons, whereas despite
its synthetic label, it is hard for Afro-Brazilian culture to be
both *Afro* and *Brazilian*, a simultaneous assertion of both the
apartness and integration of a low-income population. A contradiction of this kind is apparent in one of Bahia's most public
symbols, the famous caboclo of independence, a movable statue
housed in a chapel painted a strident yellow and green (the
Brazilian national colours) in the Praça de Lapinha, a little way
short of Liberdade. Each year on Independence Day, 2 July, the
caboclo leads a procession not in Liberdade's direction, of course,
but to the central Campo Grande. Initially he constitutes an
integrative national symbol of the union of Luso-Brazilian and
Indian against the Portuguese oppressor: in short, a negation of
pluralism, asserting a single Brazilianism. Yet, as we have seen,
this pluralism is integral to the management of Brazil's non-
capitalist relations and general social inequality. Hence the
actual figure of the caboclo who makes his way to Campo Grande is
not in fact that of the social caboclo, Brazilian peasant man,
potentially expressive of the inequality among Brazilians: on the
contrary, he is a full-blooded, thoroughly ethno-cultural Tupi
Indian, complete with feathers and bow and arrow. In this one
can see how ethnicity as a sub-cultural interpellation, rather than
an integrative one, has regained its original importance, and for
a very simple reason: the growth of the new sub-proletariat, whose
cultural dialectics subvert the traditionally dominant imagery of
its social relations of production, transforming orixás and Indians
from dependent ethno-cultural into autonomous social symbols, much
closer to a reality which to some extent they also challenge.
The workings of this dialectic can now be examined in greater
detail.

4   DOMINANT AND POPULAR IDEOLOGIES: THE SOCIAL RELATIONS OF
    PRODUCTION AND THE DIALECTICS OF POPULAR CULTURE

Dependence and autonomy as alternative interpellations: language,
social history and samba

In as much as ideology is rooted in the elements of people's
everyday lived relations, it is inherently volatile. As transformations and contradictions of the kind already outlined develop -
the changed relations and material conditions of the *new* sub-
proletariat - such people are very liable to subvert any dominant
interpellation, perhaps all the more elaborately when, by reason
of their class character, their interests are not easily translated
into social action. The popular culture of Liberdade revolves
around such dialectics. In brief, the dependent interpellation
is transformed into one of autonomy, whilst the ethnicity within
it revolves on its semantic axis, assuming a dynamic social instead
of a static cultural meaning. Though they interweave, the first
transformation will be the main theme of the present section, while
the second is central to the section which follows.
    These dialectics are not just a matter of starkly opposing sets

of symbols. In the case of Omulú, for instance, his cultural
ethnicity as an orixá and his social ethnicity among the caboclos,
associated respectively with dependence and autonomy and a host
of other connotations, are not exclusive alternatives of which
one is present and the other absent in any given manifestation,
or case of possession. Rather they constitute a spectrum on which
any particular manifestation has a position of its own; and even
this will be uncertain, since the very associations involved are
ideologically disputed. There will be a constant tendency for
the dominant ideology to appropriate the caboclo symbol and imbue
it with a cultural meaning, and conversely for the popular one
to socialise the orixás, as illustrated by the arrow in Figure 4.2.
The structural consistency lies not in the distribution of forms,
which only tend to have certain meanings: but in the dialectic
itself, as one between the reproduction and rupture, through all
available symbols, of the social relations of production.

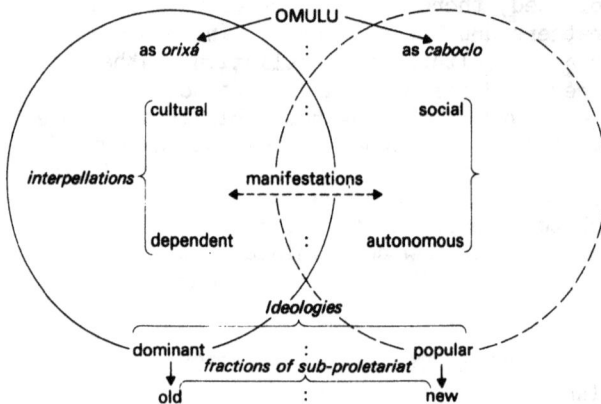

FIGURE 4.2

Correspondingly, this dialectic knows no institutional boundaries. Rooted as it is in the structure of relations, it is
also the implicit weave of the whole range of popular culture, and
no less so in instances which do not immediately afford opposing
sets of cultural symbols. Before looking at its operation within
specific institutions, this dialectic's ubiquity and independence
of cultural forms can be illustrated from a central item in the
language and the conceptualisation of social history in Liberdade:
the name itself. Officially it commemorates the emancipation of
Brazilian slaves by the Empress Dona Isabel (though other sources
associate it with Brazil's independence from Portugal much earlier
in the nineteenth century). However, some local people say that
the popular use of the name is older and has quite different
connotations: that the original Liberdade was a quilombo, or a

secret route to one, hidden deep in the then thickly wooded baixadas now crammed with makeshift low-income housing. Thus the word most central to people's daily existence is a battle-ground for the meanings of history, in which the twin themes of patronage and pluralism, with their respective dominant inter-pellations of dependence and cultural ethnicity, are both inter-woven and inverted: on the one hand a freedom given from above, on the other a freedom taken from below; a gesture of paternalism steeped in ethnic symbiosis as against an act of collective defiance by slaves towards their rejected masters.

In some sense this battle between a dominant, ruling-class history and an autonomous popular one is Brazilian culture's central theme, from candomblé to academia, not for the sake of history as such, but as an allegorical debate on the nature of present-day social relations. Thus for the present the official version of the origin of Liberdade carries the implicit connotation that it is modern state largesse in the Dona Isabel tradition which has shaped the bairro, paved its streets and provided the drains and schools, however few, and other facilities which are the stuff of Liberdade's official history and of the local politics permitted by the military. The popular interpretation of Liberdade tends on the contrary to be linked in conversation with an ethos of shared independence, with 'living in our own social style' in this socially homogeneous setting, compared to that of the older bairros: 'aqui temos uma vida propria' ('we can live a life of our own here'). Equally there is the connotation of having won the means to do so, mainly through the land invasions led by the older generation of dockers, small retailers and so on: 'ganhámos este bairro na raça. Fizemos esta rua aqui com nossas mãos'. ('We fought our own battle for this bairro. We made this street with our own hands'.) And detailed descriptions of the invasions usually follow: of how people moved in together at night, and measured house lots and future streets and fought off the police on the following morning, to create their own conditions of existence.

The question of which origin of the actual name of Liberdade is *historically valid* has little meaning. In this sense, ideology permits no history. The ideological apparatus - official records, the local schools and press and so on - preserves or rather produces and reproduces one class history, popular consciousness another. Their interest lies less in the doubtful prospect of sifting truth from ideology than in the contemporary conditions which make for two modes of thinking about the past, and their implications for present relations.

This dialectic is constant in the linguistic structuring of history at a quite everyday, popular level. In some cases it does involve opposing signs, in this context words, as distinct from one sign like *Liberdade* which points in two opposed directions. For instance, slaves in the dominant history featuring Dona Isabel are called escravos. However, among older people, often talking of relatives whom they knew, they are usually called cativos (captives). On the one hand, an absolute social status; on the other, an imposed condition, semantically pervaded by the impli-cation of its opposite, freedom. Elements of this dialectic

between dependence and autonomy still enter into the experience
of even the children of Liberdade, whose ties with this past
are becoming extended, since street names echo an alternative
history. Most of those on the official maps, which few of them
will ever see, commemorate the politician who legalised or
temporarily paved them; but those in colloquial use are quite
different, commemorating the street's first invader or aspects of
everyday social life, often with a vein of irony. Rua do Ceu
(Sky Street), for instance, is almost the lowest baixada of all,
notorious for the number of times that the mud has replaced its
electoral paving. The main street up on the escarpment even has
a name plaque to its credit, Lima e Silva, in honour of a nineteenth century statesman. Yet this is still known locally as
Estrada da Liberdade (Freedom Road).

This sociology of popular language has been surprisingly
neglected in peripheral capitalist formations, where the multiplicity of language sources, their correlations with social
structure and the natural fluidity of a mainly oral as opposed to
written language, combine to make it a touchstone of how its users
structure and re-structure the social world around them. Bahian
popular greetings are another example of this process. Many terms
of pejorative value in their originally inter-class context are
used to a contrary effect between social equals, undermining the
dominant values previously implicit in them. Thus bandido (bandit
or scoundrel), vagabundo (idler), malandro (wrong-doer) and even
descarado (shameless) are standard ruling-class epithets for those
who forget their place in society by failing to pay the respects
entailed in their ideologically dependent status. However, they
are also used as clearly affectionate intra-class greetings within
sections of the sub-proletariat most often subjected to them as
insults, like those who make a precarious but autonomous living
minding cars in the city centre, through inter-class but irregular
and potentially conflictive relations. The degree of social
consciousness in such usages is indeterminable, precisely because
they are merely expressive. They are, though, indisputably class
reappropriations of language, defying the dominant ideology. The
attachment of positive values to these terms does logically imply
that one man's or class's 'banditry' is another's reappropriation
of the surplus appropriated from him; that the vagabundo's 'idle-
ness' is a commendable withholding of underpaid labour; that it is
desirable to adopt alternative behaviour patterns (descarado,
malandro, and so on), which are seen by social superiors as a
rejection of the dependence identified here as integral to the
social relations of production.

One scarcely has to demonstrate a popular science of linguistics
to see such usages as a challenge to the dominant order and ideology, substantially rooted in shared material and social conditions. Moreover, one can often see in such contexts the interweaving and the dialectics of both the central interpellations.
Descarado, used either way, tends strongly to be linked with the
word negro; when one type of interpellation weakens, the other
tends to weaken with it. Hence negro in this context of association with descarado, as an inter-class insult, strips ethnicity
of its cultural and symbiotic implications, by locating it within

a new, antagonistic social setting. Inversely, as an affectionate
greeting, it lends this same ethnicity a cohesive intra-class
social value. This metamorphosis of dependent cultural into autonomous social ethnicity - an interpellation which reiterates the
social boundaries it previously masked - is implicit in less restricted phrases like 'na raça', used above in the context of Liberdade's invasions. Meaning literally 'in the race', its effective
translation would be something like 'struggling against the odds
together', and this without limits being imposed, by its ethnic
etymology, on its power to express a purely social and embryo-
nically class solidarity. For the rulers as much as the ruled,
ideology is a bazardous business.

It is, however, a two-way battle, fought from above as well as
below. The dominant ideology is not just present but actively
present, renewing itself and recolonising the very images which
negate it. As Sinhô, one of the best known composers of popular
sambas once observed: 'The samba is like a little bird. It belongs
to whoever catches it'. (36) Whilst this co-optive capacity of
the dominant ideology could also be shown in connection with
language, it is most apparent in the areas of popular culture based
on formal institutions, of which candomblés and the samba schools
of carnival are two of Bahia's outstanding examples. As juridical
institutions, they are directly accessible to the ideological
apparatus, with concrete needs and a corporate existence which
make them relatively easy either to patronise or coerce, through
formal or informal sactions. Moreover, the depth of consistency
in the membership and cultural content of each type of institution
enables one to correlate them and test their concomitant variations.
The extent and composition of their membership is also important.
Most candomblés and all samba schools are strongly rooted in
particular bairros; their composition is similarly sub-proletarian,
yet complementary, as participation in samba schools is predominantly young and male, whilst that in candomblés is largely
though not exclusively female, and typically lasts for life. In
Bahia, with its population of just over a million, there are some
twenty samba schools and twice that number of carnival groups with
slightly different characteristics (most of them are known as
blocks), but basically similar tendencies. The number of candomblés is usually put at well over a thousand. In Liberdade alone
there are over a hundred, in contrast to a single Catholic and two
or three small Protestant churches; perhaps half the population
is at least occasionally involved with them in one way or another.
The two institutions are also complementary for an analysis of
ideology. Whilst both illustrate the interweaving of dependence
and ethnicity and their related dialectics, the former is arguably
the key to the workings of the samba schools and the latter to
that of candomblés. Through them one can therefore see structurally
analogous tensions in their respective interpellations; their
connections with the transformation of the social relations of
production; and finally their implications for the sub-proletariat's
class nature.

For all their seeming spontaneity, the samba schools and all
carnival groups are subject to a degree of control whose stringency
suggests the importance attached to such cultural institutions.

It is also symptomatic of the increasing autonomy of the Brazilian
state apparatus, as its agencies such as the police and departments
of information and tourism take over the patronage and control
once vested largely in upper-class patrons. Whilst this is particularly marked in Bahia, the general increase of control is
common to most Brazilian cities, as carnival groups proliferate
among their growing sub-proletariat. These restrictions obviously
limit the independent self-expression inherent in such institutions.
Moreover, the incentives offered, and their associated conditions,
immediately pose the choice of whether or not to make the most
of what little autonomy is permitted. Not surprisingly, the outcome varies from one samba school to another; such variations are
closely consistent not just with each other but also with wider
social factors, and have in some cases reached the point of open
conflict with the 'system'.

First, the latter needs outlining. Though not restricted to
carnival, the life of samba schools revolves around its competition
(concurso) for the best samba de enredo (samba with a theme). This
comprises a song accompanied by an orchestra (bateria) led by
drummers (batuqueiros) and an elaborate choreography: special dance
steps and visual effects, especially costumes and a float relating,
sometimes a trifle obscurely, to the enredo. The concurso takes
place on a platform (palanque) in the main square, with a bank of
sheltered seats on one side whose price restricts them to wealthy
spectators. Others throng the square all round it, and have some
difficulty in seeing. By law each participant samba school must
be juridically constituted, with statutes and named office holders,
and registered with the police and the tourist department. This
runs the concurso, nominating a panel of judges from a local and
visiting cultural elite, whose knowledge of popular samba is slight
and thus mediated by the department. (The wealthy celebrate
carnival mainly in exclusive clubs. Whilst some middle-class
bairros have carnival blocks, these are aesthetically unambitious
and often hire batuqueiros from the low-income samba schools).

Each samba de enredo must be approved by the police and the
tourist department, and under federal legislation dating from the
1930s, its theme must deal with national history. (37) Whilst in
Rio this has led to bald reproductions of recent government propaganda, the commonest Bahian themes are those of the remoter past:
the casa grande or master's big house on the traditional sugar
plantation, emancipation, Brazilian independence, and so on. The
samba schools are divided into two separate leagues, according to
their size and resources. Although the section of Bahiana dancers
in traditional Afro-Brazilian costume is not formally required in
Bahia, the first league samba schools often include it. The
subsidies and prizes provided by the tourist department are not
a serious incentive, as they are small and usually late, if paid
at all. The real rewards are the publicity and status attaching
to winning the concurso, and consequent contracts to play in
night-clubs, or subsidised appearances on official occasions such
as presidential visits to Bahia.

The poles of Bahia's samba spectrum within this structure of
control are symbolised by the respective names of the two major
samba schools which gradually came to represent them in the popular

imagination: the Ritmistas (Rhythm-makers) and Diplomatas (Diplo-
mats). The former are something of a legend for their musical
originality and their social independence, while the Diplomatas
are a byword for conventional success. The Ritmistas were the
first in the still unwritten history of Bahia's samba schools.
Though the traditional samba de roda (samba in a circle), with
its improvisation of popular themes, was mainly northeastern,
especially Bahian and in origin Bantu, the samba schools as such
developed among the northeastern migrants to Rio. They reached
Bahia in the 1950s, preceded by an omen recorded by the local
daily A Tarde (38). 'One of the most popular turn-outs in this
year's carnival is the "Nega Maluca". With their followers all
round them, they filled the Rua Chile, scaring many good citizens',
(amedrontando a muita gente bôa). An element of class confrontation had come to the city's carnival, previously dominated by
the lavish floats and charity balls of the upper-class clubs and
societies. It was out of the Nega Maluca (literally, Crazy Black
Girl), initially based in Preguiça (Laziness, a notorious part
of the red-light zone), that the Ritmistas later developed. If
their earlier name reflects their rather particular roots in the
lumpenproletariat, the one they adopted expresses their wiser
incarnation of samba values.

For a while they were official champions of the newly instituted
concurso (this in the period of transition from populist to military
rule in the early to mid-1960s), and they long continued so un-
officially, in the popular estimation. This was not just for the
musical skill which they had so much time and imagination to
develop, but also for the satire and anti-social connotations
of which they were almost equally proud. It was well known that
many of them, thinly disguised and screened by their colleagues,
were wanted by the local police. That they rarely played without
the use of marijuana, known amongst them by its Bantu origin name,
liamba. That their choreography, like their inverted terms of
address (bandido, malandro and so on) exploited their own social
image to subvert the ideological effects of official samba regulations. One of their carnival floats, for instance, included a
map of South America with Brazil in patriotic colours, but somewhat
smaller than Uruguay. On being advised of their mistake, they
attributed it to their alleged illiteracy. This satire was specifically anarchistic. When left-wing students tried to politicise
the Ritmistas' sambas, they would have none of it, seeing this as
entreguismo, selling out to an alien language. The essence of
the golpe (coup), as they called it, was a satire so disingenuous
that it could be played to its actual targets - the local authorities, panel of judges and paying spectators at the palanque -
without their being able to censure or sometimes even understand
it, whilst the crowd in the square did so quite clearly.

However, the official fortunes of the Ritmistas changed. Often
disqualified for breaking the rules, although this lost them little
sleep, they were ousted by 'softer' samba schools, an epithet employed by all parties. These developed in the older low-income
areas, and were largely financed by their residential and working
contacts with upper-class families, and increasingly with politicians. In many cases these patrons became honorary or even

active members of these samba schools' diretorias (management committees). In the late 1960s and early 1970s, the concurso came to be dominated by the largest of them, the Diplomatas de Amaralina. The latter is a bairro which, though relatively big and new, has been settled mainly by people removed from the older ones by the expansion of luxury housing. Physically apart from the main area of low-income residential expansion, it combines a traditional with a new brand of clientelism. It was lotted and is still largely owned by a single landlord, Amaral, who is the Diplomatas' president and virtually appoints its diretoria. In addition, Amaralina is next to the local army barracks. Socially it is therefore much closer, in significantly modern ways, to the traditional low-income bairros of the old sub-proletariat than to the independent new ones formed by invasions, like Liberdade. The Diplomatas' relations reflect this. Sergeants from the neighbouring barracks liaised with the landlord-president to provide the samba school with a large and well-lit sede (rehearsal centre), plus instruments and amplification, and sambas, costumes and choreography usually commissioned in Rio. Their claim to fame, above all, was their luxo (the richness of their dramatic props), of a kind which had never been seen in Bahia.

This basis in such different fractions and associated social networks of the sub-proletariat was starkly apparent in the Ritmistas' and Diplomatas' samba styles. It also emerged in their contrasting attitudes to the official concurso, in their internal organisation, relations with other samba schools and with the general samba public. The Ritmistas became openly contemptuous of the concurso. On one occasion they diverged from their approved samba text and from any pretence at compliance with *history*, to suggest that black Bahians were still slaves; they then left the palanque to play their way through popular acclaim to Preguiça. They were, of course, disqualified. Subsequently most of their carnival outings took place in this zone, with occasional charismatic visits to low-income bairros like Liberdade and their smaller samba schools, which some of the Ritmistas joined when they later drifted apart in the 1970s. Only one or two of them succumbed to the Diplomatas' policy of wooing the best batuqueiros from samba schools outside their bairro. For them the transformation was total, since the Diplomatas focused more exclusively than any other first league samba school on the concurso and palanque. They made no exchange visits to samba schools in other bairros, regarding them strictly as rivals. Their playing style was equally different, an exhibition as against the Ritmistas' charismatic invitation to popular involvement. They marched in carefully ordered ranks, with soloists prominently displayed and their supporters behind and apart from the enredo; the Ritmistas, on the other hand, moved down the pulsing avenues in a bunch reminiscent of samba de roda, with their followers milling round them and spectators often joining in.

These contrasts began in their rehearsals. Here the Ritmistas sat composing sambas de sotaque (homespun sambas, literally 'with an accent'), improvised satires and comments on life akin once more to sambas de roda. The Diplomatas, however, were subject to almost military discipline, as their authoritarian diretoria

instilled the melody and often unfamiliar words of their commissioned samba de enredo on some textbook figure of national
history such as Dona Isabel, which few of them ever understood
fully. Such figures were much less prominent in the Ritmistas'
sambas de enredo, which tended to represent a mass history, in
a casual, bucolic way without symbiotic overtones, and to clown
the dominant historical clichés. Even their musical structures
were different, the Diplomatas' centring on solos, the Ritmistas'
on interplay. The Ritmistas were proud of these distinctions,
describing their genre as 'samba no asfalto' (street samba) in
contrast to the Diplomatas' 'samba no palanque' (platform samba),
a distinction also appreciated by their enormous following.

Anatomising an occasion as volatile as carnival might seem to
be self-contradictory and even to reflect a lack of humour peculiar
to social science; yet the net effect of these contrasts is clear-
cut and fairly widely apparent. For many Bahians, the spectrum
between the Diplomatas' dependence and the Ritmistas' autonomy,
with all their respective connotations, is every bit as prominent
as carnival's glittering turbulence and its brief suspension of
social reality. Nor does this apply only to extremes. Liberdade's
samba is clearly towards the autonomous end of this spectrum, and
if it lacks the Ritmistas' cutting, specifically lumpen style, it
has in recent years developed an increasingly clear opposition to
both the central interpellations of the dominant ideology.

Again, the names of samba schools are symptomatic. Their main
emphasis is on the bairro: the Ritmos da Liberdade and the Filhos
da Liberdade (the Rhythms and the Sons and Daughters of Liberdade).
Occasional winners in the second league, they are very similar
in nature. All their members live in the bairro, including members
of their diretorias, whose influence derives less from any external
ties than from their local social standing and experience of samba.
Though they are not averse in principle to financial patrons, there
are none of the social variety within reach, while experience with
politicians has left the usual bitter taste of broken promises for
the modest equipment they have had to build up independently.
Both schools' rehearsal centres, cramped and precariously lit like
many a local candomblé, are in their presidents' backyards. Together their members finance, design and make their own costumes
through months of saving, labour and emotion, often using their
craft skills as petty commodity producers, and materials such as
cloth and wood which are culled from their roles in the reserve
army as seamstresses, construction workers, and so on. Usually
they compose their own sambas de enredo, whose themes are fairly
conventional: for instance, Freyre's casa grande is something of
a staple diet. However, this conformity is checked by wider
influences and constraints. In local practice the casa grande
becomes the plantation and the slave range (senzala). Liberdade's
view of history tends spontaneously towards a mass focus, and away
from the grand history book figures, partly because older people
know and encourage this social history, but also because more
people enjoy it, and simply for reasons of resources. No samba
school in Liberdade could begin to afford the dazzling costumes
which the Diplomatas import from Rio for their idealised slave
ancestors and conspicuously friendly masters. What Liberdade

does afford for samba, as for the labour market, is numbers. However fortuitously, the result is relatively true to the past, with floats, for instance, overrun with field slaves, since their only expense is a cheap cotton loin-cloth. One way or another, few candidates for participation are excluded.

Both the Ritmos' and the Filhos' main feature is their sense of roots and pride in the bairro, which has often formed the theme of their sambas. For all their rivalry, their will to win the second league is strongly bound up with a common sense of defending Liberdade's prestige. Their arrival at the central planque from somewhere which is only known as a social myth to their wealthy spectators has something of the quality of the Persians reaching the Parthenon: an uneasy display of the social distance and inequality, with its close ethnic correlations, which carnival does not conceal, despite conventions to the contrary, but dramatises uniquely. Otherwise most of their carnival activity occurs within the bairro itself, or in others immediately neighbouring it. It is often said proudly that Liberdade 'has its own carnival', and its sense of samba hegemony in this low-income part of the city hangs, just like the Ritmistas', on the ranking of samba no asfalto above samba no palanque. In rehearsals they are also given to improvised sambas de sotaque, whose themes of everyday local life are often touched with social satire and accompanied by samba de roda, with its still collective dancing style.

In all, this outwardly cultural antithesis between two different types of samba, with its symbolic counterpart in the centre-bairro opposition, is intimately correlated with a spectrum of contrasting relations which hinge on each samba school's dependence on patronage or its own resources. Thus the culture is intrinsically the vehicle of these relations and their extended repercussions beyond the immediate sphere of samba. In samba schools of the dependent type, which are typified by the Diplomatas, relations are highly hierarchical: not only are decisions taken by agents of the ruling class, but their authority stems from this status rather than from a command of samba, which becomes increasingly derivative in both its sources and its standards. If the opposite applies in a random way to the Ritmistas' anarchy, this is systematically the case with decision-making in Liberdade, where diretorias are entirely local and reasonably consultative; for instance, women take part in them, by virtue of their contribution as dancers and costumiers, though not as musicians. Hence samba itself remains rooted in local skills and values, as well as material resources. In short, where relations between members are hierarchical at one end of the spectrum, they are egalitarian at the other, and the former is clearly associated with a relatively derivative as opposed to autochthonous type of samba. There is a similar contrast in the relations between participants, in that these are individualised at the dependent end of the spectrum, but more collective at the other. Indeed these various types of relations are obviously complementary, since among the Diplomatas this individualism is both rooted in and reproduces hierarchy; it rests partly on participants receiving their costumes individually from the diretoria or even the president himself, and the way in which their quality and even their reputed cost is seen as a measure of relative talent and

individual prestige. In Liberdade these differences are much
less marked, and in any case the costumes derive from largely
collective resources and labour. This same antithesis is repeated
in their respective musical styles, with the Diplomatas' emphasis
on star performers and their solos, as against the collective
interplay of the Ritmistas or Liberdade; and again in their respective pictures of a socially hierarchical history dominated by
individuals, as against the history of the masses.

A third antithesis is that between on the one hand competitive,
and on the other reciprocal relations between samba schools; like
the others, this is just a tendency, but again it is closely
correlated with the dependence-autonomy spectrum. Finally, the
contrast between intra-class fission and solidarity extends beyond
the samba schools' boundaries to their sub-proletarian samba
public, in the way in which the Diplomatas keep it at an admiring
distance, whilst others like the Ritmistas tend naturally to
incorporate it.

In terms of content, contrasts additional to that between a
derivative and an autochthonous samba accompany these sets of relations. At the dependent end of the spectrum, content is governed
by orthodoxy, and at the other it is more spontaneous, with inter-
jections and improvisation; or again, its themes are governed by
tradition, as opposed to expressing situations with clearly social
implications; and its basic genres, like samba de roda or sotaque
and enredo are in the one case kept apart in divergent cultural
categories, whereas in the other they converge as strands of a
collective creativity. Such contrasts at the level of content are
much more apparent in candomblé, where they will be discussed more
fully; suffice to say that the general effect is to give their
content a much more socially than culturally determined character.
For purposes of clarification and subsequent comparison with candomblé, these contrasts are set out in Figure 4.3, which locates
them in the overall structure of dominant and popular ideologies
and their respective interpellations.

The degree of general correspondence between these contrasts
and those which occur in the social relations of production in
the two bairros is fairly apparent, given Amaralina's association
with the sub-proletariat's older fraction, in contrast to Liberdade. In some cases the samba spectrum is directly connected with
the reproduction of these relations: the Diplomatas' inter-class
network is a frequent source of employment for members, typically
in personal services, whereas in Liberdade co-operation in samba
schools involves domestic production units and often those who work
together outside the family, usually on an autonomous basis. The
Ritmos da Liberdade even have something of a guild background, as
many of the older members used to celebrate carnival together before
founding it as a samba school, as an informal association of small
furniture makers in the bairro. At a less formal level the connections are very similar. The social networks of samba schools,
be they vertical or horizontal, are very much those on which
people rely in the event of any crisis in the day-to-day struggle
for survival, with either network producing and each of them reinforcing the other. In all, directly or by analogy as ways of
thinking social relations, the dependent-autonomous opposition and
its implications for fragmented-cohesive intra-class relations are

much the same in the sphere of samba as in its participants'
material existence, in ways which could be traced more fully and
substantiated with evidence from other cities, especially Recife.

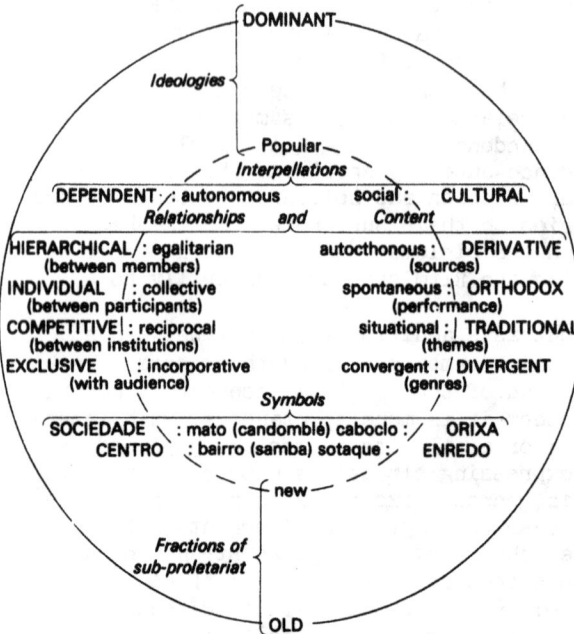

DOMINANT

Ideologies

Popular
Interpellations

DEPENDENT / : autonomous   social : CULTURAL
Relationships   and   Content

HIERARCHICAL / : egalitarian   autocthonous : \ DERIVATIVE
(between members)   (sources)
INDIVIDUAL / : collective   spontaneous : \ ORTHODOX
(between participants)   (performance)
COMPETITIVE | : reciprocal   situational : | TRADITIONAL
(between institutions)   (themes)
EXCLUSIVE \ : incorporative   convergent : / DIVERGENT
(with audience)   (genres)

Symbols

SOCIEDADE \ : mato (candomblé) caboclo :/ ORIXA
CENTRO / : bairro (samba) sotaque :/ ENREDO

new

Fractions of
sub-proletariat

OLD

FIGURE 4.3

With the passing of time this polarisation is clearly becoming
more explicit in response to the underlying tensions among the new
sub-proletariat, particularly in Liberdade; it is also increasingly
interwoven with defiance, at the level of content, of the ethno-
cultural interpellation. Though less central than in candomblé,
this has always been prominent and encouraged as a theme for samba
de enredo, through the image of the casa grande, with its symbiotic
pluralism between master and slaves. In a remarkable demonstration
of ideology's resilience, the Filhos da Liberdade, for instance,
based much of their choreography on a treasured reproduction from
the weekly magazine *Manchete* of the paintings of the French artist
Debret, whose idealised depiction of nineteenth century Brazilian
slaves is used by Freyre, Pierson and others to illustrate their
repetitions of the *friendly master* thesis. (39) However, this
image has long since been challenged by Bahian samba in ways more
direct than the Filhos' depiction of field slaves, and in significantly close correlation with defiance of the patronage structure
in which the samba schools are enveloped. For instance, the
Ritmistas' first name, the Nega Maluca, had the well-warranted

intonation of casting the archetypal black prostitute who was
the Nega Maluca in question as the Mother Courage of Bahia. To
this they added the briefly inflammatory observation to the effect
that slavery was still the lot of blacks in Bahia.

With the dampening of such deviations under the eye of the
military, ethnicity as a samba theme regained its dominant cultural
and symbiotic implications, until in the mid-1970s social tensions
re-emerged in the ideology of samba and focused on this interpellation. Young people in Liberdade began moving away from samba
schools into carnival blocks, in explicit protest at the restrictions on the former. These began to clash with middle-class blocks,
particularly one inappropriately called the Internationals, much
patronised by society figures and with a well-known policy of
allowing only blacks to take part as paid batuqueiros.

At the same time, in Liberdade a new block was formed which
simultaneously defied the patronage system, the ideological and
the legal apparatus. Calling itself the Ilé and citing the Internationals as grounds for restricting participation to blacks, it
began to portray black history as a struggle for an independent
identity within Brazilian society. Though it lapsed into many of
the contradictions of ethnic radicalism, the popular following and
official wrath which this provoked were a measure of the range of
alternative meanings implicit in ethnicity. Recaptured and re-
socialised by popular ideology, it became a sharp if inherently
ambivalent weapon.

It is in candomblé that this popular vesting of cultural signs
with social meaning has long crystallised round ethnicity in a
deeper and more complex way. Combining this with a negation of
the dependent interpellation, the divinities of Liberdade dance
the ever-shifting boundaries of sub-proletarian awareness.

From cultural to social ethnicity: the dialectics of candomblé

Whilst its historical depth has meant that the social control
of candomblé is more rooted in civil society than in the case of
samba schools, the state has also played a part in influencing
its variations, whose spetial, social and cultural features are
structurally comparable to samba's. Until the mid-1970s every
cult house had to be registered with the police and obtain their
permission and pay a small fee for each ceremony. At the same
time many of them belonged to the Federation of Afro-Brazilian
Cults of Bahia, in which police agents as well as ward-heelers
(cabos eleitorais) and members of the local cultural elite,
including academics, were active. This Federation's original
purpose, though paternalistic, was protective. By maintaining
a ritual purity defined in terms of conformity with supposedly
African traditions, it aspired to give candomblé a legitimacy
which would protect it from indiscriminate repression. In fact
its effects were more complex, as it lent an element of coercion
to the politicians' patronage and the norms of ritual orthodoxy
influenced by the cultural elite, and made them mutually reinforcing, through the mediation of the large and more traditional
cult houses which dominate the Federation. On the one hand, these

monopolise the favours from politicians and patrons, which range
from jobs and subsidies to appearances on official occasions,
publicity in the media and recommendations to the tourist department, passed on to the agencies and hotels. On the other hand,
they legitimise the association of such status with the maintenance
of the traditions revolving round the orixás, through which candomblé is moulded into an ethno-cultural, Afro-Brazilian interpellation, with its symbiotic associations. As well as marginal-
ising the smaller, less orthodox cult houses, this pattern is
heavily reinforced by rivalry among the large ones as to which are
most 'correct' in their rituals. It is on this basis and that of
their luxo (the richness of their ornaments, and hence their
material resources) that they compete for attention, prestige and
even the public ritual involvement of well-known local and national
figures, thus reproducing the interdependence of patronage and
pluralism.

As in samba, the outcome of these institutional controls is
varied, and the variations have a geographical dimension. The
largest and longest established cult houses most prominent in the
patronage network, the Federation and the public image of candomblé, are based in the older, more central districts. The best-
known and most traditional of all, the famous Menininha's Gantois,
is on a spectacular hilltop relatively close to the city centre,
overlooking valleys whose crowded low-income population has been
decimated by the new freeways of the Brazilian miracle. Liberdade's, on the other hand, are as little known outside the bairro
as they are prolific; quite apart from the deterrent of the
bairro's social reputation, few tourists could find the candomblés
like Catarina's in the unpaved, unlit baixadas where the drumming
of any number of them may mingle confusingly in the darkness.
However, like samba's these contrasts are rooted not in geography,
but in the respective social histories and current social relations
of the older and newer low-income bairros. Just as the formers'
cult houses express the traditionally symbiotic relationship with
a neighbouring ruling class, in ways evolved over generations, so
Liberdade's played a part in its antithetical expansion as the
first independent low-income bairro. In addition to their distinctive content, there is evidence that some of them, established
before the land invasions, furnished their leaders' social networks; this may partly explain the vivid local recollections of
how they were persecuted around the same time by the mounted
police, who also confronted the land invaders. So too, in the
present, their imagery and relations revolve around the autonomous
tendencies of the new sub-proletariat in contrast to the dependent
ethos of the traditional cult houses.

Just as candomblé has played a rather profounder part in more
people's lives for much longer than samba, its cultural content
is more complex, and it is at the cultural level that the contrasts
within it are most immediately apparent. The transformation of
Omulú, from an Afro-Brazilian orixá performing a traditional and
relatively solo ritual in a well-known candomblé to his spontaneous
interaction with the caboclos in Liberdade (see Figure 4.1),
reflects a general antithesis between the orixá and caboclo genres,
akin to that between samba de enredo and samba de sotaque. The

difference is that in candomblé this appears to be much more
strongly governed by distinctive cultural traditions, as relatively
independent forces. Whilst it is fairly evident that varying
relationships mould the cultural images of samba, the social
dimensions of candomblé seem more consequent in most people's
minds on its complex cultural pluralism: on intellectuals' perception of it as a series of cultural survivals; on the valorisation
within it of its traditionally Afro-Brazilian as opposed to degenerate caboclo forms, and their elaborate attribution to the
various African groups or nations like Gêge, Ketu and Nagô, with
which each cult house is associated. (40) Certainly from reading
studies of them or visiting the big cult houses - and even to a
lesser extent the smaller ones of Liberdade - one gets the
impression that candomblé is both conceived and organised above
all in terms of these categories: that given cult houses and their
rituals are more or less purely Afro-Brazilian and either Gêge or
Ketu, and so on; and that this sense of cultural identity sustains
them as social institutions. From this it would follow implicitly
that their participants' social relations are governed by similarly cultural distinctions from the rest of Bahian society and
among themselves, the urban poor, just as writers like Freyre and
Pierson have argued.

To evaluate this perspective, one must first examine its basic
premise. Do candomblés revolve around the distinctive, self-
contained cultural systems so commonly imputed to them? One's
doubts are immediately raised by a number of obvious paradoxes.
If Candomblé is essentially a series of cultural survivals, why
should involvement in it be growing, in a rapidly changing urban
society? And why should its degenerate caboclo forms be flourishing
above all others? May it not be that its cultural categories are
simply movable points of reference rather than static, self-
governing systems? That they rationalise and reproduce quite
varied sets of social relations, as opposed to reflecting the
cultural, yet somehow degenerating roots of a persistent dualism?
The cultural anthropological studies which clearly imply the contrary do little to vindicate their premise that they are describing
autonomous, stable cultural systems.

The French anthropologist Bastide is the acknowledged authority
on the subject. Yet he rarely demonstrates that any given cultural
trait is of this or that distinct origin, rather than merely
thought to be, still less that there are consistently Gêge, Ketu
or Nagô cult houses. (41) He never states if the forms which he
attributes to 'Nagô rites' are gleaned from one cult house or several,
and if so, which - in short whether these categories regulate, as
opposed to rationalising behaviour at a purely ideal level, no
doubt in the minds of certain informants as well as cultural
anthropologists. These suspicions are confirmed by direct observations. Whilst participants are aware of the concept of various
'nations' with distinctive traits, especially drum rhythms, even
traditional cult houses are not exclusively associated with any
one nation or another, as living expressions of its sub-culture.
Most have initiates with orixás of different 'nations'. If a
traditional house is described as being of a single nation, it is
generally that of the orixá of the cult head, and conveys the extent

to which the affairs of this particular cult house and its
rituals respectively are dominated by this duo. In short, it
suggests an individualistic and hierarchical social situation,
not a homogeneous sub-cultural identity, which is merely its
typical form of appearance.

Nor, if one turns to the relations between the orixás and
caboclos, are these as uniformly exclusive as the literature
again implies, in suggesting that some candomblés are caboclo,
and/or that others by definition exclude or have little to do
with caboclos. Neither is the case. Although every candomblé
initiate has one orixá (and rarely more), most also have one or
more caboclos, despite the discouragement of many cult heads in
traditional houses. Whilst the ritual attributes of these two
genres are formally distinct and their ceremonies kept apart,
their most evident relationship is that much more attention is
paid to caboclos in cult houses strongly associated with a particular nation, Angola, and these are precisely the smaller and more
numerous ones so common in bairros like Liberdade. Adepts' explanations for this affinity between Angola orixás and the caboclos are vague and varied, but tend to be more social than cultural. The Angola orixás' own adepts describe them as similar to
the caboclos - both are 'friendly' and 'lively' and tend to live in
the forest (mato). Also their rhythms are similar and Angolan
orixás often sing in the Portuguese dialect of the caboclos.
Hence it is natural that they should mutually understand, and
even occasionally talk to each other (i.e., move between the two
genres and their respective ceremonies). In the bigger, traditional cult houses, on the other hand, the view is that Angola
goes with caboclo because it is equally 'mixed up', or ritually lax
and deviant, and all in all less Afro-Brazilian. Such informants
tend not to document this, but rather to add that those involved
are 'no good', 'not serious', or even 'dishonest'. Quite often
these big cult houses apply the same epithets to each other, but
less publicly and automatically than to the Angola/caboclo complex.
Whatever conclusions one might draw, it is clear that relations
between the orixá and caboclo genres are not an unvaried, essentially cultural gulf between pure and degenerate forms, and that
the convention to this effect involves less cultural information
than socially superior attitudes on the part of the big cult houses.

This discrepancy with cultural ideals is apparent in several
other ways. Whilst one can identify many traits as being of African
origin, this is sometimes actually at odds with their prevailing
classification and the conventional belief that the bigger cult
houses are more 'traditional' (Afro-Brazilian). For instance,
'degenerate' Angola preserves some such clearly African traits which
traditional cult houses tend to exclude, on the grounds that they
are outside the rules of candomblé, or 'just an Angola custom', and
so on; on the other hand traditional houses have clearly acquired
some new traits and re-interpreted some old ones. One example of
this is their selection of office-holders known as ogans for
their protective and prestigious social influence, in short as
patrons, whereas in the past ogans were all ritual office-holders,
doorkeepers, sacrificiers and so on, as they still tend much more
to be in the mainly Angola-cum-caboclo cult houses. Another

clearly long-standing trait which traditional candomblés avoid
and Angola initiates sustain is that of erés. These are mis-
chievous, improvising and usually child spirits associated with
the return from full possession to normality, or in Mauss's terms,
the boundary between the sacred and profane. (42) Their exclusion
is also rationalised in terms of cultural origin, but this too
is based on social inference rather than accurate cultural history.
Erés are clearly more Angola, their critics say, as they don't
obey candomblé rules, and they upset people. It is clear that
this is more because of their conduct than their imputed origins:
erés are given to involving their audience in scurrilous songs
and dialogue on social and often sexual themes and occasionally
political ones, or even in libidinous sambas. Improper as such
behaviour may sound, especially to westernised ears (including
those of some cult heads), it is in fact fairly typical of liminal
deities of this kind. Whether or not it upsets you depends, in
its Brazilian context, on your social attitudes and/or station,
and perhaps on the erés' perception of them and inclination to
satirise them. Nor, in all, is it untypical of other divinities'
behaviour in small cult houses, be they orixás or caboclos; of
their lack and intolerance of pretensions, their closeness to
secular relations, their interaction with each other and with their
audience, to degrees which are unimaginable in the more serious
cult houses.

What should be made of such evidence that candomblé is rationalised, not regulated, by these Afro-Brazilian norms in general
and their sub-cultural categories? That relations between these
categories, especially Angola and caboclo, are not as exclusive
as implied, but varied in specific ways, for which there are only
vague, subjective and weakly cultural explanations? That the
candomblé rules or traditions rationalising particular traits are
often at odds with a scarcely knowable, but even less known cultural history which is supposed to underlie them? The sort of
answer for which one must look is indicated by the social character
of the factors clearly correlated with these formally cultural
variations: the authority of the cult head, the mutual sociability
of the Angola orixás and caboclos, the social status of ogans,
the erés' de-bunking behaviour, and so on. Candomblé's complex
variations are governed not by cultural history as such, however
much they draw on it, but by determinate structural principles
which govern the way in which they do so; and on scrutiny these
are as socially determined, and ideological in effect, as those
which order the content of samba.

Indeed, as Figure 4.3 outlines, the principles in both fields
are the same beneath their differing cultural expressions. Their
respective images are twin pendants in the mobile structured by
the same social relations, and are correspondingly transformed
by the same variations within them. However strongly permeated
with the aura of the sacred, candomblé is equally governed by
its cult houses' varied positions in the control and patronage
structure, which gives the images their meaning. Through culturally
expressed relations within cult houses and between them and with
the wider society, these different positions foster the ideological
interpellations (dependent, autonomous and so on) which reproduce

the social relations characteristic of the sub-proletariat's
old and new fractions respectively, in the older and newer low-
income bairros.   The main difference from samba is that in the
case of candomblé the stock of imagery is much richer, since it
derives from so many, albeit no longer distinct, sub-cultures.
Hence the much deeper interweaving between the dependent and ethno-
cultural interpellations, and the relative complexity with which
the latter masks the former.   For instance, the Omulú who sheds
his cultural ethnicity and distributes popcorn in Liberdade in
explicitly social and caboclo fashion, may in an orthodox candomblé
pay solo homage through Afro-Brazilian ritual to a wealthy, prestigious white ogan.   This relationship even derives from the
linkage of the two dominant interpellations (the dependence and
cultural ethnicity) which it also expresses, since the ogan is
the adept's or rather the orixá's padrinho (godfather), having paid
the considerable expenses of her Afro-Brazilian initiation.   In
such situations the imagery of Afro-Brazilian sub-culture is the
cement of hierarchical and individualised social relations, applied
in rituals whose different context in the Angola-caboclo cult
houses lends them the more egalitarian and collective intonations
of the sub-proletariat's new fraction.
  Why, though, should these two genres have such distinct associations?   The historical answer lies once more in the interplay
between culture and class at the heart of Northeastern social
history, with its roots in the political economy of Luso-Brazilian
colonialism.   Rather than being *pure* or *degenerate*, most cult
houses combine different proportions of principally African but
also Amerindian and even European derived traits with varying
degrees of innovation.   However, what gives them their intonations
is partly the structural divide which runs right through the Northeasterners' past, between domestic slaves and those who escaped
to the freedom of the quilombos, between rural dependents and
frontier peasants who wrested autonomy from the landowners, between
the old and new fractions of today's sub-proletariat, with all
their different characteristics.   It would seem that the roots
of the Angola-caboclo complex go back to the fact that the slaves
from Angola, of mainly Bantu origin, were those employed as field
hands in Brazil's highly pluralised slave regime, who also established the quilombos.   The Angolans were thus the main component
of the labouring and rebellious fraction of slave society, whose
ethnicity blended to varying degrees with the increasingly unified
Amerindian-cum-peasant, caboclo culture of the independent frontier
society to which so many of them escaped.   Indeed their survival
would have often depended on this convergence of sub-cultures as
the cement of a peasant resistance to large landowners and specu-
lators and the state apparatus at their disposal, (43) with structurally close analogies to Liberdade's social history.   Hence the
lasting combination of Angola and caboclo imagery to convey a
sense of autonomy whose ethnicity is essentially social, in over-
riding the boundaries of its sub-cultural components, compared to
the cultural ethnicity of the Afro-Brazilian cult houses among the
old sub-proletariat.   Rather than history revealing one as a degenerate form of the other, it suggests that they are equally deep-
rooted and Brazilian cultures, but associated increasingly with
resistance on the one hand and accommodation on the other.

Thus culture's part in social history, not cultural history itself (which has no independent existence), distinguishes the two candomblé genres revolving in ideal terms around the orixás and caboclos. This is not to imply that candomblé is governed by history, social or cultural: it is living and changing social relations which weave its semantics, as they apparently did in a past which merely suggests associations between cultural traits and social relations, as its legacy to the continuing struggle to reproduce or transform the latter. Only this can begin to account not only for the variations in candomblé, as shadows cast by the consciousness of the sub-proletariat's different fractions, but also for their constantly mobile combinations and intonations, as these same shadows flicker in response to changing class relations.

The most conspicuous expression of these relations in candomblé is the social composition of audiences in the big cult houses, and especially of their ogans, whose pluralistic patronage evokes an ethno-cultural dependence which pervades the whole fabric of relations within them. For instance, among the ogans of the largest and allegedly authentic cult houses are many high-ranking local officials, politicians and members of the cultural elite, including anthropologists; it is they who testify to these cult houses' purity and seriousness, and literally lay down the law on behalf of the Federation, which threatens to close the smaller cult houses unable to follow its ritual prescriptions. So committed are some of these patrons to the ethno-cultural interpellation of Bahian candomblé that they have even sponsored visits by cult heads to West Africa, resulting in the re-Africanisation of aspects of Afro-Brazilian ritual. Such ogans' presence at ceremonies, often seated in ornate personal chairs where they receive the adepts' homage, establishes a generally hierarchical ethos. Amongst the adepts this pivots on marked deference to the cult head and lends the traditional orixás an almost Catholic serious-ness. Indeed 'seriousness' is a common term of esteem for their rituals, whilst it is in these big cult houses that the well-known twinning of orixás with Catholic saints is at its strongest, and tends most clearly to imply that the orixás are of junior status. This hierarchy and gravity are the stuff of such orixás' ritual behaviour. In this setting they interact very little, except for their deferential greetings to the superior orixás of the cult head and her deputy. Possession by them usually occurs in a standard sequence of seniority (according to length of initiation), and their songs and dances generally follow a fixed as well as solo pattern. This outwardly ritual ethos has further social correlations. Whilst most initiates are local, and thus repre-sentative of occupations among the dependent local fraction of the sub-proletariat, there is sometimes apparent discouragement of other local peoples' attendance, or a tendency to segregate them from more distinguished visitors. In one case this has even reached the point of the audience sitting on rows of benches rather than round the cult house, as is usual, whilst most local people stand at the back or crowd round the windows, with rather less interest in orixás from Africa than in tourists from Sao Paulo or Paris.

The analogies between these details and those of the Diplomatas' performance in carnival need no underlining. Ideologically the samba palanque and dancing floors of the big cult houses are much the same expressive arena. Relations between such candomblés are also similar to those between the major samba schools. For all their mutual interest in maintaining the creed of orthodoxy, there is little direct interaction or co-operation between them. On the contrary, they tend to sustain this creed by maligning each other a good deal on the grounds of failing to live up to it. Again, these charges tend to be general (lack of seriousness, and so on), rather than culturally informed. In practice what seems to lie behind them is the competition for desirable ogans and for recognition in the wider society, whose standards influence the interplay between ethnicity and dependence which *seriousness* evidently entails. This rivalry means that attendance at each others' ceremonies by well-known cult heads is very rare: it seems rather specifically limited to those of distinctly unequal status, resulting in clearly reciprocal gains: for the superior cult head, a public demonstration of status; for the lesser one, public recognition. Those of similar standing tend to keep their distance and remark on each others' undue aspirations. Initiates are often forbidden by such cult heads to attend other houses, sometimes strongly against their wishes. In this and many other ways the structural relationships implicit in the dependent ethos - its competitiveness, its hierarchy, its individualism and its exclusive character - are mutually reinforcing, just as they also interlock with the sub-cultural imagery, whose patterns of non-convergence prevent their component ethnicity from assuming a more social meaning.

Conversely, the different class context of the Angola/caboclo cult houses is conducive to a relatively autochthonous type of candomblé, which gives their residual ethnicity precisely this more social intonation. Whilst many of these are better endowed than Catarina's, most are still in small back rooms which, like the samba schools' headquarters, are paved and lit and modestly expanded over time on the strength of members' contributions. As in the orthodox cult houses, many of these come from ogans, but in ways which echo the contrasts between samba school diretorias in the two areas and fractions of the sub-proletariat, since all these ogans are local people, of ritual rather than social distinction. Indeed, socially there is nothing to distinguish them from other participants in such cult houses, whose close-knit character is reflected in these ogans' frequently being the kin or husbands of the initiates, since here as elsewhere the initiates are mainly though not exclusively women. In practice such ogans' contributions are rarely made in cash or kind, but usually in the collective labour of maintaining and extending the cult house, using the skills connected with their typically independent livelihoods.

These cult houses are also relatively independent of the other direct sources of the dominant interpellations. Like the ogans, their audiences are predominantly local, apart from people who used to live in Liberdade but have moved to more outlying bairros, usually for economic reasons; and their contact with the Federation is generally minimal. Few small cult houses can afford to pay its fairly heavy subscription, much less to muster the resources required to meet its standards of orthodoxy. For instance, for initiation it demands a period of ritual confinement which varies according to nation, but invariably exceeds the time which a typical adept in Liberdade could afford to spend without working, even with other members' help, in the absence of the wealthy patrons who solve such problems in bigger cult houses. In all, the Federation's standards are seen at best as unrealistic, and at worst as positively oppressive, when it endeavours to impose them.

It is in the ceremonies of the Angola/caboclo cult houses that the contrast between this genre and the Afro-Brazilian one is dramatic. Whilst those of Angola orixás and the caboclos are usually separate, they often occur on the same occasion - the caboclos tend to arrive spontaneously as the orixás leave - and their incidence in the same cult houses deepens the qualitative links which history has forged between them. Orixás' festivals are referred to, as elsewhere, as obligations (obrigações), since failure to hold them brings punishments (castigos), in the form of misfortune, from the offended orixá. However, in describing these festivals in the Angola-caboclo cult houses, people often use the word brincadeira (fun), which tends to be used automatically to refer to caboclo ceremonies.

The implications of this word bring out the complex correspondence between candomblé adepts' relations with divinities and among themselves. In the bigger cult houses the orixás, like the cult head who mediates adepts' relationships with them, are severe as well as dignified, and exercise mainly negative sanctions (castigos); in the smaller ones they are more usually referred to as having afforded ajuda (help), as is almost always the case with caboclos. This is particularly so with the orixá of the cult head, through whose solution of crises rooted in socio-economic conditions most adepts and others join the cult house. The effect is one of having not just escaped a sanction exercised by the divinity, but of having overcome it actively through a substantially social network with a secular, mutual aid dimension, centring on the cult head but also involving other members. Together with the absence of socially superior ogans or spectators and concomitantly derivative standards of propriety and orthodoxy, it is these relationships and their effects which underlie the brincadeira quality - also referred to as alegria (happiness) - of the Angola ceremonies. For all the ups and downs of the intimacy of this social network, its rituals are implicitly, among other things, a celebration of having collectively overcome the problems which all participants share by virtue of their class position. Indeed, in their creativity, the rituals themselves are part of this process. Hence their most conspicuous feature in any bairro like Liberdade: the zest with which people participate in them and the extent to which they enjoy them.

From the outset packed audiences join in the singing, clapping in time. Men and boys vie for the enjoyment rather than just the status of drumming, and pride themselves on their musical ability to induce possession. This, too, is much more socialised than in the orthodox cult houses, where it is often brought about by the cult head. In the smaller ones it is strongly encouraged by audience participation, and is greeted with shouts and rounds of applause. This in turn encourages the orixás to bless and embrace every person present, which often includes other local cult heads; though by no means free of rivalry, they seem no more able than anyone else to resist the lure of the brincadeira. As successive orixás arrive, they themselves exchange greetings and dance together much more than in larger candomblés. The seniority rule concerning order of possession is usually set aside for the particular adept(s)/orixá in whose name the ceremony is being held and on whom it tends to focus, for all the cult head's command of the ritual. In general his or her behaviour toward adepts and audiences alike is much more egalitarian than that of the well-known cult heads, whose distinctly authoritarian style appears by contrast to mediate the inescapable hierarchy between the performers and an audience of partly different social status. In Liberdade the relationship of adept to cult head, both ritual and secular, involves a respect based not so much on awe as on affection, gratitude for help received, and often on both parties' intimate knowledge of each others' everyday social lives. These egalitarian, collective and incorporative qualities are especially marked toward the end of the ceremony, when food is often shared and members of the audience begin to dance with the orixás, by invitation or spontaneously, sometimes as a result of possession, sometimes as a prelude to it, and often independently of it. The reciprocity of relations between these different cult houses is also underlined by the care with which such gestures are extended to visiting cult heads or adepts. Occasionally, too, the orixás engage in dialogue with the audience; in particular they call men to account for their social, especially their family, behaviour. This is usually accepted without a murmur. It constitutes one of the few junctures at which authority is displayed, and this to egalitarian effect, in using the sacred to temper the secular inequalities of relationships between men and women. Finally, when the erés arrive as the licensed, improvising scourges of every discernible pretension on the part of even the cult head, and again, particularly of males, the interaction and above all the fun are total, albeit in ways shot through with such social intonations.

It is in the caboclo festivals, also referred to literally as festas, that these qualities emerge most fully. These ceremonies are also often for a particular caboclo, but following his or her arrival the atmosphere is one of almost complete inventiveness and interaction. Whilst adepts do have established relations with specified caboclos, these can be of any number, and though they revolve around standard figures, each one has its own variations. This allows wide scope for improvisation. Moreover, on any occasion a new caboclo may arrive, perhaps singing unfamiliar songs and demanding that the audience learn or even help him or her to compose them. From this unpredictable, often spectacular performance, allusive life histories and popular maxims usually emerge, on which people speculate endlessly. (Adepts themselves officially have no recollection of their states of possession, nor any responsibility for them.) This combination of audience involvement and spontaneity is highly infectious. A persuasive caboclo may induce possession among several apparently reluctant spectators, whose antics (or those of their caboclos) are then equally unforeseeable. Any situation can be improvised, from a seeming fragment of social history to a samba de sotaque or compulsory challenge to ritual battle (capoeira) with male members of the audience who, in due deference, must lose it. However much orthodox cult heads may cite this 'carrying on' (esculhambação) as their grounds for avoiding the caboclos, their apprehension clearly turns on its inevitable threat to the delicately hierarchical webs of social-cum-ritual relations of which they are the exclusive centres in their particular cult houses.

Who then are the caboclos and related Angola orixás, in comparison to the traditional ones whose Afro-Brazilianism reproduces dependent inter-class relations and also structures them cognitively around the cultural dualism which rationalises inequality? Within their more reciprocal, egalitarian, collective and incorporative patterns of behaviour, they too could be seen as the dramatisation of another Brazilian sub-culture, since each generic caboclo figure is an idealised representation of the life-style and material traits of a particular type of peasant.

For instance, Martim Pescador, as his name suggests, is a fisherman, complete with paddle and fishing line. Vaqueiro, the cowboy, dances in a characteristically galloping style; clad in leather hat and breeches, and reining in his imaginary horse in front of the pounding candomblé drums, he sings of his dusty journey from the backlands' far-flung cattle ranges. The Indians, who appear alongside these more literally peasant caboclos, have an equally sub-cultural appearance. Their often ethno-cultural names - Tupí and Guaraní are among the commonest - are supplemented with feather anklets and head-dresses and bows and arrows, not without a touch of Hollywood alongside that of Amazonia, and they usually dance in hunting style. Equally the association of particular orixás with the caboclos has an undeniably sub-cultural dimension. For instance Omulú shares with them a knowledge of herbal remedies which he often dispenses amongst his audience, along with healing rituals of a distinctly Amerindian nature. Oxóssi, the other orixá who is even more commonly conceived of as having a caboclo aspect, has comparable affinities with the life style of Indians and caboclos: like the former he is a hunter and therefore shares the forest with them, exulting in its lushness and the beauty and plenty of his quarry. The most conspicuous feature of their relatively spontaneous ritual with its autochthonous quality, in ignoring external criteria of propriety and purity, is a process of acculturation in which both the genres and their various Amerindian, African, peasant European and rural Brazilian sources converge, in contrast to their marked divergence within the orthodox cult houses.

Yet, as indicated in Figure 4.3, the actual collective representations of all these figures - their songs and dances and interaction and the ways in which people talk about them - suggest that this convergence is construed in essentially social terms, to which many of their cultural traits are relatively incidental, whilst others are strengthened by virtue of their symbolising certain common social values. The fact that poverty often limits their ritual ornaments and costumes apparently causes few

inhibitions, and the types of theme which they dramatise are not
legendary traditions about far-removed divinities like the Afro-
Brazilian orixás; they deal instead with situations of an essentially human stamp, shot through with echoes of popular history
and of the social experiences and relatively independent values
of most of today's low-income Brazilians, both rural and urban.
For instance, the Indians present a Utopian picture of life in the
forest, its space and freedom, its physical health and food in
abundance: in short, of material and social conditions diametrically opposite to those familiar to their adepts, in ways which
are often quite explicit in both formal and informal ritual. On
one occasion Catarina's Guaraní drew to his audience's attention
the contrast between his circumstances and those of his adept
Catarina, condemned to ill-health and poverty in a tumbledown home
in a crowded bairro beyond which she could hardly travel, whereas
he (Guaraní) could simply transport himself at will from Amazonas
to Bahia; and whilst here, he added, he wasn't staying in Liberdade,
but would take a trip around the night-clubs to dance and down a
few cold beers before going back to his forest freedom.

In countless ways like this the spontaneity of the caboclos
conveys not the individualism of the orthodox orixás' performance
but rather, through this creative freedom, a collective sense,
however fantastic, of alternative conditions of existence. At
times the images are almost surreal, as when the caboclo Sete
Estrelas (Seven Stars) balances a star on the fingers of one hand
and plays with a snake on the wrist of the other, as if Amerindian,
African and peasant Europe's mythology are combining to stress
the remoteness of his apparently untroubled world from that of his
adepts. At other times they seem to be a more literal reversal of
reality. Martim Pescador, philosopher of an imagined freedom,
is able to fish to his heart's content in a way which seems to
emphasise that in this natural economy his time is not a commodity
to be put at the disposal of others. Vaqueiro's particular independence is slightly different again. It represents one of the
few situations which have historically permitted a fraction of
the Northeastern poor to better their lot, since it consists in
his building up a herd of his own from the fifth of the calves
which pay for his labour. In other cases the imagery is even
haunted with the actual chapters of a popular history which is
almost unrecorded elsewhere, with allusions to the slave ranges
(senzalas) and the routes from Bahia to Minas Gerais along which
so many slaves were sold, when the axis of the economy shifted from
the cane-fields to the diamond mines, as long ago as the eighteenth
century.

Within this universe most which remains of the once cultural
ethnicity so sanctified in the big cult houses acquires a common,
social value. The Indians', orixás' and caboclos' forest becomes
a single world of freedom, the hunting an image of food in plenty,
the encyclopaedic geography a portrait of the richness of the
country's natural resources, as familiar in the imagination, from
their enjoyment as use values, as they are known in reality from
the centuries of labour migrations involved in exploiting them
for others. Hence the convergence of the cultural traits which
are so distinct in the bigger cult houses, where the Indians, when

they do occur, are almost ethnographic exhibits. In the smaller
ones they are much less Indian than social symbols of a natural
economy, in direct contrast to the process whereby the national
caboclo of the Independence Day procession is ethnicised into the
guise of a conspicuously cultural Indian. In some of the primitive paintings of Indians found in Angola-caboclo cult houses,
they are even black as well as white figures, an echo perhaps
of the quilombo and frontier formation of a unified rather than
hybrid culture of the Northeastern Brazilian people.

Moreover, differences of dialect between the Indians and
caboclos, even on occasions the Angola orixás, are few. Even
the latter often use the same rustic speech which is known as
sotaque de caboclo, with traces of Tupí-Guaraní, Iberian peasant
Portuguese and also Bantu phonology, to communicate in a social
idiom whose often satirical overtones are unintelligible to users
of more conventional Portuguese. In short, the effect is not
just one of convergence or acculturation, but of unified social
ethnicity, selected as well as interwoven and positively played
upon to express a class-like identity, historically accumulated
but so strongly rooted in present concerns that often the divinities are drawn right out of their cultural backgrounds. For
instance, just as Guaraní frequents the night-clubs of Bahia, so
Boiadeiro the cattle-driver (closely related to Vaqueiro) may reach
back into social history to proclaim himself 'son of Ganga-Zumba',
chief of the famous Palmares quilombo, or forward both in time and
class structure, with the galloping of his horse's hooves becoming
the rhythm of an engine, to join the Bahian proletariat:

Sou empregado da Leste,	I work for the Western railroad,
E maquinista do trem	I'm the one who drives the train,
Vou embora par'o sertão	I'm heading for the backlands,
Aqui não passo bem.	As this isn't my domain.

Whether anyone is aware at such moments of the historical role
of the rail-workers' union in the Northeastern labour movement,
with its mobilisation of scattered peasants with whom their work
brought them into contact, like Bahia's cattle-drivers/boiadeiros
before them, is an unanswerable question. What does seem certain
is that this explosive imagery is a collective allegory of the
multiplicity of social relations, conditions of existence, connections between them and imagined metamorphoses of them which
the Northeastern poor have shared in the face of Brazilian capitalism; and that this power of imagination, far from being literally
rural, is specific to the relatively new but now majority fraction
of the Bahian sub-proletariat, whose conditions are most acutely
determined by the present mode of accumulation.

In what sense then is this the imagery of a class in itself or
for itself, with a sense of the possible transformation of its
relations of production?

5 PASTORALISM: THE BOUNDARIES OF SUB-PROLETARIAN SYMBOLISM

What is clearly implicit in this growing popular dialectic with

the dominant interpellations is a statement of social identity
on the part of people without the means, in view of their productive relations and the political conjuncture, to activate this
identity economically or politically, as opposed to ideologically.
So does the imagery suggest, in its perceptible effects or the
logic of its implications, any answers to the basic question of
its protagonists' class nature?

Certainly the social identity of the new sub-proletariat is
given by its shared conditions of existence and also by their
being governed, in ways outlined in Section 2, by Brazil's peripheral capitalism; and certainly through this imagery the actors
are not merely expressing a sense of this collective situation,
but conceiving of alternatives to it, and not just allegorically
but concretely, within the limits imposed on the poor by the
Brazilian miracle. Cult heads like Catarina are in effect socia-
lising skills which are scarce but generally required in order to
optimise conditions of existence in low-income bairros like Liber-
date, particularly among the women who are their disproportionate
victims. In part this is done by such cult heads' examples, as
sheer models of the will to survive. Almost all of them, like
Catarina, have brought up families single-handed, and overcome
tuberculosis, mental disorder or some similar affliction connected
with their deprivation, by means explicitly imputed to their
candomblé associations, particularly with the caboclos. It is such
situations which they have since resolved for their adepts
as the basis of the bonds between them, and for many more casual
associates, through the effective psychiatric and even medical
(herbal) treatment which the social wage does not provide.

Moreover, the cult houses, as economic and social as well as
expressive institutions, have maximised the collective means at
the sub-proletariat's disposal of dealing with these situations.
Most adepts have lived in the cult houses in the course of one
crisis or another, when abandoned by their family's main earner,
ejected by one of the large-scale landlords of Liberdade's poorer
housing, or in a period of illness or prolonged unemployment.
These independent mutual aid networks ramify among the adepts,
especially those who have been initiated together, or in candomblé
idiom, 'shared the same boat'. In many cases they have been a
source of stable employment or self-employment, through mainly
intra-class contacts, advice and co-operation in independent petty
commodity production, a preference for which is slightly more
marked than in the population at large and also somewhat correlated,
as an ideal and in practice, with the incidence of possession by
and general relationships with caboclos. (This is also in distinct
contrast to the pattern in the bigger cult houses, where this
preference appears to be somewhat less than in the general population, and the candomblé-derived employment of the old sub-
proletariat is largely through the vertical networks, often
including high status ogans and much more exclusively centred on
the individual cult head.) For those with a permanent spouse,
these stabilising effects have been deepened by a marked reduction
of the inequalities prevalent between men and women. From the
comments of adepts of the Angola-caboclo cult houses, it is quite
clear that many of them regard all aspects of candomblé, ritual

and secular, expressive and concrete, as having been both a
means of survival and the source of a sense of identity which
might otherwise have been still more elusive.

This functional autonomy, in countering the immediate effects
of the sub-proletariat's class relations, is not in itself a
measure of awareness of them. The test of this presumably lies
in how their causes are conceptualised, and here the picture is
more ambiguous. Indeed it might well be argued that in substituting the social wage, candomblé is relieving a contradiction
of Brazilian capitalism; that the autonomous interpellation and
relationships in these cult houses, in apparently fostering petty
commodity production, are still reproducing a widespread form of
articulation with the capitalist sector, and this a less proletarian
one than engagement in the reserve army, with a lower level of
awareness; that the sacred in candomblé mystifies the contradictions
which it confronts, in imputing them to supernatural rather than
to class relations; and, finally, that at best it confines whatever
awareness it may involve to the expressive, symbolic level rather
than that of social action. The validity of these comments varies,
but the general answer is simply that, contrary to Marcusian
assumptions, any ideology must ultimately be bounded by the objective relations in which it is rooted; (44) and these relations, in
even the case of the new sub-proletariat, preclude concerted
collective action of an economic or political nature, short of a
wider class alliance and more open political situation, to perhaps
an even greater extent than is also the case with the peasantry.
Hence in the immediate circumstances the awareness is necessarily
confined to the ideological level.

As to the possible mystification, the evidence suggests that
this varies with positions on the candomblé spectrum. At the
dominant end it would indeed seem that orixás are conceived of
as the absolute causes of social effects, with only sacred remedies;
but at the other end the sacred is relatively complementary to
concepts of social and scientific causality, and of human agency.
The social basis of inequality and medical causes of illness,
for instance, are quite explicitly referred to; if caboclos per
se have a causal role, it is in explaining the individual's relative capacity to overcome them, whilst the means they afford for
doing so are the highly social and secular ones which their per-
sonalities, behaviour and expressive symbolism foster in the Angola-
caboclo cult houses. As to their relationships facilitating petty
commodity production, these cult houses are simply affording
certain social and economic conditions for realising an objective
choice from limited alternatives: contrary to one stereotype of
developmental sociology, it is not *pre-industrial attitudes* which
deter the sub-proletariat from engagement in the reserve army
rather than in self-employment, but conclusions drawn from experience of its forms and rates of exploitation, to which such
sociologists pay relatively little attention. (45) This preference
does reproduce relations still indirectly linked with the mode
of capital accumulation; but all that this proves is the point
that in any predominantly capitalist formation the mode of accumulation directly or indirectly governs all relations of production,
despite confusion of the issue by concepts like those of Gunder
Frank. (46)

Where the boundary of awareness in this imagery does seem to
lie is in the type of alternative existence of which it apparently
conceives, which is only dialectical in the sense of posing a
symbolic escape from existing relations and conditions, and more
from their effects than their structure. The most striking instance
of this is the symbol of the mato, the forest, as the central motif
in the interweaving of the sub-cultural components of this popular
imagination. For all its conceptualisation of alternative conditions of existence, and the symbolic, historical, social and
explicit grounds for seeing it as an image of freedom from the
labour market, it is no more than one of escape and the optimi-
sation of autonomy, as opposed to a transformation of relations.
Essentially pastoral in its projection of a natural economy, it
is like the communitarian element of candomblé, an other-world
island in the reality of Brazil's peripheral capitalism and the
competition for survival amongst the poor of Liberdade. Its less
conspicuous attributes underline this unreal quality: for instance
the mato is often described as a world apart, impenetrable and
closed, cerrado.

Yet there is also a strong suggestion that its promises, perhaps
like those of the independence of petty commodity production and
even the interdependent relations of the candomblé community, are
frail in the face of realities to which even they are eventually
subject. This theme emerges consistently as one looks more closely
at the details. Even the freedom of the Indians is ultimately
a poignant one, destroyed as they are hunted down by the colonising
Portuguese. So, too, Martim Pescador is in the end a Lear-like
figure, more impotent than independent: perpetually drunk, he
spends less of his time in fishing than in trying to paddle back
to shore and forever going round in circles. Vaqueiro, too,
laments the death of his waterless cattle as often as he exults
in their beauty, reflecting the outcome of the dreams of many a
Northeastern peasant. And so on, as if despite the resort to this
idealised pastoralism, its limitations are perceived in ideology
as in life, suggesting the need for a link with a stronger ideology and social identity, like that assumed by Boiadeiro, to lead
the way out of these contradictions.

It is here than an answer begins to emerge. Certainly the new
sub-proletariat's relations to the means of production constrain
its scope for social action and even expose its ideology to co-
option: more sophisticated politicians within the expanding state
apparatus already patronise caboclos as symbols of Brazilianism
and get a positive response. Yet, for all this, the imagination
of the urban poor reveals a power to keep alive a people's history
and counter the dominant ideology's dialectics of expansion from
the older to the new fraction: through it, the mass of the urban
poor do build alternative relations and conceive at least of wholly
different conditions (however much they may have to look to relationships with other classes for any prospect of their fulfil-
ment), in ways beyond the boundary (though even this appears to
be sensed) of their own particular ideology. The dialectics of
this imagination distinguish the sub-proletariat's different
fractions in ways which social scientists have hardly yet begun
to do as Lenin did for the peasantry, say, as a precondition of

the task of defining the popular alliance entailed in the transformation of any specific social order. In Lenin's thinking, this was not only strategically but almost philosophically vital. His activists, like those now looking to prospects of real change in Brazil, 'must go along all classes of the population', not just to build a new power bloc, but because only an awareness of the problems of all these different classes would give their political purpose its universalistic scope. (47)   Hence in Brazil some understanding of the popular imagination is far from marginal to the task of defining such a political purpose and the alliance to achieve it, despite contemporary Marxism's being so ill-equipped in this direction.

It is not unsymptomatic that the last time I saw Catarina, in the late 1970s, having kept in touch with her for a decade, much of her frail world had crumbled. The Federation had brought pressure on her candomblé for what it considered an impropriety which struck at the heart of its communitarian essence: the use of part of its limited space for adepts to stay in the cult house, as well as for ritual purposes. Without any influential patrons and unsure of the Federation's status, but knowing it to be well connected with the media, police and distinguished cult heads, she had felt unable to confront it, and suspended some of the festivals of both the orixás and caboclos. In these uncertain circumstances some of her adepts had already left, together with the most senior of them, who was opening her own cult house. In the end, the real world was more powerful than that of the imagination, and even the relations wrested from it were subject to its harsher dictates. Catarina felt a deep sense of betrayal and, as poorly off as ever, she was ill again and doubted now if even her caboclos could help her. Yet this was not the only development. One of her younger former adepts, still involved in candomblé but growing into a wider world, was now active in an association defending a new land invasion, an organisation like hundreds which are springing up all over Brazil, perhaps as the seeds of the class alliance fore-shadowed by the transformations of Omulú and Boiadeiro.

ACKNOWLEDGMENT

I would like to thank a number of colleagues for their comments on early drafts of this paper, in particular John Humphrey, Colin Murray and John Peel.

NOTES AND REFERENCES

1 The state of Bahia is the southernmost and one of the largest states of the Brazilian Northeast; its main traditional products are sugar, tobacco and cocoa. Its capital, Salvador, has a population of just over a million and is one of the region's industrial growth centres, led by its petro-chemical industry. The capital of colonial Brazil until the 1760s, it is known locally as Bahia rather than Salvador. Since this paper makes little reference to the state of Bahia, as opposed to the city, this popular usage is followed throughout.

2 The fullest ethnographic studies of Bahian candomblé are
   EDISON CARNEIRO, *Candomblés da Bahia* (3rd edition, Rio de
   Janeiro, 1961); and ROGER BASTIDE, *O Candomblé da Bahia* (São
   Paulo, 1961). The most comprehensive survey of Afro-Brazilian
   beliefs in general is BASTIDE's *As Religiões Africanas no
   Brasil* (São Paulo, 1971).

3 For instance, whilst Carneiro is one of the few to have paid
   much attention to the candomblés de caboclo, he views them not
   in social but in strictly cultural terms and thus as 'formas
   religiosas em franca descomposicão' ('clearly degenerate religious phenomena'): EDISON CARNEIRO, *Negros Bantus* (Rio de
   Janeiro, 1937), p.33.

4 ANDREW G. FRANK, The Sociology of Development and the Under-
   development of Sociology, in *Latin America: Under-development
   or Revolution* (New York, 1969).

5 ROBERTO CAMPOS, cited in *The Brazilian Gazette*, Year 2, No. 10,
   (London, May/June 1975), p.3.

6 CHARLES WAGLEY, *Introduction to Brazil*, (3rd edition, New
   York, 1965), pp.120-1.

7 JACQUES LAMBERT, *Os Dois Brasis* (Rio de Janeiro, 1959).

8 BERTRAM HUTCHINSON, The Patron-Client Relationship in Brazil:
   a Preliminary Examination, *Sociologia Ruralis*, vol. 6, 1966.

9 S.N. EISENSTADT, *Modernisation: Protest and Change* (Englewood
   Cliffs, New Jersey, 1966), p.88-9.

10 DESAL, *Marginalidad en América Latina: un Ensayo Diagnóstico*
    (Barcelona, 1969), pp.377ff.

11 ERNESTO LACLAU, Feudalism and Capitalism in Latin America,
    New Left Review, 67, 1972. See also LACLAU, *Politics and
    Ideology in Marxist Theory* (London, 1977).

12 JOSÉ NUN, Superpoblación Relative, Ejército Industrial de
    Reserva y Masa Marginal, *Revista Latino-Americana de Sociologia*,
    No. 2, 1969.

13 ANIBAL QUIJANO, The Marginal Pole of the Economy and the
    Marginalised Labour Force, *Economy and Society*, November 1974.

14 FRANCISCO DE OLIVEIRA, A Economia Brasileira: Crítica à
    Razão Dualista, *Estudos CEBRAP* 2, 1972.

15 ALISON MacEWEN SCOTT, Capitalism and Petty Commodity Production
    in Peru, (mimeo., Department of Sociology, University of Essex,
    1977).

16 The most noteworthy of these authors is, of course, GILBERTO
    FREYRE in his *Casa Grande e Senzala* (Rio de Janeiro, 1933:
    The Masters and the Slaves, New York, 1946); *Sobrados e
    Mucambos* (São Paulo, 1936: *The Mansions and the Shanties*,
    New York, 1963). His analysis is closely followed with
    reference to Bahia by DONALD PIERSON, *Negroes in Brazil:
    a Study of Race Contact at Bahia* (revised edition, Southern
    Illinois University Press, 1967); and also by THALES DE AZEVEDO,
    Povoamento da Cidade de Salvador (Bahia, 1969); and *As Elites
    de Côr: um Estudo de Ascenção Social* (Sao Paulo, 1955).

17 The sources for this local history of Liberdade are almost
    exclusively oral, modestly supplemented by the Bahian daily,
    A Tarde.

18 PHILIPPE SCHMITTER, The Portugalisation of Brazil? in ALFRED
    STEPHAN (ed.), *Authoritarian Brazil* (New Haven, 1973), p.197.

19   LOUIS ALTHUSSER, Ideology and Ideological State Apparatuses,
      in *Lenin and Philosophy and Other Essays* (London, 1971).
20   JOHN MEPHAM, The Theory of Ideology in Capital, *Radical
      Philosophy*, 2, 1972.
21   ALTHUSSER, op.cit., pp.160ff; LACLAU, op.cit., 1977, Chapters
      3-4, where 'interpellation' is preferred to 'interpolation'.
22   HUTCHINSON, op.cit.
23   FLORESTAN FERNANDES, *A Integracão do Negro na Sociedade de
      Classes* (São Paulo, 1965: The Negro in Brazilian Society,
      New York, 1969), passim.
24   GEORGES BALANDIER, The Colonial Situation, in PIERRE VAN DEN
      BERGHE (ed.), *Africa: Social Problems of Change and Conflict*
      (San Francisco, 1965).
25   VICTOR NUNES LEAL, *Coronelismo, Enxada e Voto: O Municipio
      e o Regime Representativo no Brasil* (Rio de Janeiro, 1949:
      *Coronelismo: the Municipality and Representative Government
      in Brazil*, Cambridge, 1977).
26   For a fuller account of these structures and a more com-
      parative analysis of the historical data which follow, see
      COLIN HENFREY, Imperialism and Race Relations as a Dimension
      of Social Control: Brazil and Guyana, in DAVID STANSFIELD
      (ed.), *Perspectives on Dependency* (Amsterdam, 1974).
27   MAURICIO GOULART, *A Escravidão Africana no Brasil* (3rd edition,
      São Paulo, 1975), pp.163-4 and 219.
28   CARNEIRO, op.cit., 1961, p.55.
29   PIERSON, op.cit., pp.40-1.
30   EDISON CARNEIRO, *O Quilombo de Palmares* (São Paulo, 1947).
31   SETH AND RUTH LEACOCK, *Spirits of the Deep* (New York, 1972),
      p.45.
32   RENÉ RIBEIRO, *Cultos Afro-Brazileiros do Recife: um Estudo
      de Ajustamento Social* (Recife, 1952), p.24.
33   KATHARINE REAL, *O Folclore no Carnaval do Recife* (Rio de
      Janeiro, 1967), p.23ff.
34   FREYRE, op.cit., 1933, especially chapters 4 and 5.
35   LUIS GARDEL, *Escolas de Samba* (Rio de Janeiro, 1967), p.54.
36   EDIGAR DE ALENCAR, *Nosso Sinhô do Samba* (Rio de Janeiro,
      1968), p.57.
37   GARDEL, op.cit., p.42.
38   *A Tarde*, Bahia, 20 February 1950, p.2.
39   J.B. DEBRET, *Voyage Pittoresque et Historique au Brésil*
      (Paris, 1835); cited both by FREYRE, op.cit., 1933, pp.43-4,
      and PIERSON, op.cit., pp.76-8.
40   CARNEIRO, op.cit., 1961, for instance, classifies the cults
      in this way, as do most other authors, including BASTIDE, op.
      cit., 1961, as is implicit in the book's sub-title: *Rito
      Nagô* (a Nagô Ritual). The latter nation is in fact very much
      a historical hybrid, Nagô having developed, albeit mainly
      from Yoruba, as the lingua franca of Bahian slaves (PIERSON,
      op.cit., p.7), whilst the other categories are Brazilian-
      isations of West African place and tribal names. Gêge, for
      instance, derives from Ewe, and Ketu is a sub-category of
      Yoruba (ibid., chapter 2).
41   BASTIDE, op.cit., 1961.
42   MARCEL MAUSS and HENRI HUBERT, *Sacrifice: its Nature and
      Functions* (London, 1964).

43   The vigour and frontier autonomy of this peasant resistance
in the modern period is documented, for example, in CLODOMIR
MORAES, The Peasant Leagues in Brazil, in RODOLFO STAVENHAGEN
(ed.), *Agrarian Problems and Peasant Movements in Latin
America* (New York, 1970), especially pp.458-61.

44   Unfortunately such assumptions dominate what is almost the
only published work to attempt the analysis of an aspect of
Afro-Brazilian religion in an ideological light: GEORGE
LAPASSADE and MARCO AURÉLIO LUZ, *O Segredo da Macumba* (Rio
de Janeiro, 1972). The effect is to consider the antithesis
between umbanda and quimbanda almost wholly in terms of the
latter's relative negritude, as a relatively autonomous and
authentic idiom, without assessing the semantics of this
ethno-cultural idiom within the wider framework of Brazilian
ideology and social relations of production. Like most such
analyses it therefore leads to little more than paternalistic
radicalism, despite its convincing and interesting empirical
content.

45   See, for example, BERTRAM HUTCHINSON (ed.), *Mobilidade e
Trabalho: um Estudo na Cidade de São Paulo* (São Paulo, 1960),
especially chapter 12; JUAREZ RUBEN BRANDÃO LOPES, O Adjus-
tamento do Trabalhador à Industria: Mobilidade Social e
Motivacão.

46   The valid but rather static critique by LACLAU (op.cit.) of
FRANK'S *Capitalism and Under-development in Latin America*
(London, 1967) on the nature of non-capitalist relations within
predominantly capitalist formations, has been much clarified
by JAIRUS BANAJI, Modes of Production in a Materialist Con-
ception of History, *Capital and Class*, 3, 1977. His insistence that it is the predominantly capitalist mode of production which governs the content of these relations, as
distinct from their form, is the synthesis underlying the
conclusions of Section 2 (above) on the class position of the
urban poor, as the point of departure for the rest of this
paper.

47   LENIN, What is to be Done? *Selected Works* (Moscow, 1977),
vol. 1, especially pp.152-6.

Chapter 5

ON THE RELATIONSHIP BETWEEN THE SUBSISTENCE SECTOR AND THE MARKET ECONOMY IN THE PARNAÍBA VALLEY

Regis de Castro Andrade

This is a brief study of the coexistence of a capitalist extractive sector and a peasant economy of subsistence in the Parnaíba Valley, in Northeast Brazil. Though the region remains largely undocumented in comparison with other parts of the Northeast, the available evidence suggests that, in a broad perspective, the Parnaíba Valley is a social economic formation made up by two morphologically independent and partially articulated modes of production, which, as will be shown, are interwined (a) during the harvest time in the extractive sector when the labour force is paid a wage substantially inferior to the subsistence minimum; and (b) as the food staples surpluses of the subsistence sector are commercialised at prices which do not reflect market conditions. The extraction of a surplus, whatever its form, is in both cases accomplished by methods whereby the capitalist extraction of surplus value and trade gains are supplemented and reinforced by the operation of subordinated non-capitalist relations of production.

The relationship between the two sectors, thus synchronically stated, may also be seen as the outcome of a process of increasing subordination of the local economy to extra-regional capitalist centres. Should we speak here of a situation of *regional dependence*? The local landowners had for many decades drawn most of their revenue from the exploitation of the palm forests. (1) As time passed, however, their situation was affected by falling international prices and by a fiercer extra-regional competition for the commercial gains in the business. The various phases of the extractive economy were progressively taken over by extra-regional industrial or commercial firms, supported by stronger financing agencies. The landowners survived as they could, and managed to secure an income by renting the land to sharecroppers, or to firms or agents devoted to the extractive activities. The history of such changes is engraved in the crumbling dignity of the buildings and streets of Parnaíba, the aristocratic former economic capital of the state of Piauí. The structure of the land tenure was nevertheless maintained through a process of adjustments between the local landowners and extra-regional interests.

The overall result of the integration of the backward regions of Brazil into the capitalist economy has been that of a steady draining of resources generated in those regions away to the industrial centres. Data on this are abundant though fragmentary, and they show that both the specific mechanisms whereby resources are syphoned off and the relative magnitude of such resources vary greatly from region to region. As a total process of value transfer, however, such interregional flows have played a major part in the intense capitalist expansion of Brazil. (2) The economic exploitation of the Parnaíba Valley fits in well with this general pattern, as is illustrated in Section II by figures on the distribution of the total value of production among the primary, secondary and tertiary phases in each of the extractive activities carried out in the region.

The main focus of this study, however, will be on the specific modality of surplus generation in the extractive sector and the problem of wage determination in that sector (Section III). This, and some remarks on the commercialisation of food surpluses (Section IV) will provide the basic elements for the formulation of some hypotheses on the *resistance to change* exhibited by the socio-economic formation of the Parnaíba Valley over a long period.

Some general descriptive features (Section I) will help to situate the region within the national context.

I BASIC REGIONAL DATA

The official territorial unit in the government documents dealing with that part of Brazil under discussion is the Parnaíba Basin, which comprises the state of Piauí, part of the state of Maranhão on the left bank of the Parnaíba river, and a small part of the state of Ceará. Such a natural partition of the territory, however, is not very useful: in fact, there is no precise coincidence between the geographical region (the Basin) and the socio-economic region of the Valley (which encompasses economic activities and population along the Parnaíba borders or near them). (3) Some parts of the Basin could rightly be considered as extensions of neighbouring socio-economic units.

Macro-economic data are available with regard to the Basin and to the state of Piauí. Due to the lack of information on the Valley region itself, the general figures used in this paper will refer to the state rather than to the Basin. This is not likely to distort the picture seriously, for most of the population and economic activities of Piauí are concentrated in the Valley itself. Detailed data on the activities under study, on the other hand, come from very specialised literature and direct local research.

1 Ratio of rural to total population

In September 1970 the population of Piauí reached 1.7 million (something less than 2 per cent of the Brazilian national figure). About 1.2 million, or 67 per cent, lived in the rural areas. Taking all the states of the Brazilian Federation, this is the highest rate of rural to total population in the whole country. (4)

2   Sectoral per-capita income

Rural per-capita income is the lowest in the country, according to the national accounts for 1968. For the state of Piauí the average figure is C$149.00 (149 cruzeiros), which represents 56.8 per cent and 44.5 per cent respectively of the rural per-capita income of the Northeast and of Brazil. (5)

TABLE 5.1   Sectoral per-capita income in the state of Piauí, Northeast Brazil and Brazil, 1968 (in cruzeiros)

Sectors	Piauí	Northeast	Brazil
Rural	149	262	337
Urban	412	598	1,236
Total	233	402	839

Source: Censo Demográfico de 1970 and Anuário Estatístico do Brasil, FIBGE, 1972.

The gap in urban per-capita income between Piauí and the Northeast is not important as in the rural averages because the figure for the urban Northeast is lowered by the huge marginal sector in its main cities. In the Parnaíba Valley, immigration towards the urban centre is not, and never was, very significant within the region (although a fairly large population movement towards the Centre-South has been taking place).

3   Degree of industrialisation

The ratio of industrial to total output at factor cost in the state of Piauí was 5.3 per cent in 1968. For the Northeast as a whole, this proportion is 10.6 per cent. As a regional figure the Piauí percentage is, again, the smallest in the country.

TABLE 5.2   State of Piauí, gross domestic product, 1968 (in millions of cruzeiros)

Aggregate	Product
Industrial domestic product	20.8
Agricultural domestic product	168.8
Domestic product of services	200.7
Gross domestic product	390.3

Source: Anuário Estatístico do Brasil, FIBGE, 1972.

4   Main agricultural products

Extractive activities excluded, regional agriculture is highly specialised in some few staple crops such as rice, beans, manioc and corn, the only non-staple exception being cotton. Production is for the most part consumed by the producers themselves. The circulation of food surpluses is restricted to the regional market or even to municipio markets.

TABLE 5.3 State of Piauí, main agricultural products, 1970 (1) (in thousands of cruzeiros)

Products	Value of Production
Manioc	27,503
Rice	23,895
Beans	22,262
Cotton	19,553
Corn	14,637
Total	107,850

Source: Anuário Estatístico do Brasil, FIBGE, 1972. (1) Production of 1969 adjusted to 1970 prices.

5 Relative importance of extractive production in terms of value of output at primary level

Extractive products count for almost 30 per cent of the total value of output of the five main products mentioned in Table 5.3. Most of the extractive production meets an extra-regional and foreign demand. Further data on this are presented throughout thie paper.

6 Relation of subsistence to commercial agriculture in terms of estimated monetary value

As is shown in Table 5.4, even in relatively large holdings more than 50 per cent of total production was consumed by the producers themselves in 1972, according to the Land Office of the State of Piauí. This clearly indicates the predominance of the subsistence economy over commercial agriculture from the point of view of the local peasantry. But these figures also underline the similarity of social conditions prevailing in small and large holdings. In the latter, land productivity is probably higher, but production is carried out by small sharecroppers using the same primitive techniques as the independent peasants, mostly for subsistence purposes. Marketable surpluses, therefore, are scarce in small as in large holdings.

TABLE 5.4   Proportion of *lost, consumed or stocked* production
to total agricultural production (%)

States	Holdings of 100 hectares or more	Holdings of 10 hectares or less
Piauí	50.4	62.9
São Paulo	20.3	12.5
Rio Grande do Sul	33.3	40.1
Pernambuco	17.1	71.2
Goiás	41.3	51.9

Source: Cadastro do INCRA, 1972, quoted by Juarez Brandão Lopes.

7   Labour force outside the market economy

According to a study published by the Brazilian Secretary of
Planning, those 'economically active who, in 1970, earned less
than C$150.00 monthly in the Centre-South region, and less than
C$100.00 in all other regions' should be considered 'outside
the labour market and the market economy'. (6)   The concept is
certainly better than those of *unemployment* or of *disguised unemployment*. For the whole country, 14,283,000 were found to fall
within this category, 9,661,000 of them living in the rural areas.
The serious disadvantage of taking average annual earnings as a
criterion to determine whether people are included or not in the
labour market is that it conceals the seasonal inclusion of most
of the rural workers in that market.

II   INTERSECTORAL INCOME DISTRIBUTION IN THE EXTRACTIVE ACTIVITIES

The Parnaíba Valley is commercially connected to the external
world (foreign countries and other regions of Brazil) through the
regional exports of primary products. Available statistical reports
give account of exports of three products only: carnauba wax,
babassu oil and seed-cake, and cotton. But local inquiries revealed
that other products have been exported which do not figure in the
record. Being shipped or commercialised in Fortaleza, in the
neighbouring state of Ceará, those products are merged into the
much bigger production of this state. Thus, to the three commodities mentioned above, the following products must be added:
oiticica oil, for various industrial uses; resin of jalapa, used
in the pharmaceutical industry; pigment of urucú, which is an
industrial colouring, used for instance in the USA to redden
frankfurter sausages; cashew nuts, whose production in Piauí has
multiplied ten times in recent years. Such productions are carried
out in conditions very similar to those prevailing in the three
branches analysed below, and my conclusions will be thereby reinforced. (7)
   It was possible to find some national figures on the exports

of pilocarpine, which is a substance extracted from the leaves
of a shrub, jaborandi. This and other data collected therefore
allow us to form a clear picture of the importance of this particular branch in the Parnaíba Valley. Cotton is cultivated outside
the strict limits of the Valley. My subsequent remarks, therefore,
will allude only to babassu, carnauba and pilocarpine.

TABLE 5.5 Brazil, labour force outside the labour market and
the market economy, 1970 (as a percentage of the economically
active population)

States	%
Brazil	48.3
Distrito Federal	14.5
Guanabara	20.8
São Paulo	29.7
Rio de Janeiro	30.8
Amazonas	34.2
Pará	36.9
Acre	37.5
Mato Grosso	37.6
Goiás	43.9
Rio Grande do Sul	45.7
Espírito Santo	47.7
Pernambuco	56.0
Paraná	58.1
Baía	59.3
Santa Catarina	61.4
Minas Gerais	62.8
Alagoas	62.9
Sergipe	64.0
Maranhão	64.9
Rio Grande do Norte	70.5
Paraíba	73.3
Ceará	73.4
Piauí	79.4

Source: Censo Demográfico, FIBGE, 1970.

1 Carnauba wax

Carnauba wax is the product of the industrial processing of the
powder which covers the leaves of this palm. The complete cycle
from primary production to final consumption comprises three
stages.
   In the first stage, at the beginning of the dry season, the
leaves are cut out from the palm and sub-dried. The powder is
removed by beating the leaves, or (sometimes) by industrial vacuum-
cleaning. The product is sacked and taken to the processing unit
by traders. In the second stage, the powder is processed. A
wax plant contains a storeroom for the powder, a boiling floor, a
moulding floor, and a warehouse for the final product. Finally,

the wax is sold to wholesale traders and/or to brokers in Fortaleza, being exported for the most part.

Demand in the wax market is a function of industrial development, and it seems to be positively affected by the expansion of modern technology. In fact, apart from the traditional uses in the manufacture of soaps, cosmetics and polishing products, the wax is employed for the following industrial purposes: high-quality carbon paper, photographic films, protection of aircraft parts exposed to attrition, optical instruments, computers, electric cables, paper waterproofing, metal casting moulds and medicine capsules. The main importers are the USA, Japan, UK, Italy and West Germany, out of a total of 46 countries.

In 1970 wages (and commercial margins) at the extractive stage retained 41.6 per cent of the total value of production. (8) The industrial sector, composed of a considerable number of small and rudimentary units, received 11.7 per cent, and in the third sector 46.7 per cent of the value of production reverted to commercial agents. (For sources and absolute figures, see Table 5.6.)

The small share falling to the industrial sector indicates low industrial profits in relation to monetary values involved in the business as a whole. This partly reflects the technical simplicity of the equipment and the low value of constant capital in the secondary phase. But the main reason for this lies in the weakness of local manufacturers as opposed to the export sector. Industries are small in size, some are mere craft units, settled in remote places near the sources of raw materials; the export business, on the contrary, is tightly organised in Fortaleza, in the state of Ceará, and firms operating in it dominate the complexities of both the worldwide international connections and the bureaucratic channels in the country.

The evolution of prices in the various phases demonstrates with striking clarity the dominance of the commercial sector within the branch. Over the period 1961-3 to 1970, production of carnauba wax increased 75 per cent. (9) Exports grew 30 per cent in volume. (10) These successes were, nevertheless, marred by a drop of about 45 per cent in the export price per ton of wax. As a consequence, total value of exports fell some 30 per cent, (11) and the relative share of the industrial and commercial sectors was substantially altered. In the first place, the industrial price per ton of wax suffered a sharp decline of 56 per cent. Thus, as opposed to the exporters, industry was hit by an absolute and relative loss of income. Second, commercial margins in the export sector went up from about 30 per cent in 1961-3 to 46 per cent in 1970. A simple handling of the available statistics reveals that throughout this period, exporters managed to secure for themselves a constant C$1500.00 (in real terms) per ton of wax, despite the severe fall of international prices.

2 Babassu

Though statistical data on the babassu branch can only be used with reservations, there is some evidence of a rather different pattern of intersectoral income distribution in it. The largest

aggregate share goes to the primary sector; industrial added value
fluctuates around 35 per cent of the total value of production,
and commercial benefits in the third stage seem to be smaller
than in the carnauba business.

Organisational features in the extractive and industrial stages
of the babassu branch are similar to those of the carnauba. The
coconuts are picked from the palms and manually split with a stick.
The nuts themselves are bought by a trader and sold by him to the
industry which presses the nuts and refines the oil. The oil makes
up 60 per cent of the nuts in terms of weight. The by-product is
the seed-cake, used as poultry food. The oil has several industrial uses, as in the manufacturing of soaps, shaving cream,
candles, lamination, metal tinning (blanching), lubrication of
precision instruments. But it has been mainly consumed as a low-
quality edible oil. (12)

As in the carnauba industry, babassu pressing units are dispersed over the region. But while the wax is exported, 85 per cent
of the oil is sold locally. Only the seed-cake is exported, at
very low prices. The commercial sector is deployed across many
states and includes a variety of wholesalers and retailers through
whom the product is brought to intermediate or final consumption.
Dealing with a mass consumption product, however, the commercial
sector in the oil branch is probably more dispersed than the
industry, at least as far as the cooking oil is concerned. For
this reason, benefits in the third stage are not likely to be so
high as in the carnauba branch.

3 Pilocarpine

This is the chief alkaloid obtained from the leaflets of South
American shrubs known as Pilocarpas jaborandi, or simply jaborandi,
and is used in the preparation of collyriums. The processing unit
in the Valley, set up a few years ago by a Brazilian firm, was
bought by Merck, which dominates the world market of the drug.
Apparently, the Parnaíba Valley is the only spot in the world
where this species of shrub, in natural state, contains the substance.

Production of pilocarpine is abou8 10 tons annually, almost
entirely exported. Distribution of the product is carried on by
Merck sales office in Rio de Janeiro. Total exports amounted to
US$2.4 million in 1974, at a price of US$240 to 260 a kilogram.
In 1971 international quotations were almost half below that level
and total sales reached US$1.4 million. Out of that total, 80
per cent corresponded to the vertically integrated industrial and
commercial sectors; the remaining 14 per cent went to the primary
sector.

4 Types of economic activity

These three branches may be regarded as types of economic activity
in the region according to the way in which certain elements are
combined in each of them. These elements are the magnitude of

constant capital and degree of concentration in the industrial
sector, degree of concentration in the commercial sector, and the
market wherein the product is sold.

TABLE 5.6   Parnaíba Valley, intersectoral distribution of total
value of production in three extractive branches, 1970 (in
thousands of cruzeiros)

Products	Value of primary product		Industrial added value and commercial margins		Total market value of production	
	C$	%	C$	%	C$	%
Babassu (1)	20,140	57.2	15,050	42.8	35,190	100.0
oil					33,030	
seed-cake					2,160	
Carnauba wax (2)	9,650	41.6	13,500	58.4	23,210	100.0
Pilocarpine (3)	1,060	14.0	6,490	86.0	7,550	100.0
Total	30,850	43.7	35,100	56.3	65,950	100.0

Sources: Various State and Federal statistical publications, SUDENE
reports and local research.
(1)   Volume of primary production taken from the bulletin of the
      *Escritório de Estatísticas Agrícolas do Ministério da Agri-
      culture* (EAGRI) and DEE of Piauí and Maranhão.   Prices are
      provided by *Estudo de Mercado de Produtos Agropecuarios do
      Nordeste: Babacu*, SUDENE, Recife, 1972.   Industrial added
      value is estimated in the latter report as amounting to
      35 per cent of value of production for the oil and seed-cake.
      A narrow commercial margin of 15 per cent was estimated for
      the oil; seed-cake is accounted for in its export value.
(2)   Total value corresponds to export value, even for internal
      sales.   In this branch direct data is available for all
      sectors.
(3)   Figures of 1971 adjusted to 1970.

   In the babassu branch, industrial technology is rudimentary
and the magnitude of constant capital per industrial unit is low;
total output in the processing stage includes the contribution
of many small plants; the commercial sector is competitive and
traditionally organised; for the most part, the oil is sold to the
internal market.   This is the situation in a few other branches:
tanning, tucum oil and traditional fishing.
   A second type characterises a situation in which the product
is manufactured in small-size industrial units, using poor technology, and sold to the external market through very specialised
commercial channels based outside the region.   This is clearly
the state of affairs in the carnauba branch.   But some other
branches exhibit the same general pattern, such as jalapa resin,
cashew nuts, pigment of urucú and oiticica oil.
   The pilocarpine branch is a good example of a regional enclave.
Industrial processing is capital-intensive, both industrial and

commercial sectors are concentrated, and the product is exported.
Apart from pilocarpine, only perhaps deep sea fishing, recently
undertaken by a firm in the municipio de Luiz Correi, could be
included in this category.

Three points should be made as a conclusion of this section.
In the first place, all three types of economic activity have in
common the extensive and seasonal use of immense quantities of
local labour force at extremely low wages. This crucial feature
of the extractive economy of the Valley will be discussed in the
following sections. Second, it is interesting to note that the
more integrated the branch is in the outside world in terms of
the market for local production or in terms of control of the
secondary and tertiary phases by extra-regional firms, the smaller
the proportion of the total value of production of the branch
is retained in the region. Third, as will be shown below, extra-
regional firms operating in the region have been able to transfer
to the region part of the losses they have incurred as prices
fell or, inversely, to retain outside the region the gains stemming
from international trade.

III   WAGES AND THE ECONOMIC SURPLUS

The deeper meaning of the patterns of income distribution presented in Section II can only be visualised when wages, employment
and the evolution of the economic surplus are brought into the
picture. In fact, a labour share of 40 or 50 per cent in a
particular branch of activity involving industrial and commercial
stages, could seem, on the face of it, quite large. If we take
into account the current wage rates and the low capital-intensity
of industrial and commercial units in the region, however, those
figures appear in a very different light.
1 In all branches of activity investments are extremely labour-
intensive. Indeed, the total amount of capital required to carry
out the extractive business is very low in relation to aggregate
sales. There is hardly any investment in land, since for the most
part shrubs and palms spread over unoccupied areas. No expenses
are incurred in cultivation or in the improvement of work conditions, although deforestation and the clearing of pathways might
raise labour productivity. Machinery, equipment and buildings
in processing plants are very simple, locally manufactured for the
most part, and do not require large provisions for replacement.
Commercial expertise and good connections, finally, represent the
bulk of the 'commercial assets'.

The labour-force employed in all branches is enormous in relation to value of production. In the cutting of leaves and
removal of powder of carnauba, some 70,000 men are employed during
two months a year. In the picking and crushing of babassu coco-
cuts, at least 50,000 are required during three months a year; if
women and children engaged in the extraction of nuts were all
counted, that figure would probably be higher. (13) In the pilocarpine branch, 3000 to 5000 people are required to collect and
to dry jaborandi leaflets.

Wage levels are far below the regional officially stipulated

minimum. In the babassu and carnauba extractive sector, daily wages
were C₵3.50 in 1972. Monthly earnings, therefore, assuming a 30-
working-day month in the harvest time, would amount to C₵105.00.
This sum counts for only 58 per cent of the local official minimum
wage, which was C₵182.00 in 1972. It should be noticed that the
salário mínimo for Piauí and Maranhão was the lowest in the country.
For other states of the Northeast, for instance, the figure was
C₵206.40 and for São Paulo and Guanabara it was C₵268.80. (14)
Workers in the extraction and drying of jaborandi leaflets were
paid C₵2.10 a kilogram in 1974. It is difficult to say how much
a full-time worker could make during a month; but assuming that
harvest time lasts three months, monthly earnings would not be
higher than half the regional minimum. In any case, it clearly
emerges from these figures that wages do not cover the cost of
means of subsistence necessary for the replacement of labour-force
during the harvest time, even if we take the concept in the strict
sense of means of material subsistence.
2 The intertwining of the peasant economy of subsistence and the
capitalist extractive sector affects simultaneously the way variable capital is financed and wages are determined, conveying to
the regional system its inability to evolve and expand along capitalist lines. A simple model of capitalist development in a
situation of very elastic supply of labour may help to clarify the
argument.

Let us assume that the mass of economic surplus depends on (a)
the number of labourers employed and (b) the rate of surplus
value. In a given backward and closed national or regional system,
in which labour supply is very elastic, investment would naturally
be labour-intensive, and since the cost of necessary labour is
relatively high (due to a generally low level of productivity),
surplus value rates will be low. As long as the *labour surplus*
is not absorbed, (15) the obvious way of increasing the total
economic surplus is the incorporation of manpower, this being done
at a low rate of exploitation. But when the extension of employment becomes for some reason difficult (general or selective scar-
cities of manpower, unionisation, etc.) the increase of the mass
monetary surplus will depend, ceteris paribus, on the reduction
of the cost of labour as a result of productivity improvements in
the sector producing means of subsistence. As the process goes
farther in this direction, the relative rate of surplus value
increases; in the short and medium run, in all probability both
real wages and surplus value rate will rise.

In the Parnaíba Valley the situation is that of the worst of
all possible worlds. It is a backward sub-system with a large
labour surplus in which the cost of reproduction of the labour-
force is indeed high in terms of necessary labour time. Land
productivity in terms of yield per hectare is very low - the lowest
in the country actually - due to natural aridity. Since investment
in irrigation and other improvements is virtually nil, labour
efficiency is likewise low. All this would not constitute, however,
an absolute obstacle for the development of the model. In the
process of incorporation of wage labour, the system should be
expected to expand the internal outlets for its increasingly diversified production, becoming therefore less dependent on external

demand. The real problem is of a different kind. It has been
pointed out that employers in the Valley do not pay the workers
wages corresponding to the cost of reproduction of the labour-
force. A large proportion of the means of subsistence is produced
by the workers themselves. All the capitalist needs to do in order
to enjoy the privilege of paying them well below the bread-line,
is to lay off the men working for him during some months of the
year; but given the seasonal nature of the extractive business in
the Valley, this does not constitute a *sacrifice*. What must be
stressed, in this respect, is that the difference between the
official minimum wage (C$182.00) and the effectively paid wage
(C$105.00) roughly measures the part of necessary labour non-paid
by the employer, who, in these circumstances, is straightforwardly
given 43 per cent of his variable capital in the form of foodstuffs previously accumulated by the workers. (16)

   This is a basic element of the explanation why the process of
capital accumulation at the national level, although feeding on
the regional sources of manpower and regional resources, has not
introduced in the region, through its local ramifications, any
dynamic element. The use of manpower was vastly increased, but
in such a context that the urge for the reduction of the necessary
labour is not triggered; the industrial sector, producing goods
for local consumption, remains very feeble and stagnant. Excepting
babassu oil, all main activities in the capitalist sector remain
orientated towards extra-regional markets.

3 In theory, wages are incompressible beyond a certain limit
which is posed by the necessity of replacing the labour-force; in
the Valley it would be reasonable to expect them to be at this
strict limit level. As we know, even this level is not attained,
for a substantial portion of the means of subsistence is produced
by the workers themselves. Since wages do not keep any apparent
relationship with the cost of the labour-force, the question arises
of how they are determined in the region. Before an answer is
proposed to that question, some alternative explanations must be
discussed.

   Let us first examine the relationship between wages and the
profitability of the extractive sector. Although land productivity and labour efficiency in real terms are low as compared
with other regions (whenever comparisons are possible), productivity of labour in the sector is high in monetary terms. A
distinction must then be made between the rate of surplus value -
which measures the ratio of the value of necessary labour to total
value produced in a given industry - and the rate of economic
surplus. The rate of surplus value, or the rate of exploitation,
despite the high cost of necessary labour in terms of labour time
(as a consequence of low land productivity and labour efficiency)
is certainly high, for that cost is partly covered by the workers
themselves (as indicated in Section III. 2). The estimate of the
rate in the region presents some obvious difficulties, and the
concept itself could only be used in an approximate sense, due to
the overlapping of two different modes of production in the region.
The rate of economic surplus, on the other hand, indicates here
the relationship between wages in the primary sector and all other
sorts of payment in industry and commerce within a given branch.

This rate is probably higher than the rate of surplus value, because one of its elements - the total monetary value of extractive production, as given in the most part by export prices - is determined not only be its real value, but also by hazardous market conditions and monopoly practices. Table 5.6 provides the elements for a rough estimate of the proportion of surplus in relation to total market value of production. The surplus corresponds in each sector to the remuneration of the secondary and tertiary phases, less wages paid in industries (which are relatively unimportant) plus a margin of commercialisation and rent of 8 to 16 per cent of the value of primary production. It is clear that the low level of wages in the region could not be explained either by low rates of surplus value, nor by insufficient economic surpluses.

Attempts to associate wages to marginal productivity of labour in such a situation, moreover, are bound to fail. Even a superficial glance at Tables 5.7 and 5.8 shows that, over ten years, sharp increases in the volume of production (which correspond to increases of employment) are accompanied by equally sharp declines in the price of the products with no proportional changes in the real earning per worker as estimated by prices in the primary phase. In fact, wages lag so far behind labour productivity, and the fluctuations of total employment are so independent from labour productivity, that conditions of production at the margin would be hardly relevant.

In a well-known study, Lewis suggested that wages in the larger capitalist holdings are determined by productivity on the smaller holdings, devoted, partially at least, to subsistence cultivations. (17) Wherever jobs in capitalist farms are permanent this makes sense. In the Parnaíba Valley, however, employment in the extractive sectors is seasonal, and wages seem to be differently determined.

In such a situation wages in the capitalist sector correspond to the market value of those non-primary commodities which the worker cannot produce himself in the subsistence crop, but which are nevertheless necessary to him and his family, such as clothes, oil, household utensils, tools, etc. Significantly, some moradores families living far away in the palm bushes are reported to be paid in kind. Wages in the capitalist sector are not dependent on, or related to, medium yields in the subsistence sector, because harvest time in the capitalist activities corresponds to the idle season in the subsistence crops, the cost of opportunity of labour being zero in such a period. The real determinant of wages is, in the last resort, the cost of reproduction of the labour force, which is partly covered by autonomous and non-commercial production of subsistence foodstuffs, and complemented by monetary earnings in the form of seasonal wages.

It should be stressed, however, that such mechanism of wage determination could be dealt with only as a tendency. Strictly speaking, the social cost of reproduction of the labour force is not covered in the region. The total yearly amount of means of subsistence consumed by the workers is just sufficient to keep them alive for a small number of years, in appalling health and nutritional conditions. This is expressed in the high rate of mortality (total and infantile). In such an economy, constant

and intensive labour is the condition of survival; inability or
inefficiency to work due to age or illness means starvation. One
way of avoiding this is to have many-children families.
4 The analysis of some figures on the extraction and processing
of babassu nuts corroborates this interpretation. Although there
is no direct evidence of the evolution of wages in the primary
phase of any of the extractive branches, it is possible to estimate
an index of per-capita monetary earnings of the workers in the
babassu branch by taking into con8ideration the value of production
per ton of nuts. This is a precise indicator of wage evolution
in the primary sector, because changes in real output accurately
reflect changes in total employment, and because rent and the rate
of commercial margins between primary producers and the industry
are not likely to vary substantially according to production or
industrial prices.

TABLE 5.7 Brazil, indices of production and of values per ton
of nuts and babassu oil

Years	Volume of production of nuts	Value per ton	
		Nuts (1)	Oil (2)
1961	100.0	100.0	100.0
1962	116.4	87.0	63.1
1963	121.0	98.5	76.7
1964	132.1	108.2	102.5
1965	145.4	101.6	77.4
1966	147.1	70.9	64.9
1967	148.9	84.7	67.7
1968	150.5	85.0	72.6
1969	153.6	83.4	59.8
1970	154.0	89.7	71.6

Sources: *Escritório de Estatísticas Agrícolas do Ministério da
Agricultura* (EAGRI), for production and *Estudo de Mercado de
Produtos Agropecuários do Nordeste: Babacu*, SUDENE, Recife,
1972, for prices.
(1) Deflator: index for agricultural products.
(2) Deflator: general index for industrialised products.

Production of nuts rose 45 per cent over the first quinquennium,
and 6 per cent over the second. Wages, by comparison, oscillated
around index 100 over the first five years and around index 85
over the following period. In the long run, therefore, labour
earnings are quite inelastic to changes in production. But these
figures also suggest that there exists a ceiling close to which
these earnings are brought when production is vigorously expanding;
such a slight upward trend probably represents a necessary encouragement to the supplementary tens of thousands of workers
required each year. When production becomes stable, or slowly

expanding, wages are brought down to a sort of floor, a lower
limit, below which the workers would refuse to work and break all
links with the labour market. As related to industrial prices,
wage elasticity is again quite low. As a general trend, the
worker's share floats according to industrial prices, but not at
the same proportion. As can be seen in Table 5.8, high industrial
prices (in 1961 and 1964) are not proportionally reflected in wage
rises in the primary production; also when market prices went
down (1962 and 1969) wages were only slightly affected.

TABLE 5.8   Brazil, prices of babassu nuts and oil (in cruzeiros
of 1970 per ton)

Year	Nuts (A)	Oil (B)	B/A
1961	682	2036	3.0
1962	594	1285	2.2
1963	672	1557	2.3
1964	738	2088	2.8
1965	693	1577	2.3
1966	484	1323	2.7
1967	578	1379	2.4
1968	580	1480	2.6
1969	569	1218	2.1
1970	612	1458	2.4

Source: As for Table 5.7.

The utilisation of the labour-force is subjected to the same
conditions in all extractive branches. There is a large, homogeneous reservoir of labour-force purveying all activities. Given
the unstructured nature of the labour market and the similarity
of the work to be performed in all branches, wages are likely to
behave in the same way in the whole capitalist sector. In so far
as it is possible to generalise the observations concerning the
babassu branch, then, it might be suggested that the work-force
does not benefit in terms of eage increases from trade gains
falling to the branch in the international or internal market.
But, on the other hand, industrial and commercial sectors do not
succeed in transferring all their trade losses to the workers,
although wages do decline to a certain extent in periods of falling
prices. This seems to confirm the hypothesis that wages are
determined by a fraction of the cost of reproduction of the labour-
force, as stated in Section III.3.

IV   THE TOTAL MONETARY INCOME OF RURAL WORKERS AND THE PRICES
     OF MARKETABLE SURPLUSES

In addition to wages in the extractive sector, the total monetary income of rural workers includes earnings from the selling of food surpluses. Available data do not provide information on the relative weight of these two major elements of the monetary income. But they certainly suggest some general considerations on this matter.

Table 5.4, on the proportion of *lost, consumed or stocked* production to total agricultural production, offered a direct measure of the marketable surplus in relation to production. The total value of such a surplus would be derived from the total monetary income, as shown in Table 5.9, by subtracting the total value of wages paid in the extractive sector. A definite set of figures is naturally impossible to produce, since we do not have the average income for each bracket and we cannot establish the proportion of people working in the extractive sector during harvest time. But data in Table 5.9 are telling enough. The Census takes into account the total number of workers and the autonomous, who are cropholders working on their own land (as proprietors or occupants) or on someone else's land (as tenants or sharecroppers), even though they are occupied in extractive activities in the dry season. The difference between the autonomous and the total gives (presumably) the number of workers making an income exclusively from wages, on a temporary or permanent basis. If we consider that the official regional minimum was C$124.80 in 1970, we must conclude from these data that about 90 per cent of the work-force is engaged in varying degrees in subsistence activities in crops, livestock, farming and fishing. In fact, 91.8 per cent at least of the work-force earned either no monetary income at all (first bracket or stratum) or an income substantially inferior to the minimum wage (second and third brackets).

TABLE 5.9 State of Piauí, monthly earnings of workers in agriculture, cattle raising, forestry, extractivism, hunting and fishing, 1970

Income strata	Number of workers ('000)	
	Total	Autonomous
No monetary income	86.0	
to C$50,000	102.0	90.0
from C$51.00 to C$100.00	124.0	111.0
from C$101.00 to C$150.00	20.0	18.0
from C$151.00 to C$200.00	8.0	6.0
from C$201.00 to C$250.00	1.3	1.2
from C$251.00 to C$300.00	1.3	1.1
from C$301.00 to C$400.00	0.6	0.4
C$401.00 and more	(...) (1)	(...) (1)

Source: Censo Demográfico do Estado do Piauí, FIBGE, 1970.
(1) Negligible.

Assuming that the average income of each bracket is not far from the medium value within the bracket, the total monthly per-capita income of the rural workers would be around C$50.00, to which wage earnings contribute with about C$10.00 (as calculated from Table 5.7). Such an extremely low figure does not seem to reflect only the small size of the marketable surplus. Indeed, as shown in Table 5.4, the surplus represents something less than 50 per cent of total production in volume, whereas in value it would be less than 30 per cent (conservatively assuming that the market value of total output in the crops would amount to the minimum wage, or C$124.80 monthly). The conclusion is that prices paid to primary producers are also extremely low. Some figures on the commercialisation of fresh-water fish, collected on the field, will illustrate the point.

According to the Demographic Census, there were 1686 fishermen in the Parnaíba Valley as a whole in 1970. The Statistical Year-book and the Department of Economic Statistics of the various states, however, give a much bigger number, something like, 19,000 fishermen. This apparent inconsistency is due to the use of different concepts in those publications. The Demographic Census consider only fishermen registered in their official organisations (Colônias de Pescadores), who are supposedly full-time fishermen. The other sources contemplate occasional fishermen as well. The difference between the two figures (17,400) may be taken as an estimate of the great number of people for whom occasional fishing is a way of supplementing their protein diet and/or of increasing their monetary earnings. Data presented on Table 5.10 compare prices paid to the fishermen in the Boa Esperança Dam and prices paid by the consumers in Terezina in January 1974. It must be noted that the commercialisation of fish in the dam is assisted by the local administration, which centralises the dealings with traders. The situation of fishermen in other parts of the Valley is likely to be even worse.

TABLE 5.10   Commercial margins in fresh-water fisheries, (*artisanal* fishing) (1), Boa Esperança Dam (Piauí), January 1974

Type of fish	Producer price per kg. (C$)	Consumer price per kg. (in Terezina, Piauí) (C$)	Commercial margins %
1st class	2.50	15.00	600.0
2nd class	2.00	10.00	500.0
3rd class	1.00	7.00	700.0
4th class	0.60	5.00	833.0

Source: Local research
(1) Fishing by individual fishermen using primitive techniques, partly for subsistence purposes.

In such circumstances, prices of marketable surpluses could hardly be said to be determined by market conditions: the difference between prices paid to the producer and prices paid by the consumer are unjustifiable by mere economic reasons. If extraction of surplus value constitutes the basic (but not the exclusive) modality of exploitation in the capitalist sector, underpayment of food staples is the mechanism of surplus expropriation in the peasant sector. Here again the two modes of production overlap. To the producers, agricultural products are just use values, necessary condition of their own survival, and means of keeping the right to cultivate the land. Whenever good rains or otherwise favourable conditions permit, a surplus is generated that could be exchanged against some manufactured goods, the operation requiring, however, the previous selling of the surplus under trade terms, which are to a great extent imposed by the traders or by the landlords, who sometimes commercialise the production. The small crop-holders are isolated, unaware of the general situation of the market, usually in debt to the landowner, and frequently unable to preserve, to transport or to sell the products themselves in the main urban centres. They are, indeed, directly dependent on the landowners and/or the traders to commercialise their products. (18) To the traders, however, the surpluses are commodities. They collect them wherever they are available and put them into general commercial circulation. The regularity of their capitalist trade links up with the uncertain production of food surpluses, and the resulting prices reflect, on the part of the producers, the need to acquire some supplementary consumer goods, and on the part of the traders, a necessary encouragement to the production of surpluses within a cycle of reproduction of poverty in the rural areas. This is made possible through the utilisation, by traders, or legal, political and ideological forms of domination in order to make a profit in the capitalist market.

V   REMARKS ON THE REPRODUCTION OF THE PEASANT ECONOMY OF SUBSISTENCE

A descriptive approach would immediately discover that the old social and economic order exhibits a remarkable resistance to change. Some partial, though interconnected reasons for that have been pointed out at the structural level: weakness of the industry as opposed to the export sector, low wages in the extractive sector, low prices of surpluses of food staples, etc. All this has been analysed in the light of the coexistence and articulation of two modes of production in the Valley. Some final observations should now be made to explain tentatively the functioning of the system, with emphasis on its conservative effect upon the local economy. Why, in fact, has an all-pervading, fast-growing Brazilian capitalism not disrupted the peasant economy and the peculiar operation of the extractive sector in the region?

The pertinence of such a question is enhanced by the striking evidence of an expanding agricultural production in the region. Primary output grew at twice the national rate over the period 1955-68. In current prices, agricultural produce in Piauí, Maranhão and Brazil went up from index 100 in 1955 to, respectively, indexes 151.53, 144.42 and 831.7 in 1968. (19) Partly this is a consequence of the demographic growth in the rural areas. We may also think

that production of the remotest parts of the state has been progressively taken into account by the official statistical agencies.
The same phenomenon, however, has been observed in all states of
the Northeast: this in a way attaches some verisimilitude to the
regional data and associates the trend with the major processes of
capitalist development in the country as a whole. In Piauí, moreover, as well as in other parts of the Northeast, the increase of
agricultural output is accompanied by the multiplication of the
minifundia (in the sense of small, family holdings on previously
unoccupied land or on someone else's land for the most part). The
outstanding feature of this evolution, however, is the increase
of sharecropping, suggesting that the marketable surpluses have
considerably grown throughout the process.

Sá Jr associates the growth of primary production in the Northeast precisely to the growing number of minifúndia, resulting from
pressure on the land and expressing the extension of the subsistence economy. (20) 'Demographic pressure on subsistence activities proved to be more efficient in increasing production than
investments and the modernisation of imports and equipment', he
says, comparing the Northeast and Centre-South regions. The strong
pressure on land is expressed in the rapid multiplication of minifúndia all over the Northeast; the binomial minifúndia-latifúndia
would characterise a system in which people expelled from plantations due to falls in international prices try to make a living
in subsistence crops, without any alteration of economic and political power based on large land holdings.

In Piauí and Maranhão, the number of minifúndia has, indeed,
substantially increased over the last twenty years, throughout a
process of expansion of both the external frontier (occupation of
vacant land), and the internal one (expansion of land-renting to
small-holders). (21) The reasons for this seem to be different
from that proposed by Sá Jr, who was mainly concerned with the
coastal regions of the Northeast. In fact the situation in the
Parnaíba Valley is quite different from that of the sugar cane
region. It must be remembered that production has been vigorously
expanding in the extractive sectors in spite of falling international prices. So the expansion of the peasant sector is not
a consequence of lack of seasonal jobs in the extractive sector.
It also could not be explained by excessively low wages in the
sector; as we have seen, the workers' income, at the current levels,
is incompressible and has remained stable for a decade. Another
conceivable cause would be the improvement of technical and/or
market conditions in the peasant sector, if this were big enough
and sufficiently widespread to attract people to it. As to the
technical conditions, there is no evidence at all of any improvement in the cultivation techniques. Rural workers in the Valley
are, as they have always been, trabalhadores de enxada (hoe
workers). And as poorer land became occupied, productivity of
practically all crops fell substantially during the 1960s. (22)

Strictly speaking, rural workers in the region have not been
expelled from the latifúndia. Demographic pressures are visible
in the occupation of new land. But the most important trend is
the landowners' shift from direct exploitation of the natural resources to land-renting from 1950 onwards. (23) This process seems

to be closely related to the penetration - or interweaving - of capitalism in the very core of the old society based on primary exports. Broadly speaking, there are grounds to believe that the growing importance of land-renting is part of a long process of accommodation taking place between landlords and extra-regional capitalist interests, during which the landlords, losing control of most lucrative phases of the extractive activities and part of their political power, were nevertheless able to keep control over the land and to secure a revenue by sharing in the growing production of food staples. This arrangement, on the other hand, nicely served the capitalist interests. By maintaining the old mode of production based on the concentration of land, property and seasonal extraction of natural resources by an extensive labour force otherwise occupied in subsistence crops, it was possible to carry out the extractive business at extremely low cost (by paying wages below the subsistence level) and to extract a cheap and growing marketable surplus. It is interesting to note the two-fold influence of capitalist penetration in the region: it has at the same time promoted the multiplication of surplus-yielding mini-fúndia inside the latifúndia and also developed the outlets for the expanded production, as the urban market for food staples grew.

Some of the contradictions inherent in such a social formation are immediately apparent. First, the expansion of the marketable surplus is based on the expansion of small holdings primarily engaged in subsistence production. Second, the extractive sector is based on the exploitation of a labour-force that is available at such low wages only because it is occupied in non-capitalist activities during most of the year. The emergence of a capitalist peasantry has been so far hindered by the persistence of the land tenure structure, and the maintenance of the traditional conditions of production. The peculiarities of the seasonal work in the extractive sector, on the other hand, have so far prevented the emergence of any kind of unionisation. Economic trends in the last decade, however, suggest that the proportion of production sold to the market is bound to increase in relation to total production. Pressures for a better share of regional income and land may follow as cities grow and the process of integration of the regional economy to the market develops. In any event, the evolution of the socio-economic formation of the Parnaíba Valley will be determined by that of the industrial centres. Moreover, judging by what has happened in other regions in Brazil, the formation of a healthy capitalist peasant economy in Piauí is unlikely; wherever primary production on a fully capitalist basis has become profitable, the number of minifundia have decreased and small land-holders have turned into wage-earners.

NOTES

1   The two main extractive products of the region are carnauba wax and babassu oil. In 1918 the export value of carnauba wax represented 2 per cent of total Brazilian exports, against 1 per cent in 1957 and 0.3 per cent in 1970. This is chiefly due to falling world prices of the product. In 1923, the

price per ton of wax was inferior to that of skins, cotton
(raw) and wool. (*Commercial Encyclopedia*, British and Latin
American Chamber of Commerce, Birmingham, 1924). As to babassu,
the Encyclopedia pointed out that

> After the coconut, the babassu palm is the most important
> of Brazilian oil-bearing plants. It grows extensively in
> the States of Maranhão, Piauhy and Goiaz ... (...) Babassu
> oil is used in superior margarine, for illuminating, in
> the making of fine toilet soaps, and as a combustible for
> internal-combustion engines. (...) The chief difficulties
> in the exploitation of these oil-bearing palms has hitherto
> been the crushing and the transport to the nearest sea
> port. After many years of experiment, however, a crusher
> has been patented. (...) Upon the solution of the transport
> problem now, in a measure, depends the development of this
> valuable industry.

New roads have shortened the distance to the port of Fortaleza
in Ceará; but the crusher turned out to be another failure in
a very long series of failed attempts to crush the shell by
mechanical means.

2   It would be misleading to conceive the economic stagnation of
the region as the natural state of an inert society by empha-
sising its traditional institutional or cultural features.
The dynamic possibilities inherent in the extraction of surplus
through capitalist methods or for capitalist purposes are,
in fact, realised outside the region. By the same taken, the
vicious circle approach – which ascribes under-development to
poverty (hence shortage of savings) and then proceeds the
other way round – proves to be totally sterile in the analysis
of the Brazilian Northeast's social realities.

3   A *socio-economic region* is an abstract, undetermined notion,
be it taken in the sense of an economic field induced by a
growth pole (a polarised region) or as an economic space whose
homogeneity is defined by the similar behaviour of some chosen
variables along the various parts of that space. As a first
attempt to organise the available descriptive materials,
however, the notion is instrumental to further analytical
purposes.

4   Censo Demográfico do Piauí, 1970. The ratio for the Northeast
as a whole is about 58 per cent.

5   Obtained by dividing the value of agricultural production
by total rural population. In strict terms, this procedure
could be challenged on grounds that a certain proportion of
people living in the rural areas work in non-primary activities. But this is certainly not true for Piauí. A serious
limitation of the use of value of production per-capita as an
indicator of per-capita income, however, is that the former
figure incorporates the estimated value of subsistence production which has not been actually transformed into monetary
income; compare, for instance, this figure for 1968 with those
on Table 5.9, for 1970, which are much lower. But in inter-
regional comparison with the Northeast, the intervening bias
is partly neutralised.

6   *Industrialização e Emprego no Brasil*, Instituto de Planejamento
    Economico e Social (IPEA), Presidencia da Republica Secretaria
    de Planejamento (Rio de Janeiro, 1974), p.113.

7   The *branch* denotes in this paper a set of primary, secondary
    and tertiary activities associated to a specific product,
    regardless of the degree of vertical integration or the geo-
    graphic position of industrial or commercial firms operating
    in the business. Each branch is schematically analysed in
    three *sectors*: primary production, industrial processing, and
    commercialisation of the industrialised product.

8   A certain number of assumptions and adjustments had to be
    introduced in these calculations in order to sort out a handy
    set of aggregate figures. Commercial benefits between the
    primary producer and the industry - amounting to about 8 per
    cent in the carnauba branch - were not con8idered, neither
    were rent payments wherever the carbauba palms were situated
    on private properties. Fragmentary information reveals a 16
    per cent retention over the value of production by the landlord
    as rent and commercial margins. These aspects of income dis-
    tribution had to be ignored because the proportion of total
    production coming from private lands is not known, the assum-
    ption being, however, that it is low. Depreciation funds,
    moreover, are not contemplated, because there are no estimates
    of the monetary value of fixed capital in any branch. But
    this omission is definitely not important in view of my present
    purposes, since investments in those branches - excepting the
    industrial sectors of pilocarpine - are negligible.

9   Source: Escritorio de Estatísticas Agrícolas do Ministerio
    da Agricultura (EAGRI) and Departamentos Estadnais de
    Estatística (DEE of Piauí, Ceará and Maranhão), various years.

10 Comercio Exterior do Brasil, Ministerio da Fazenda.

11 Estudos de Mercado de Produtos Agropecuários do Nordeste:
    Carnauba, SUDENE (Recife, 1972).

12 More recently attempts to solve the problem of mechanical
    crushing of the nuts have brought about the possibility of
    large-scale use of the shell as cheap fuel.

13 These figures were obtained by taking into consideration the
    total production and average daily productivity per worker
    during harvest time in both branches as provided by SUDENE in
    the Estudos de Mercado de Produtos Agropecuários (Recife, 1972).
    Data on pilocarpine were directly collected. Another way of
    estimating the total work-force in the extractive activities
    is to divide the value of production in the primary phases by
    earnings per worker. The result is circa 100,000 workers,
    which fairly approximates to the previous one. Of course,
    these are not precise figures. They only allow a broad estimate
    of the relevant aggregates.

14 Wages being simply the price of manpower, they do not neces-
    sarily express the value of the labour-force, which is given
    by the value of means of subsistence necessary for its repro-
    duction. It is assumed, moreover, in these inter-regional
    comparisons, that the working day is comparable everywhere
    in terms of its intensiveness and extensiveness. As to this
    latter aspect, it is worth noticing that the working day in the

region is quite long, as a consequence of low productivity
of land. In fact, it would be misleading to consider the
unemployed in the Valley as a mass of idle and easily dis-
posable people. Subsistence and extractive activities demand
hard and constant work, absorbing a large amount of female
labour.

State of Piauí, weekly hours worked in the primary activities,
1970

Weekly hours worked	Men	Women	Total	%
less than 15	2,113	2,443	4,556	3.3
15-39	11,902	14,830	26,732	19.6
40-49	51,122	20,421	71,543	52.5
50 and more	23,365	9,745	33,110	24.3
Total	88,502	47,439	135,941	100.0

Source: Censo Demográfico, Série Regional, Piauí, 1970,
FIBGE.

15 For most of the year the bulk of the rural workers are engaged
in very hard work in low-productivity crops. The expression
labour surplus, therefore, does not imply here the existence
of structural unemployment of a certain proportion of the
labour force whose productivity is supposed to be zero, etc.
The labour surplus exists only from the point of view of the
capitalists, who are in a position to increase the monetary
earnings of the workers even by paying them very low wages.

16 It is assumed that the minimum official rate expresses the
monthly value of the labour-force. But it must be noted that
this is a conservative assumption, for the official minimum
wage is calculated on the basis of local practices and traditional local standards of living, from which medical care,
education, proper housing, etc. are excluded. As a result
of underpayment and lack of public services, life span in the
Valley is short as compared with national standards.

17 W.A. LEWIS, Desarollo Economico en condiciones de oferta
ilimitada de mano de obra, in *El Trimestre Económico*, No.108,
FCE, Mexico, 1970.

18 Fruits, vegetables, animals, etc. are also sold in the local
feiras by the producers themselves. One cannot minimise the
importance of this trade throughout the Northeast of Brazil:
but for the most part the feiras are circumscribed to a local,
petty commerce, which by no means alters the general situation
in the region.

19 Brazilian National Accounts, F.G.V.

20 F. SÁ JR., O Desenvolvimento da Agricultura Nordestina e a
Função das Atividades de Subsistência, *Estudos CEBRAP 3* (Rio
de Janeiro, 1973). In Sá's study, peasant economy in the
Northeast is that of 'small proprietors and sharecroppers',
(p.116).

21   It was not possible to get the figures for 1970; trends
in other Northeast states and local research, however, suggest
that the expansion of the subsistence crops continued after
1960. Figures below refer to the number of holdings in the
states of Piauí and Maranhão.

Holdings with less than 5 ha.	1950	1960
privately owned	12,941	14,544
occupied	57,592	122,291
rented	5,305	107,186

Source: Sá Jr., op.cit.

22   Produção Agropecuária do Estado do Piauí; DEE, several years.

23   JUAREZ BRANDÃO LOPES, in a preliminary study on the class
structure in the Northeast (in manuscript), estimated the
number of peasants in the State of Piauí as follows (in
thousands):

Categories of peasants (1)	1950	1960	1970
Proprietors	13.5	10.1	14.0
Arrendatarios (tenants)	0.6	7.0	9.6
Occupants	0.4	1.0	9.0

Sources used by Lopes: Censos Agrícolas, 1950 and 1960;
Sinopse do Censo Agropecuário of 1970.
(1) Non-paid members of the peasant families are excluded.

Chapter 6

STAGNANT PEASANT CAPITALISM: THE CASE OF INSHORE FISHERMEN IN NORTHEASTERN BRAZIL

Simon Mitchell

During the last twenty-five years inshore fishing in many developing countries has been radically altered by the introduction of larger hulls and engines to replace boats propelled by oar or sail. Techniques have changed with the mechanisation of vessels and catches have, as a consequence, been increased. Technological innovation and increased wealth have, moreover, had effects upon the social organisation and general culture of inshore fishermen and their families. Ready examples of recent changes may be found on the West African coast, in Malaya, India, Taiwan and Hong Kong. (1)

This paper is concerned with the comparative lack of technological change in inshore fishing in the Northeast of Brazil. A striking characteristic of the technology employed by inshore fishermen of Northeast Brazil is its static and extremely primitive state. To exploit the waters of the continental shelf up to twenty miles from the coast, fishermen have continued to use jangadas, crude log sailing rafts which have changed very little since the seventeenth century, small hulled sailing boats, and canoes. Only very rarely are motor boats encountered along the 1800 miles of the Northeast littoral, and even more rarely are these boats owned by fishermen producers themselves.

It is jangadas which perhaps most vividly ememplify the unchanging economic situation of fishermen between the states of Alagoas and Ceará: lying on coconut palm rollers on the beaches of the state capital cities against a backcloth of neon lights, expensive apartment blocks and luxurious tesselated pavements, they are as surrealist as an ox-cart would be in Manhattan. Irony has been added to surrealism in recent years with the introduction of brightly coloured sails advertising commercial companies and their products. These sails have been given free to grateful fishermen who are now able to fish by Stone-Age means and advertise thrusting manufacturing concerns at the same time.

In this paper I suggest reasons for the backwardness of this inshore fishing sector and for the continuing poverty of fishermen and their families. My basic assumption is not that technology alone will solve the problems of inshore fishermen; improved methods of fishing, if widely distributed, would almost certainly, given the present number of fishermen, destroy existing fish stocks. Technological improvements, both spontaneous and induced, can and have taken place with disastrous consequences, an appropriate example being the over-extraction of fish from the North Atlantic. My working supposition is, however, that people endeavour to improve their technology if they can see a way to do so and that governments, in general, if only to decrease imports, wish to increase production of basic commodities. My query in this paper is a neutral one. Why have neither fishermen nor governmental agencies improved the technology of fishing?

I will argue that there are at least three elements which are central to an understanding of an almost unchanging situation: the nature of the inshore fishing economy itself, the social organisation with that economy, and the arrangement of non-institutional and institutional credit. All three will be briefly considered; and discussion of the last, credit, leads to broader conclusions which I would argue are as relevant for other small-scale producers as for fishermen.

Over 100,000 fishermen and their families (2) live from fishing the waters of the continental shelf of Northeast Brazil. Most of them are caught in a classic low-level equilibrium trap of low production and small-scale investment and can do little about it. Continuous investment is necessary in fishing; a sailing raft's hull lasts one or two years at the most, nets are frequently damaged, fish traps are often lost, and fishing gear, in general, is very quickly worn out. The technology ensures that catches are small. Boats propelled by sail or oar often cannot reach the best fishing grounds, or take so much time to do so that only a small proportion of time can be spent fishing. The level of profits is such that it is not only a struggle for most fishermen to maintain ownership of a raft and its gear from year to year; it is all too easy for intervening circumstances, in the form of medical expenses or some other crisis, to change radically a fisherman's fortunes over a winter. The tenuous position of these people is made very clear from the fluctuating patterns of ownership in any particular community from year to year. (3)

This low-level economy is sustained by certain elements in the social organisation of fishing families. One marked feature of their organisation is the lack of co-operation between individuals in investment and economic activity. Owner-producers operate financially as individuals. Joint ventures are almost never undertaken. Apprenticeship in fishing is of short duration; a man can learn to become a competent fisherman in two or three years and, after that period, generally hopes to become an owner of a raft, boat or canoe. Few manage this, but any member of a crew sees himself potentially as an owner. The largest temporary co-operative group in inshore fishing is the crew of a boat, composed of between two and five men; but these crews tend to be unstable, with men changing from one boat to another from week to week, or even daily.

A strong ethnic of individualism and egalitarianism is also to be discerned in social relationships. Individuals, irrespective of their material status, will not readily tolerate direct orders from another, and decisions on a boat at sea, for example, are almost always made collectively. Men earn for their households,

which are the units of production and consumption. Outside the
household neither kinship nor any other principle provides a
basis for recruitment of stable groups over time. This type of
organisation is not surprising, for few fishing communities have
a stable past. Families are almost invariably squatters on the
land on which they have built their huts. Many are migrants from
the interior of the region and there has been a considerable degree
of mobility of families from one fishing community to another.

This somewhat atomised type of organisation has two serious consequences for the economy. The first is that savings are fragmented; the small quantity of capital available for productive
investment is employed by individuals rather than groups, and very
few people are able to make significant investment in improved
equipment such as hulled boats or motors. The second consequence
is that fishermen producers are easy prey for middlemen. Individuals can be picked off one by one by an incoming entrepreneur,
whether trader or aspiring rich producer. This vulnerability was
clearly demonstrated during the lobster boom of 1958-65 when fleet-
owning entrepreneurs from the cities were able to persuade fishermen to leave their rafts and fish on motorised boats. Crews' pay,
generally calculated on piece-work, was low and ingeniously based
very slightly above the scale of wages earned from jangada fishing.
The profits, however, from the export of lobster tails to the USA
and elsewhere were high, and fleet-owners prospered while a plentiful supply of lobster was available. As stocks were depleted, the
discarded crews returned to raft fishing worse off than they had
been before the boom, with neither savings nor productive equipment.
Exploitation was all too easy; fishermen were contracted individually and at no stage during the years of the boom was any
collective action organised by the labour force.

Another example of fishermen's collective weakness is apparent
in their relationship with local traders. Fishermen themselves
sell a proportion of their catch directly to individual consumers
and small traders on the beach. Some also sell their fish in the
local markets. But a high proportion of the profits on fish sales
is absorbed by traders with lorries and ice who have made contact
with individual producers. Some of these traders, usually from
the coastal towns, have succeeded in exercising a near monopoly
on the catches of fishing communities by binding producers to
themselves by a careful programme of favours, small loans of money,
or presents. The forging of dyadic ties with individuals is
highly effective; and although fishermen individually may realise
that traders make considerable profit at their expense, they lack
the capacity to organise collectively against outside buyers.

Yet neither the cyclical impasse of low production and low
investments, nor fishermen's socio-economic organisation are enough
to explain the continuing poor technology and stagnancy of the
fishing sector. There are other factors which are of direct
relevance.

Why do not those with available capital invest in inshore
fishing, other than in fishing for lobster, the single, very highly
priced species of catch? (We may leave aside for the moment the
question as to why investment is invariably made in company-owned
equipment, rather than through credit to existing producers.)

Is demand for fish in the Northeast sufficient to warrant investment? Are there enough fish to make investment worthwhile?
Would increased production, higher catches, be of advantage to
traders and retailers? Is it easier for middlemen to control
individually dozens of small producers catching limited quantities,
rather than allow a body of producers with better equipment to
catch more, and perhaps risk the possibility that with improved
catches they might organise themselves into a powerful body with
more clearly defined interests at stake?
    These questions are not easy to answer. It may well be the
case that on purely economic grounds entrepreneurs do not deem
investment worthwhile. Although one study in Recife calculates
that demand is much greater than supply, (4) the question of
general demand remains an open one; the interrogation of urban
retailers is not itself sufficient to gauge the situation, and, in
any case, potential demand in the huge interior is an unknown.
One indicator of demans is that the price of sih in urban centres
is very high relative to other types of protein food, and it is
certainly the case that large quantities of dried cod are imported
by Northeast Brazil from Scandinavia and Portugal. However, it
does not follow that a conservative taste for imported dried fish
indicates short supplies of fresh fish. One strongly suspects
that demand for fish throughout the Northeastern region is habi-
tually low, but that increased supplies of fish would have the
effect of raising it sharply.
    Concerning the quantity of fish stocks on the continental shelf,
research which has been done by personnel of SUDENE (Superintendencia do Desenvolvimento do Nordeste), SUDEPE (Superintendencia
do Desenvolvimento da Pesca) and FAO (Food and Agriculture Organisation) points to there being neither a special abundance, nor
a marked dearth, of fish. Fishing technicians have also noted
that there are various pelagic species of fish in commercial
quantities which are not exploited. It is plausible to argue
therefore that a partial answer to the general lack of investment
in fishing is that fishing does not offer a guarantee of high
return, that money is better employed in real estate or manufacturing.
    On the other hand, it would seem of direct benefit to retailers
and traders, those already making money from fish, to increase
their turnover. However, it might be argued that the present
organisation of production, with large numbers of small-scale producers employing equipment requiring very low capital cost, allows
traders to reap very high profit margins, and that, if they were
to invest in technological improvement, they would simply be involving themselves in an unnecessarily risky enterprise. The
situation at the moment allows a numerous body of traders and
middlemen to profit from a weak and divided production work-force;
even a few strong producers fishing with motor vessels and improved
gear might alter the picture.
    These factors may to some extent explain the general lack of
investment by entrepreneurs, traders and middlemen, but there is
a further dimension which has a direct bearing upon the unchanging
character of the fishing economy. If we examine the organisation
of credit, both non-institutional credit (that arranged with the

fishing sector itself) and institutional credit (that arranged
by banks and federal, state or private aid agencies) we can find
suggestive differences between the situation in Northeast Brazil
and elsewhere.

There seems to be a marked contrast in the kind of economic
agreements made between socio-economic classes in Northeast Brazil
(and, to some degree, I suspect, in Brazil at large) and other
countries which have successfully developed their inshore fishing
industries. In other countries credit flows between different
classes and occupational groups involved with fish; it does not
appear to do so in Northeast Brazil.

On the east coast of Malaya, for example, Firth describes how,
even before technological changes occurred, fishermen-producers
were highly sensitive to the market and were able to constrain
and to some extent control fish traders and middlemen. He also
describes how credit was given by middlemen and Chinese entrepreneurs to fishermen to improve their equipment. The industry
responded, was able to respond, when technological improvements
became available; within fifteen years between 1950 and 1965, the
inshore fishing sector was transformed. Sailing boats were superseded by larger motorised vessels owned by single men or small
syndicates, most of them fishermen or ex-fishermen. The ownership
of production was left in the hands of producers, although the
credit which improved production techniques was supplied by dis-
tributors and others not directly connected with first-stage
extraction of fish from the sea.

Ward reports a similar story in Hong Kong. There, fishermen
were able to motorise their junks with credit from a British funding
agency established in the early 1950s, but also from traders and
fish merchants who competed with the fund. She describes the
rapidity with which development took place and stresses that
fishermen remained wholly in control of their vessels and catch.
The same kind of rapid technological change has occurred in Twiwan,
and in West Africa, where, largely through non-institutional
credit, inboard and outboard motors have been fitted to traditional
fishing canoes.

It is by comparing technological changes elsewhere with the
situation in Northeast Brazil that one realises that there are
two stark disadvantages suffered by fishermen in the latter region.
Non-institutional credit is very limited in its range and scale,
and institutional credit is non-existent. The lack of either
type of credit can be explained in large part by the polarised
nature of class relations in the Northeast.

Let us begin with non-institutional credit. Small quantities
of money are lent or given by pombeiros (5) or raft- or boat-
owners to crews. These loans are essentially attempts to acquire
loyalty, or given with an expectation of some future reciprocal
favour. They are never large - they cannot be - and the notion
of interest is rudimentary. The only loan of any significant
size is that given most often by a pombeiro to a fisherman wishing
to own his own raft. The debtor will be lent the cost price of a
new raft and will be expected to pay back the sum during the life-
time of the raft, that is to say, within one year or eighteen
months. In addition, the debtor is compelled during the raft's

working life to sell his catch to the creditor, who will then market the fish for a price which is much higher than his buying price. This is the one type of loan demanding interest; other loans are nearly always, in effect, non-commercial favours. Small traders, those who buy fish on beaches and transport the catch by bicycle to local consumers, are not able to lend.

Traders on a larger scale, those who operate with trucks and ice, will, as mentioned earlier, give small loans to fishermen producers in attempts to bind them with ties of obligation, but never give clear-cut loans entailing mutually agreed rates of monetary interest, to allow producers to invest in long-lasting equipment such as boats or motors. And those who are richest in the inshore fishing sector, the urban fish retailers, merchants and entrepreneurs, never lend money to those involved in production.

The essential difference then, in non-institutional credit arrangements, between those countries which have experienced rapid technological change in inshore fishing and Northeast Brazil is that, in the former, credit seems to flow downwards to the production sector from above. It is doubtful that creditors anywhere are motivated by altruism; interest and the potential goodwill of the debtor in future retailing of catch are ready advantages in themselves. A significant point, however, is that credit even from the wealthiest operators in inshore fishing allows the producer autonomy in improving his productive capacity.

In Northeast Brazil, on the other hand, there is highly restricted linkage between personnel involved with fishing. Loans are circulated among the poorest levels; fishermen, pombeiros and small traders. Loans from larger traders are specific and instrumental, and tie the producer closely to the retailer. Those with the ability to make significant loans are totally uninvolved in credit relationships with producers.

Turning to institutional credit, the situation in Northeast Brazil is most remarkable. In other parts of the world public credit or bank loans have been made available to inshore fishermen; but the authorities in the Northeast, despite being recipients of massive inputs of aid money over the last twenty years, have never provided any effective credit scheme to small-scale producers. Instead, both state and federal authorities have endeavoured to control fishermen (without total success), and have undertaken various sporadic and short-lived assistentialist measures to provide medical aid and pension schemes.

The history of the state's action is worth briefly describing. In 1864 inshore fishermen were officially divided into groups known as capatazias occupying specific districts; one has little doubt that their approximate number was calculated by the authorities anxious to exercise a degree of bureaucratic control over 'peasant' fishermen who were considerably more free than their counterparts working on the land. Nothing more was done until the 1930s when, under the first Vargas administration, the capatazias were changed in name to colonias. The government, stating its concern about fishermen's material conditions, also planned schemes to provide medical and dental help, to unionise fishermen, and to set the foundations for co-operatives. No plans, however, were put into effect.

In the 1950s another governmental initiative was made with the establishment of SUDEPE, an agency designed to be responsible for the development of inshore and deep-water fishing. Its bureaucracy grew rapidly in its early years, but it did nothing for inshore fishermen except to count their numbers yet again, *fiscalise* them (a central function of much of the Brazilian public bureaucracy), and insist ineffectually that fishermen should acquire appropriate papers to have the legal right to fish. In Northeast Brazil the SUDEPE agency was awakened briefly from its torpor in the early 1960s by the energetic example of SUDENE under Furtado. (SUDENE was also to fall into institutionalised inertia after Furtado's exile in 1964.)

An alliance was formed between the fishing division of SUDENE and SUDEPE; a programme of marine biology research was got under way; technicians in the two agencies planned pilot co-operative schemes in several locations off the Northeast littoral. However, during a period when it would have been easy to find money from the USA and other foreign sources, no funds were found to provide credit schemes for fishermen to invest in gear.

The co-operative pilot projects were expensive in terms of the number of personnel involved, vehicle cost, and the hours spent in elaborate theoretical planning. The various operations were markedly paternalistic in character, involving technicians talking down to fishermen, explaining over-simplistically why they should form co-operatives and what was expected of them. No serious attempts were made by the aid people to understand the culture and organisation of their recipients, and day visits were often made by personnel with office girls in tow wanting to see the curious and outlandish jangadeiros of the interior. It was not at all surprising, given the socio-economic structure of fishing communities, that all the pilot co-operatives failed and in doing so reinforced the general assumption of aid personnel that fishermen were childish, irresponsible and ignorante. This writer even found written confirmation of this common perception in an internal note distributed within SUDEPE in 1966 by its sub-head; his subject was inshore fishermen; his comments were that they are 'lazy, irresponsible, promiscuous and drunken' (sic) and that there was little that could be done for them. A part of SUDEPE's brief was to develop inshore fishing; but with this attitude toward their human material their own model of development could hardly accommodate the possibility of fishermen themselves improving their lot with direct material help. Indeed, there was an occasion in 1967 when more than 25 small diesel engines of various sizes were in the hands of SUDEPE to be sold on very favourable hire purchase terms. Only two of these engines were sold to small-scale owner-producers (around the corner from the SUDEPE building); the rest were sold to urban entrepreneurs for their own proposed fleets of motorboats.

Although it had become clear that co-operatives were failing by 1965, no alternative schemes were attempted, and small-scale efforts to start co-operatives continued into the 1970s. SUDEPE continued meanwhile the time-honoured process of *fiscalising* fishermen, counting their numbers, checking whether they had appropriate papers, and manifesting in general a disproportionate concern for bureaucratic trivia. Nothing was done to improve catches, incomes or living standards.

Another development in this rather sorry history was effected in 1973 with the setting up of a new aid organisation known as PESCART (Plano de Assistencia a Pesca Artesenal). This body announced in its publicity pamphlet that it intended to devote its first three years to: recruiting fishermen to the colonias, with the possibility of medical and dental treatment; training fishermen to conserve and utilise fishing resources; and conserving lobster stocks (for the sake, the pamphlet states, of inshore fishermen). There is bitter irony about this programme, given the previous performance of state agencies in relation to fishing. Medical and dental treatment was given for a brief period in the 1960s, but these services faltered and died in most places from lack of organisation, lack of will on the part of medical staff, and lack of funds. To ask fishermen to be concerned with conserving re-sources when their technology is barely adequate to catch sufficient fish to support their families would hardly seem a suitable first-phase priority. To conserve lobster stocks means simply to allow wealthy urban entrepreneurs to continue their lucrative trade with the USA; it is their motorised fleets which catch lobster in sig-nificant quantity, not the inshore fishermen owner-producers and their crews.

What emerges from this institutional story is that all the agencies from the past to present which have been concerned with fishing have never offered direct material help to those engaged in the sector. Moreover, the behaviour of agencies (SUDENE, SUDEPE, PESCART) with regard to credit has been remarkably similar to agencies like the BNB (Banco do Nordeste), BB (Banco do Brasil), BNDE (Banco Nacional do Desenvolvimento), and PROTERRA, responsible for helping small-scale agriculturalists.

In neither the public nor the private sector will individuals, or groups of individuals, loan money directly to producers. The state concerns have been prepared to engage in piece-meal social engineering, to patronise, instruct and control the human resources whose condition they are charged with improving. They are not, however, prepared to allow autonomous development to occur, offering direct credit, perhaps the simplest type of aid. Private entrepreneurs and rich fish retailers are similarly not willing to embark upon schemes in which producers, while agreeing to sell catch to their creditors, remain financially independent. Instead, they have invariably invested in their own productive equipment and hired skilled labour for wages.

Why is this the case? I suggest that the attitudes, assumptions and values of personnel in state agencies regarding the poor working population at large are central to an understanding of the agencies' past and present behaviour. Moreover, the lack of flow of credit in the fishing sector itself is partly explained by attitudes held by different classes. The class structure in Northeast Brazil is highly polarised. This polarisation is not only readily observable in the material differences between classes but is also very clearly reflected in cognitive terms. The author of the internal note in SUDEPE, mentioned above, was doing no more than reflecting suppositions generally held by the middle class and petty bourgeoisie about the poor working masses. The working poor, in general, are perceived to be ignorante (rude) and

childlike, likeable and simples (a creditable quality), innocent
and emphatically incapable of sustained responsibility, a set of
attributes not dissimilar to those which cotton plantation owners
in the USA applied generally to their slaves. Given this perspective, it follows for the Northeast executive class, the bankers,
aid men and entrepreneurs with capital that the poor are not able
to cope with the intricacies of credit or to be trusted to pay back
their debts within a given period.

These assumptions, and the non-action which results from them,
have a direct effect upon the socio-economic structure of the
society. The very limited opportunities open to small-scale producers are perpetuated. At the same time the public money made
available for credit schemes is channelled to those who are, whether
in fishing, agriculture or other productive sectors, already in
a relatively powerful position. The types of aid operation which
have been effected since 1960 in the Northeast offer no promise
of changing the attitudes of either the planners or the wider
elite. Educated Northeasterners (the region's executive class)
have no empirical examples which would make them doubt their
beliefs in the irredeemable backwardness of the peasant, whether
sharecropper, tenant, small landowner or fisherman; yet they will
offer no chance and have no vision that things might be otherwise.

A paradoxical element in the picture is that rotating credit
schemes are discussed, and are part of the repertoire of the
planning agencies at a federal and state level. Yet on the ground
it is the bank staff and the bureaucrats responsible for deploying
public funds who refuse to implement them. Their most frequent
overt excuse is that there is insufficient security offered by
the poor client against any proposed loan, even though anticipated
profit from production in fishing or agricultural activity makes
this demand largely irrelevant. The basic covert motive behind
refusal (and one which is often conceded orally) is that it is not
possible to trust a small-scale producer to honour, or be responsible about, any financial contract. That this attitude has a
self-fulfilling effect is all too clear. I would maintain that
it is central for an understanding of public aid and private
investment in the region.

A further misfortune is that the class conceptions of those
with executive influence are wholly compatible with present governmental economic intentions. Since 1964 federal policy has been to
foster large-scale production against small-scale enterprise.
There has been no sign of a national development policy envisaging
direct systematic help to small producers, one way, it might be
argued, which might lessen the extreme material differences which
exist between classes.

In a sense development agencies in Northeast Brazil suffer
from basic mauvaise foi. They have all too rarely confronted
directly the sectors most in need of help. It is also striking
how countless reports and feasibility studies (paid for handsomely
with public money) fail to take into account the vital, if not
easily measurable, factor of attitudes and their effect upon the
working of institutions.

There is every likelihood, from past showing, that independent
inshore fishermen in Northeast Brazil will remain technologically

impoverished. The most probably future development is the increase
of fishing companies employing crews as sharecroppers at sea,
and so perpetuating in this particular sector the inegalitarian
economic structures from which the Northeast has been suffering
in other sectors since the arrival of the Portuguese in the sixteenth century.

NOTES

1 See, inter alia: R. FIRTH, *Malay Fishermen: Their Peasant
   Economy*, Routledge & Kegan Paul, 2nd edition, 1966; B. WARD,
   Chinese Fishermen in Hong Kong; Their Post-Peasant Economy,
   in *Social Organization* (ed. M. Freedman, Frank Cass, 1967);
   Report of FAO technical conference on Fisheries in West African
   Countries, Report R50 - E 1967; KLAUSEN ARNE MARTIN, *Kerala
   Fishermen and the Indo-Norwegian Project* (Oslo, Universitets-
   forlaget, 1968).
2 The Third Master Plan of SUDENE (1965) estimated that 100,000
   fishermen work with primitive methods on the Northeast littoral.
   This estimate was probably too low, and it has been estimated
   that numbers have grown steadily since that time (cf. De Souza
   Brasil JP., Apontamentos para O Estudo do *Campesinato Pescador*
   Nordestino, *Revista de Ciências Sociais*, vol. 4, No. 2, 1973).
3 The author gathered detailed information on changes of ownership in a fishing community in Pernambuco, and also found in
   other fishing centres in the Northeast states that patterns
   of ownership were invariably unstable from year to year.
4 CLÓVIS CAVALCANTI, O Mercado de Pescado do Grande Recife
   (SUDENE, 1967, mimeo.).
5 The term pombeiro is applied to people who trade in fish and
   also to men owning one or two rafts who make contacts with
   other fishermen to crew them. The term here is applied to the
   latter category.

Chapter 7

INNOVATION AND SOCIAL STRUCTURE: THE SUGAR INDUSTRY OF NORTHEAST BRAZIL
Anthony Hall

Discussion of agrarian reform in Northeast Brazil has frequently stressed the importance of a traditional, non-innovatory mentality among landowners as a major factor in explaining resistance to change. One recent observer.commented that certain value-orientations of those involved in the sugar industry, such as 'the rejection of nature as a viable partners, the rejection of innovation, the rejection of co-operation and a rejection of long-range planning', are incompatible with modernization. (1) Others have condemned the 'lack of an entrepreneurial mentality' among sugar producers and have stressed the need for 'intellectual investment'. (2) Unfortunately these observations are not accompanied by explanations why such conservative values arose in the first place and, more importantly, why they persist to the present day. I intend to concentrate on one major set of factors which, I believe, helps to explain why Northeastern sugar producers have not only failed to keep up with their more industrially efficient counterparts in the Centre-South, but also why they have strongly resisted government attempts to introduce agrarian reforms.

I shall argue that, in resisting innovation within the sugar industry, sugar producers are acting in what they regard as their own best interests. As the virtually absolute holders of power since colonial times to the present day, plantation and mill owners have dominated a rigid, basically two-class social structure in the zona da mata (the sugar-producing humid coastal zone) which has provided them with an abundant, cheap and subservient labour force. As long as landowners can count on such a cheap and plentiful supply of manpower, they see no need to change existing methods. Furthermore, the social circumstances which have brought about such a situation have had important repercussions on the response of sugar producers to proposed reforms within the industry. Although by no means revolutionary in nature, such reform proposals have been received with apathy and even hostility. I argue that sugar producers dislike such proposals, especially when they imply social or political change, because they would inevitably threaten their dominant position at the apex of the social pyramid, giving more economic, social and political independence to the rural mass.

It is worth sketching briefly the relative decline of the

Northeastern sugar industry. Sugar production was established
in the zona da mata by the Portuguese in the early sixteenth
century and, apart from minor fluctuations, provided a stable
economic base for the whole region throughout the colonial period.
Plantation owners (senhores de engenho) prospered, Many built
sumptuous houses, engaged in ostentatious consumption such as
importing fine European silver and glass, and províded a steady
flow of revenue for the Portuguese crown. (3) During the nineteenth
century, however, Brazil began to lose its pre-eminence in world
sugar markets for several reasons, including the technological
backwardness of production even at this stage, which drove up costs,
and competition from beet sugar on the international market. (4)
Since the 1950s São Paulo has surpassed the Northeast as Brazil's
main sugar-producing region, both for the domestic market and for
export. São Paulo's share of the domestic market has risen from
15 per cent (2.5 million sacks) to 60 per cent (40 million sacks)
over the past thirty years. The cost of production per ton of
cane has increased rapidly in the zona da mata to more than double
the São Paulo figure. Cane yields in the Northeast barely reach
40 tons per hectare, whereas in the Centre-South the average is
60 to 80 tons. (5)

In the zona da mata labour costs form 70 per cent of total
production costs, more than double the figure for São Paulo, where
much greater use is made of machine power and fertilisers to
increase productivity. It is estimated that in São Paulo seventeen
times as many machine hours and one quarter as many man or animal
days are used to produce one hectare of sugar cane compared with
the Northeast. (6) Landowners in the zona da mata always complain
that they are at a strong disadvantage with regard to increasing
mechanisation because of the hillier topography of the region.
This seems to be exaggerated, for the highest cane yields in the
world are obtained in Hawaii, where 60 per cent of the terrain is
classed as hilly and irregular. (7) The lack of technological
sophistication has led landowners in the Northeast to cultivate
increasingly marginal lands rather than attempt to increase productivity of existing areas under production, driving up costs of
production and transportation to the mills even further.

Decisions whether or not to introduce technological changes and/
or more far-reaching agrarian reforms have always been completely
voluntary. The Brazilian government has never obliged Northeastern sugar producers to adopt innovative techniques, although
the urgent necessity for this has long been officially recognised.
Such a need was stressed with the formation of the Superintendency
for the Development of the Northeast (SUDENE) in 1959 and in its
subsequent master plans for the economic development of the region.
(8) A strongly worded inter-ministerial report several years later
recommended fundamental changes in the obsolete economic and social
structure of the sugar industry in the zona da mata, (9) which led
to the formation of the Executive Group for the Rationalization
of the North-Eastern Sugar Industry (GERAN) in 1966. GERAN
survived until 1971, when it finally gave way to rather less ambitious proposals regarding the redistribution of idle land to
workers, known as PROTERRA. (10) In fact, only 12 per cent of
PROTERRA funds were devoted toward land redistribution in 1973,

decreasing to 4 per cent in 1974. Most of the money has gone into
providing large and medium-sized property owners with subsidised
agricultural credit for buying cattle and modern inputs. The
record on land redistribution is diappointing. In the first four
years of its existence, PROTERRA redistributed almost no land to
agricultural workers and, on balance, seems to have created more
unemployment than jobs. In Pernambuco, for example, INCRA, the
national land reform agency in charge of PROTERRA, bought 3170
hectares of land from the Usina Central Barreiros, which it redistributed into twenty-seven plots of land. Only three of the
new property owners were in fact rural workers. As a result, the
usina also dismissed 209 workers the majority of whom have remained
unemployed. Similar cases can be quoted from other parts of the
zona da mata. (11)

The question that is more directly relevant to the present
argument is why the more wide-ranging GERAN plans failed so miser-
ably. The GERAN proposals were the most carefully thought out and
comprehensive reform plans ever presented to the sugar industry
in the Northeast, embracing social as well as purely technological
changes in the organisation of sugar production. GERAN tried to
persuade the class of sugar refinery owners (usineiros) of the
need for technological innovation in order to ensure the survival
of the industry. Modernisation was to be based on greater capitalisation, more intensive land-use and lower-cost production
methods, in order to make Northeastern sugar more competitive
with that produced in the Centre-South. In return for modernisation loans, usineiros would sell a proportion of their surplus
land for colonisation; this would absorb displaced excess labour
and resettle it on family farms orientated towards food production.
(12) The scheme met with little enthusiasm from sugar producers,
and when GERAN collapsed in 1971 it had only three modernisation
projects on its books.

Although GERAN's failure may undoubtedly be attributed to
several factors, including a lack of political power to back up
reform plans, a fundamental reason must lie in the almost total
lack of support it received from the usineiros themselves. Landowners are cautious of any major innovation, since genuine reforms
would certainly have to give rural workers greater economic and
political independence. I would argue that this conservative
mentality is a direct product of the type of social structure which
has grown up around the sugar industry. Traditionally accustomed
to dominating a cheap, abundant and for the most part subservient
labour force, landowners in the zona da mata fear changes in traditional methods of production and view them as threats to their
vested interests as undisputed holders of economic and political
power.

The rigid, polarised class division which characterised the
sugar industry throughout the colonial period is still its basic
feature. The relatively wealthy, landowning elite of plantation
owners (senhores de engenho) and refinery owners (usineiros) is
still visibly and sharply divided from the impoverished work-force
that provides a plentiful supply of cheap labour for sugar production. Because of their political weakness in the absence of
an organised and effective rural labour movement, sugar workers

have been forced to bear the high costs of inefficient methods of production in the form of low wages and abysmal living standards. Sugar producers have a monopsony over the labour market in the zona da mata; that is, they are the only large employers of rural labour in this densely populated coastal zone and have the power to control wage rates personally in the absence of any effective public authority to enforce minimum wage laws. Through abuses of the law and via mechanisms of debt-dependency and patron-clientage, landowners are able to minimise their labour costs, which, even so, still account for some 70 per cent of total production costs.

Landownership in the zona da mata is heavily concentrated into a few hands. Properties of over one hundred hectares in size account for 9 per cent of the total number, but occupy 82 per cent of the total area. (13)   Sugar-cane plantations, both independent and those run directly or rented out by sugar refineries, occupy an estimated 84 per cent of total cultivated land in the zona da mata. Sugar is still the mainstay of the Northeastern economy, and it is calculated that in Pernambuco sugar producers control 50 per cent of the state's wealth. (14)   Sugar provides the state government with 30 per cent of its tax revenue and accounts for 21 per cent of the region's exports, as well as 14 per cent of Brazil's total foreign exchange earnings. In Pernambuco, the most important sugar-producing state in the Northeast, 170,000 workers are dependent on the industry, or 36 per cent of the rural labour force in the zona da mata, one and a half million people including dependents. (15)

Independent plantations (fornecedores) cover some 40 per cent of the total area occupied by rural establishments in the zona da mata, while usina plantations occupy a further 44 per cent approximately. It is therefore important to examine the social structure of these two basic rural institutions, the engenho and the usina, in order to show how its development has affected landowners' attitudes towards change. From 1535 land grants known as sesmarias were made to Portuguese colonisers by the crown. On each piece of land an engenho (sugar plantation) was established. From the outset, then, landownership conveyed wealth and power to a small number of white families, these privileges having been made hereditary by the Regal Letter of 1530, given to the first Governor General of Brazil, Tomé de Souza. (16)   The engenho was a more or less self-sufficient economic unit which formed a small community in its own right and evolved its own type of social organisation. Based on the Portuguese extended family, it consisted of paterfamilias, wife, children, sons- and daughters-in-law, other relatives, unrelated dependants, and slaves.

The landowner extended his patronage not only to blood relatives but also to servants, slaves, hangers-on, and even to other families living on or near the property, who supported the senhor de engenho in exchange for his protection against other powerful landowners. Similarly, the church strengthened the paternalistic ethos by evoking humility from workers, stressing the *harmony of interests* shared by master and slave, and teaching the rural mass that their own interests were commensurate with those of the landowning class. The dependency of the freeman was thus added to the forced dependency of the slave. (17)   Bonds amongst landowning families were also reinforced by ancestral and marriage links, leading to the formation of blocks of economic and political power. The polarisation of the social structure was well established by the end of the nineteenth century.

The twentieth century saw the eclipse of the enhenho as a completely self-sufficient production unit which cultivated its own cane and manufactured its own sugar. The industrialised usina took over the taks of producing sugar and, at the same time, sought to cultivate for itself an increasingly large proportion of the sugar cane it needed, leaving the remainder to be supplied by independent producers, the old-style senhores de engenho in their new role as fornecedores or suppliers of cane to the mills. However, the abolition of slavery in 1888 and the advent of the industrialised mill did little to alter the fundamental social pattern established during the colonial period. Although some slaves left the plantations most were, in effect, tied to the production of sugar since there was no other source of employment in the area. Economic vicissitudes and persistent traditions of patron-clientage continued to make them strongly dependent on landowners. The legal freedom of ex-slaves was practically meaningless since their ability to exercise economic and political control over their own lives remained negligible. Wealth and power were still overwhelmingly concentrated in the hands of a landowning elite, perpetuated along family lines through inter-marriage amongst families or European, mainly Portuguese, descent. Although miscegenation between white plantation owners and their black slaves was common, racial mixing was not accompanied by any filtering down of economic rewards nor a more diversified class structure. Few legal bonds of marriage were ever established between master and slave. (18) White families always were, and still are to a large degree, careful to preserve their *racial purity* and corresponding monopoly over wealth.

Unable to compete with the new usinas in the grinding of cane and manufacture of sugar, most plantation owners not already bought out by the refineries continued in business as independent suppliers to the mills. The changed role of the engenho in the zona da mata did not result in any changes in its basic social composition. Still relatively isolated from the mainstream of national life, the sugar plantation is regarded by the owner very much as his personal domain, of which he and he alone is the boss. The senhor de engenho still exercises a domineering, paternalistic form of authority over his workers, both directly and through his admini-strator. The work-force consists mainly of landless, resident labourers (moradores), augmented during the cutting season by migrants from the interior who work in the zona da mata during periods of seasonal unemployment in the agreste and sertao. (19) Caught in a vicious circle of poverty, malnutrition, debt-dependency and paternalistic subordination, the rural worker has little or no ability to influence the conditions of his working existence.

In Pernambuco some 40 usinas control 517,000 hectares of land, or 44 per cent of the total area under rural establishments. (20) The usina consists of two basic sections, the factory nucleus and the cane fields which supply a large proportion of the cane used

by the factory. Cane is also supplied by fornecedores and by
plantations which, although privately managed for a proportion
of the profits, are actually owned by the usina. The area around
the factory forms the nucleus of the whole usina complex; this
includes the milling and defibring machinery, unloading bays,
shipping and storage rooms and all the other plant involved in
producing sugar from cane. Nearby are the offices which house
the small administrative staff, the company store (barracão),
schoolroom and chapel.

The usineiro, when in residence, lives in a large house next
to the factory, which in many ways resembles the casa grande of
the traditional engenho. Not far away are the administrators'
houses, fairly smart and comfortable buildings which reflect the
superior power, income and status of their occupants as second-
in-command to the mill owner himself. Rows of workers' houses
situated at varying distances from the factory nucleus form the
small village around the factory. The surrounding cane fields
belonging to the usina often extend over thousands of hectares.
These are composed of formerly independent plantations which have
been absorbed by the sugar mill. They frequently keep their
original names and in many respects are identical to independent
plantations. Work performed by the labour-force is purely agricultural and is divorced from the actual process of sugar manufacture. Most field workers live in isolated groups of huts
scattered over the plantation. The arrival of usinas on the
landscape of the zona da mata brought little change in land
settlement patterns since the new factories were established
on the sites of former plantations; no new nuclei were formed,
the older centres of activity were merely enlarged.

The slave-plantation complex centred around the colonial engenho
encouraged the dependence of the rural worker on the benevolence
of the master for his major social, economic and even religious
needs. Some observers argue that on the modern usina, particularly
in the factory nucleus where workers are engaged in the industrial
process of sugar manufacture, such features of patriarchalism
as patron-client relationships have been eliminated by the penetration of market forces originating in the urban economy; the
landowner is thus transformed into a capitalist, the rural labourer
into a proletarian worker. (21) However, there is little evidence
to substantiate this theory in the zona da mata. The social
structure of the usina displays many of the basic features of the
colonial slave-plantation complex. At the apex of the socio-
economic pyramid is the controlling elite of landowners and their
families, usually descendants of colonial senhores de engenho.
Usinas in the Northeast are generally dominated by one family and
are closed to outsiders. Concentration of control over property
is even greater than statistics suggest, not just because of the
criteria used to define rural properties in the Agricultural
Census (see below) but also because many plantations not actually
owned by the usinas are controlled by them through long-term leases
and inter-locking families. (22)

Immediately below the landowning class is the small class of
administrators (no more than two or three on any usina) who super-
vise the day-to-day running of the mill in the owner's absence,

since the usineiro himself is likely to spend much of his time in
the city attending to other business or professional interests.
The administrators are more skilled, better educated and usually
far better paid than the workers over whom they exercise their
authority. It is not uncommon for an administrator to be related
to his employer.

By far the largest and weakest group is the work-force, which
may be divided into two basic sections: the factory workers
(operários) and the resident field hands (moradores) who live
scattered all over the factory's plantations. Independent day
labourers and seasonal migrants from the interior supplement the
permanent labour force. Differences in wealth and life styles
and in the degree of power possessed by landowning/administrator
groups and rural workers are still very great indeed. Class
divisions are as distinct as they ever were, and the dominant
group makes every attempt to continue this tradition in work,
family and social activities. Wealth, power and status are still
almost totally ascribed. Almost no opportunities exist for upward
social mobility by the rural work-force. The closely-knit network of usina-owning families monopolizes sugar production and acts
as an influential pressure group at national level, chiefly through
the Sugar and Alcohol Institute (IAA), which enable it to promote
its own interests.

Sugar workers are poor, illiterate, undernourished and, above
all, constantly dependent upon the benevolence of the master or
patrão for their basic needs. The persistence of patron-clientage
has been an important factor in perpetuating and reinforcing class
divisions. The senhor de engenho, usineiro or even the admini-
strator grants favours on a discriminatory basis to his workers
who, because they need this additional support given their weak
and vulnerable position, are dependent upon him and offer their
loyalty in return. Such favours will include, typically, loans
of money, food, credit, gifts of old clothing, and medical assistance. Within a rigid class-structure based on land ownership
and characterised by extreme inequalities, patron-clientage has
compensated for some of the more severe injustices of the plantation
system, while giving the patrão an economic and political *following*,
features shared by similar class structures in parts of Spanish
America and Southern Italy, for example. (23)

During the colonial period it is generally agreed that master-
slave relationships did not exhibit quite the same degree of
repressiveness and brutality as that shown on North American
plantations, for example. This can be carried too far, however,
and one must be extremely wary of painting too idyllic a picture.
One optimistic observer has written:

> The curious observer of today has the impression that they
> (masters and slaves) have grown up fraternally and that,
> rather than being mutually hostile by reason of their antago-
> nisms, they complement one another with their differences. (24)

Such analysis appears to ignore evidence which points to obvious
signs of conflict, such as the frequently harsh treatment of
slaves and the rejection of plantation life by numerous runaway
slaves throughout the whole colonial period. The sugar museum in
Recife has on prominent display a frightening assortment of various

types of shackles and instruments of torture used to punish slaves, and pictures of executed dissident slaves. But despite the brutality it is probably fair to assume that the legitimacy of the patrão's authority went unquestioned by most. The horizons of the work-force were kept safely narrowed by total isolation from the outside world.

In this century there has been a significant change in the nature of patron-client relationships in the zona da mata. The formerly unquestioning respect of slave towards master, of worker towards employer, of client towards patron, has been changed to resentful and begruding obedience by the pressures of economic hardships, by the inability of a system based on the remains of colonial paternalism to cope with economic and social pressures for change, and by the penetration of new ideas into the rural sector. (25) Even the most illiterate workers are becoming more politicised, more aware of the changes occurring in the wider society. The penetration of ideas into the previously closed plantation society has been due to the expansion of the media, increased geographical mobility, better transport and improvements in all means of communication. The inevitable effect has been to diminish the authority traditionally enjoyed by rural patrons. This erosion of traditional bonds in the zona da mata is paralleled by developments in other areas of the under-developed world such as the Mekong Delta, Central Luzon and Lower Burma in South-East Asia. (26)

It was the introduction of such external pressures as trade union propaganda by word of mouth and over the radio that was a catalytic agent in the upsurge of peasant activity before the 1964 coup. In 1963, at the height of the confrontation between rural labour unions and landowners, a strike of 200,000 agricultural workers succeeded in raising wages by 80 per cent. Whether such mass movements represented genuine class action or whether rural workers were merely being led by charismatic and ambitious leaders chiefly for their own ends (27) is not of crucial importance to the present argument. What is important is that for the first time they were given the hope that collective action might enable them to better their lot and correct some of the blatant injustices of the system.

Aside from the question of better communications, one of the principal economic pressures that has contributed towards the loss of traditional authority has undoubtedly been a gradual decline in real living standards of rural workers. The virtually endemic poverty of sugar workers has been accentuated by price inflation, and by the overall decline in productivity of cane lands due to inefficient production methods, which has led landowners to pass on the effects to their working dependants. Historical evidence suggests that there certainly has been a significant deterioration in the living standards of the rural masses over the past century. (28)

More recent evidence seems to confirm what longer-term trends suggest. The price of a kilo of carne de charque (a dried, salted meat which forms a basic part of the peasant diet) rose by 218 per cent from 1964 to 1967, while daily wages rose by only 104 per cent. (29) This trend was aggravated considerably by the landowners' policy of devoting an ever-increasing area of marginal land to the cultivation of sugar cane, partly at the expense of lands formerly used by workers to grow subsistence crops, a right preserved from colonial times. The Rural Labour Statute (1963) established legal minimum wage levels for rural workers; but, in compensation for the landowners, removed the traditional right enjoyed by employees to cultivate their own subsistence plots. Unfortunately, many landowners withhold payment of the legal wage; on the Usina Caxangá a survey found that only 20 per cent of workers were receiving the full amount due to them. (30) A nutrition survey also revealed that from 1962 to 1968 the calorific intake of the rural population had decreased by some 20 per cent. (31) A contemporary observer noted that:

The immediate result of this is all too clear - a visible increase in their misery. Faces are more pinched and limbs of children are as thin as rakes, although their stomachs remain swollen due to untreated worms and an unrelieved diet of manioc flour. The clothes of adults are in rags, and the children usually go naked. (32)

Changes in the landownership structure and in patterns of employment within the zona da mata have occurred over the past decade which are likely to have profound repercussions on the rural labour force. These will affect its standard of living, its subservient position within the social structure, and the con-sequent strength of its economic bargaining power in the labour market. The average size of minifundios in the zona da mata of Pernambuco appears to have decreased in recent years. From 1964 to 1970 the average size of properties under ten hectares in size has gone down from 5.55 to 3.63 hectares. (33) Over the same period the average size of latifundios over 1000 hectares also seems to have decreased slightly from 1503 to 1411 hectares, but at the same time their share of rural land has risen from 18 to 21 per cent. (34) The 1970 figures taken from the Agricultural Census for the state of Pernambuco are also likely to understate the degree of concentration of property ownership at the top end of the scale, because it uses as its unit of classification *rural establishment*, which is an administrative division, not necessarily bearing any relationship to who actually owns the land.

If some costs of production have gone up, such as fertilizers and transport, there seems to be ample scope for cutting to a mini-mum other costs of production, such as labour. Both statistical and more impressionistic observations suggest that landowners in the zona da mata are gradually replacing permanent workers (mora-dores) with temporary labourers (trabalhadores volantes). In addition, the use of middlemen or empreiteiros to contract such labour on the landowner's behalf exempts him from having to fulfil many legal obligations towards his workers which he would otherwise have to meet. These practices allow the landowner to cut down his labour expenses per head considerably. Between 1950 and 1960 the number of permanent workers in the zona da mata of Pernambuco fell by 28 per cent from 82,536 to 57,916. (35) These figures reflect the expulsion of moradores from sugar properties to the outskirts of the small towns and to the roadside. More and more landowners are using empreiteiros to sub-contract temporary

labourers for work on the plantations from bearby towns and
villages, as well as those who come from the interior of the state
(the agreste and sertão) during the period of seasonal unemployment.
The whole process offers a number of immediate cost- and time-
cutting advantages for the employer. The 1963 Rural Labour Statute
does not consider temporary labour employed on a piece-work basis
as officially *salaried*. The landowner does not, therefore, have
to pay a regular wage, nor supply housing and other services;
neither is he under any obligation to observe labour laws regarding
the health and welfare of his workers. While some landowners do
look after their workers, the system is subject to widespread
abuse. (36)

The fact that such treatment is possible reflects the yawning
social and economic gap which still separates plantation and mill
owners from their workers in the zona da mata. The availability
of cheap labour, I argue, is one of the main factors which dis-
suade producers from adopting innovative techniques. Furthermore,
the social circumstances which permit such economic advantages to
be obtained condition landowners' attitudes towards reforms. They
have come to regard even the mildest and most favourable reform
proposals with great apprehension as a precursor of social and
political upheaval which would be bound to weaken their dominating
position in the class structure.

There is, however, another important set of factors which helps
to explain the survival of the Northeastern sugar industry in the
face of its inefficient methods of production. Apart from the
question of internal social structure dealt with above, is the
fact that the whole archaic system is protected and subsidised by
the Brazilian government through the Sugar and Alcohol Institute
(IAA). This institution was set up in 1933 to protect fornecedores
from the rapid expansion of usina cane fields which grew rapidly
during the present century by taking over the lands of engenhos
or independent plantations. The annual production of sugar cane
was divided into fixed quotas, and shared out amongst refineries
and plantations. Production of sugar itself was similarly divided
up amongst the usinas. Several years later in 1941 the Estatuto
da Lavoura Canavieira stipulated that 40 per cent of all sugar
cane was to be supplied by fornacedores. It prohibited the growing
of cane by newly-formed usinas, as well as establishing further
quotas and prices for sugar cane. (37)

The mistrust between usinas and fornecedores which arose from
this conflict of interests and necessitated the formation of the
IAA is a feature of their present day-to-day relationships. For
example, it would be more of an incentive to cane growers to
increase potential sugar yield per hectare of cane if they were
paid according to sucrose content rather than the current practice
of usinas paying by the ton. Fornecedores argue, however, that
this would leave them open to being cheated, since it is much
easier for them personally or their administrator to check the
weighing process rather than an analysis of sucrose content.

Two sets of quotas and prices are set by the IAA for the production of sugar cane and refined sugar, one for the Northeast
and another for the Centre-South. The Northeast enjoys a guaranteed share of the domestic market at prices substantially higher

than those obtained by prdoucers in the Centre-South. The price
per ton of cane during the 1975-6 harvest was set at C$98.70 in
the Northeast and C$80.16 in the Centre-South, a difference of
23 per cent. Similarly, the price paid per sack of unrefined sugar
(demerara) was C$96.11 in the Northeast, while Centre-South
usineiros received only C$82.06, a 17 per cent difference. (38)
These subsidies for Northeastern prdoucers are paid for by additional taxes on Centre-South sugar and are designed to compensate
for higher costs of production in the more backward region.
Without this support many producers would undoubtedly experience
considerable difficulty.

Brazilian sugar, Northeastern sugar in particular, is also
subsidised by exporting to the USA on preferential terms. Under
the Sugar Act the USA purchases 11 per cent of its total sugar
imports from Brazil. These 700,000 tons (1974) account for one-
third of all Brazilian sugar exported, having risen from the figure
of 15 per cent in 1973. Over 250,000 tons come from the state of
Pernambuco along. (39) Not only is this market guaranteed, but
prices paid by the USA have tended to substantially higher than
average, up to three times the price obtained in the free world
market. (40) These various forms of subsidy given to Northeastern
producers help to sustain high-cost production methods and do
nothing to stimulate change. With the improvements in US-Cuban
relations it is possible that the Cuban sugar quota will be res-
tored at the expense of sugar bought from Brazil, and this could
have serious repercussions for Brazilian sugar export earnings.
Another form of government support for particularly inefficient
usinas is that of intervention by the IAA. Several refineries in
Pernambuco on the point of collapse have been placed under the
supervision of the IAA, with the intention that the Institute's
technical advisers restore them into normal working operation,
control eventually to be replaced into the hands of the owners. (41)

Sugar producers in the Northeast also recently started receiving
additional government support in the form of subsidised rural credit
under the PROTERRA programme, already remarked upon for its limited
achievements with land redistribution. Landowners in the zona da
mata receive credit, for the purchase of modern inputs such as
fertilisers, which is totally interest-free. This represents a
saving of 15 per cent, equivalent to the already subsidised rate
of interest which they would have to pay for loans from the IAA.
In 1972 50 per cent of all zero-interest modern input credits under
PROTERRA went towards the purchase of fertilisers, three-quarters
of this amount going toward sugar. (42) The intended five-year
duration of funds under the programme (1972-6) when it was started
has tended to favour short-term profit-making, such as the concentration of assets into cattle-rearing, rather than the longer-
term emphasis given to the modernisation of Northeastern agro-
industry in PROTERRA's terms of reference. (43) It has been
suggested that one result of this short-term bias has been the
diversion of capital away from sugar production, aided by the
availability of subsidised credit and the various other forms
of support, into higher profit-yielding commercial and industrial
activities.

In summary, then, the dependent state of the rural work-force

in the zona da mata and the consequent cheapness of labour relative
to capital has been one of the major disincentives to technological
innovation by sugar producers. As the dominating minority in a
rigid, two-class social structure, landowners have come to fear
change. Any major innovation is viewed with considerable apprehension. The proprietary class derives its wealth and power from
estates which are still quasi-independent entities, governed auto-
cratically by the patrão. Rural workers remain powerless as long
as there are no unions to represent their interests effectively.
To the landowner 'agrarian reforms' suggest changes in the system of
production which must inevitably weaken his personal control over
the labour market, giving workers greater economic benefits and
more political power, and resulting eventually in a more diversified social structure.

In the meantime sugar producers are guaranteed an income by
the quota- and price-fixing system of the IAA, which offers little
incentive to change existing methods. In order to increase
total production of sugar cane it is easier for fornecedores and
usinas to expand the area of land under cultivation, ignoring the
more challenging alternative of improving productive efficiency
and undertaking concomitant social reforms, an opportunity which
was offered under GERAN. This facility is aided by the fact that
in Pernambuco, for example, only 15.3 per cent of the land actually
owned by sugar producers is devoted to cane cultivation in the
zona da mata. (44) However, as increasingly marginal lands are
cultivated production costs are driven up and yields decrease.
Evidence suggests that this process has been taking place in
Pernambuco (45) and it is reasonable to assume that the same thing
is happening in other states such as Paraíba and Rio Grande do
Norte. This might eventually force the more inefficient producers
to modify existing techniques or, alternatively, could result in
the transfer of production to other areas which offer cost-reducing
advantages. Several usinas in Pernambuco have, for example, transferred production to the neighbouring state of Alagoas, whose
government has provided the incentive of exempting them from
payment of ICM taxes. (46)

In hanging on to out-moded techniques and in exploiting the
cheap labour market, Northeastern sugar producers may be acting
in what they regard as their own best interests. The long-term
effects, however, can only be harmful to the development of the
sugar industry, and pose even greater obstacles to future attempts
at reform.

NOTES

1 H.W. HUTCHINSON, Value Orientations and Northeastern Brazilian
   Agro-Industrial Modernization, *Inter-American Economic Affairs*,
   21 (4), 1968, p.88.
2 ALBERTO FIGUEIREDO, *Organização e Produtividade: Aspectos do
   Problema da Produtividade na Agro-Industria do Açucar* (Recife,
   1963).
3 See, for example: *The Masters and the Slaves* (Knopf, New
   York, 1956).

4   M.C. DE ANDRADE, *A Terra e o Homem no Nordeste* (São Paulo, 1964), pp.71-2.
5   HUTCHINSON, op.cit., p.80.
6   A Concentração Económica da Agro-Industria Canavieira, *Brasil Açucareiro*, November 1968.
7   J.M. DA ROSA E SILVA NETO, *Contribuição ao Estudo da Zona da Mata em Pernambuco* (IJNPS, Recife, 1966), p.80.
8   SUPERINTENDÊNCIA DO DESENVOLVIMENTO DO NORDESTE (SUDENE); *IV Plano Diretor* (Recife, 1968); SUDENE: *Plano de Desenvolvimento do Nordeste, 1972-74* (Recife, 1971).
9   GRUPO DE TRABALHO INTERMINISTERIAL DO AÇÚCAR (GTIA); *Documento Sobre a Agro-Industria Canavieira do Nordeste Apresentado Pelo GTIA ao Governo Federal* (Recife-Rio de Janeiro, 1965).
10 *Programa de Redistribuição de Terras e Estimulos à Agro-industria do Nordeste*, instituted by Decree-Law 1179 of 6 July 1971.
11 *Jornal do Brasil*, 26 October 1975.
12 *Programa Geral do GERAN* (Recife, 1966).
13 NETO, op.cit., p.21.
14 BELDEN PAULSON, *Local Political Patterns in North-East Brazil* (Land Tenure Centre, University of Wisconsin, 1964), p.2.
15 JARBAS VASCONCELOS, *Uma Análise da Economia Canavieira de Pernambuco* (Recife, 1973), p.21; and Agricultural Census, 1970.
16 FERNANDO DE AZEVEDO, *Canaviais e Engenhos na Vida Política do Brasil* (IAA, Rio de Janeiro, 1948), pp.182-5.
17 B. HUTCHINSON, The Patron-Client Relationship in Brazil: a Preliminary Examination, *Sociologia Ruralis*, v, (1), 1966.
18 See, for example: JULIO BELLO, *Memórias de um Senhor de Engenho* (José Olímpio, Rio de Janeiro, 1938).
19 The agreste is the transition zone between the humid coastal strip and the semi-arid interior or sertão.
20 VASCONCELOS, op.cit., p.27; Agricultural Census, 1970.
21 See, for example: OCTAVIO IANNI, A Constituição do Proletariado Agrícola, *Revista Brasileira de Estudos Politicos*, 12 October 1961, and *O Colapso do Populismo no Brasil*, Civilização Brasileira (São Paulo, 1968), p.84; also CHARLES WAGLEY, A typology of subcultures, in C. WAGLEY (ed.), *The Latin American Tradition* (Columbia University Press, New York and London, 1968).
22 NETO, op.cit., p.109.
23 G.M. FOSTER, The Dyadic Contract in Tzintzuntzan, II Patron-Client Relationships, *American Anthropologist*, 65, 1963, pp.1280-94; S. SILVERMAN, The Community-National Mediator in Traditional Central Italy, in POTTER et al., *Peasant Society: A Reader* (Boston 1967); J. BOISSEVAIN, Patronage in Sicily, *Man*, 1 (1), 1966, pp.18-33.
24 FREYRE, op.cit., p.iii.
25 ANTHONY HALL, Patron-Client Relations, *Journal of Peasant Studies*, I (4), 1974; FANNY MITCHELL, Visit to an Enhenho, *Institute of Current World Affairs Newsletter*, FM-4, 1967.
26 J.C. SCOTT and B.J. KIRKVLIET, How Traditional Patrons Lose Legitimacy: a Theory With Reference to South-East Asia, *Cultures et Developement*, 5 (3), 1973.

27 BENNO GALJART, Class and *Following* in Rural Brazil, *America Latina*, VII (3), 1964; and A Further Note on *Followings*; Reply to Huizer, *America Latina*, VIII (3), 1965; G. HUIZER, Some Notes on Community Development and Rural Social Research, *America Latina*, VIII (3), 1965.

28 JAIME REIS, Hunger in the Northeast: Some Historical Aspects, in the present volume.

29 GRUPO ESPECIAL PARA A RACIONALIZAÇÃO DA AGRO-INDUSTRIA CANAVIEIRA DO NORDESTE (GERAN): *Diagnostico Socio-Económico da Zona da Mata* (mimeo., Recife, no date).

30 HERALDO SOUTO MAIOR, *Levantamento Socio-Cultural de Caxangá* (IBRA, Recife, 1969), p.54.

31 ALBERTO TAMER, *O Mesmo Nordeste* (Herder, São Paulo, 1968), p.123.

32 FANNY MITCHELL, Trouble in the Zona da Mata, *ICWA Newsletter*, FM-11, 1967.

33 Calculated from CONDEPE statistics in NETO, op.cit., p.21, and the Agricultural Census, 1970.

34 Ibid.

35 VASCONCELOS, op.cit., p.26.

36 JOAQUIM PEDRO FERREIRA, O Capitalismo no Campo, Movimento, 27 October 1975; and Visão, 21 July 1975.

37 VASCONCELOS, op.cit., p.26.

38 INSTITUTO DO ALCOOL E DO ACUCAR (IAA): *Valores de Remuneração aos Produtores de Cana de Acucar* (Rio de Janeiro, May 1975).

39 IAA: *Relatorios*, 1973 and 1974, *Jornal do Brasil*, 4 May 1975; F.O. LICHT, *International Sugar Report*, 107 (5), 13 February 1975.

40 For example:

Consumption of sugar produced in Pernambuco

Markets	Quantity (sacks)	Price (C$)
USA	7,000,000	21.274
Europe	2,000,000	6.530
Brazil (internal)	12,000,000	12.665

Source: Bento Dantas, *A Agro-Industria Canavieira de Pernambuco* (SUDENE, Recife, 1968).

41 Examples include the usinas Treze de Maio, Serrazú and Maria das Mercês.

42 Figures from the Bank of Brazil, Recife, 1973.

43. JORGE COELHO, *Proterra: Relatório Analítico* (SUDENE, Recife, 1974). PROTERRA envisages, 'financing for projects designed to expand agro-industry, including sugar: financial assistance for the organization and modernization of rural properties', PROTERRA Statute, cited in Coelho, p.8.

44 NETO, op.cit., p.95.

45 Ibid., pp.77-8.

46 *Diario de Pernambuco*, 14 May 1975. These usinas include Muribeca, Santo Inácio, José Rufino, Siberia, Timbó-Assú, Cachoeira Lisa and Aribipú.

Chapter 8

IRRIGATION IN THE BRAZILIAN NORTHEAST: ANTI-DROUGHT OR ANTI-PEASANT?
Anthony Hall

For the peasants of the sertão, the semi-arid interior of North-east Brazil, farming is risky at the best of times. In addition to serious structural problems of agrarian poverty and under-employment, periodic droughts create havoc among the low-income population. Rainfall shortages cause the production of subsistence crops to be drastically reduced; landlords temporarily dispense with their hired labourers; and peasants are forced off the land to seek employment, either in the already overcrowded cities or on emergency work fronts set up by the government during drought periods in an attempt to provide short-term relief. In 1970 half a million drought victims or flagelados were employed in this way building roads and dams. (1) At the height of the latest drought in July 1976, 140,000 men were working on emergency fronts, (2) out of a rural population of some 12 million in the sertão. Less fortunate farmers who, deprived of their normal staple food supply, are unable to find alternative means of supporting them-selves and their families, are often forced into ransacking markets or warehouses in order to avoid starvation. (3) When beans, rice or manioc flour are unavailable, or simply too expensive, cactus roots are eaten instead. Increased malnutrition, disease and suffering are the by now familiar and seemingly in-evitable by-products of the drought.

Yet successive Brazilian governments have attempted to develop anti-drought strategies capable of tackling these problems on a broad scale. The first of these was based principally on reservoir construction (acudagem) and formed the basis of anti-drought policy for over half a century until the late 1960s. It failed to have any substantial impact in alleviating the effects of the drought because, although an enormous volume of water was accumulated in hundreds of public and private reservoirs, little or no attempt was made to distribute the water for crop irrigation to farmers at risk through the drought. Only those fortunate few in the immediate vicinity of the reservoirs saw any benefit. The failure of these measures to strengthen the rural economy in any signifi-cant way against the erratic climate was made tragically evident with each drought. This culminated in the calamitous events of 1958, when 20 per cent of the population in the interior was

affected by drought, and half a million refugees were employed
on emergency fronts. (4)

The impotence of DNOCS's acudagem philosophy during and after
the catastrophic 1958 drought finally led to major policy changes.
Until then DNOCS (the Departamento Nacional de Obras Contra as
Sêcas) had successfully resisted pressures to place greater
emphasis on irrigation. In the first place, DNOCS has traditionally
been dominated by civil engineers who measured their success by
crude additions to the volume of stored water rather than by any
other criteria. Second, irrigation on any significant scale would
have necessitated expropriation of private farmlands and thereby
endangered the close political ties developed between local bosses
and DNOCS bureaucrats. (5) After 1958 the newly formed Superintendencia do Desenvolvimento do Nordeste (SUDENE) laid emphasis
in its regional development plans on the urgent need for irrigation
as an integral part of a comprehensive strategy for the Northeast.

During the mid-1960s SUDENE experimented with irrigation, but
only in 1971 was the first systematic plan for Brazil published,
prepared by the Grupo Executivo de Irrigação par o Desenvolvimento
do Nordeste (GEIDA) in conjunction with Tahal, an Israeli firm of
consultants. The proposals were highly ambitious and envisaged
the irrigation of 195,000 hectares of land in the Northeast by
1980, requiring a total investment of 6/3,188.7 million or US$759
million at 1971 values. Under the plan DNOCS was responsible for
36 projects covering 78,000 hectares. The Companhia de Desenvolvimento do Vale do São Francisco (CODEVASF) would irrigate
112,000 hectares in seventeen schemes in the São Francisco valley,
the largest in the Northeast. (6) Not content with these targets,
DNOCS set itself the even more ambitious goals of irrigating a
total of 100,000 hectares and settling 22,000 families on its
projects by the end of the 1970s. (7)

Irrigation was certainly never intended as a panacea for the
agrarian problems of the sertão; but the official targets, if
taken at face value and realised, would undoubtedly help to
alleviate the suffering associated with the drought and give more
protection to the rural population. The plan had three basic
objectives: (a) to stabilise the rural population by giving employment to families which would otherwise be forced off the land
because of drought; (b) to increase family incomes, thus attacking
the problem of rural poverty; and (c) to increase production of
high-value fruits and vegetables on projects, thus providing some
return on the heavy capital expenditure involved and enabling
irrigation farmers to earn high incomes. (8)

It appears, however, that these objectives are a long way from
being met and, indeed, that current irrigation strategy may be
of no more use in fighting the drought effects than DNOCS's
original policy based on reservoir-building. Central aspects of
current strategy are directly counter-productive. Furthermore, it
seems clear that most of the beneficiaries of the irrigation programme up to now have, for one reason or another, never been at
risk from the drought. The evidence for this was collected from
three case-studies of DNOCS schemes selected as representative of
the twelve projects in operation during the time that fieldwork
was undertaken in 1974-5. Since then, further documentary

information has become available concerning irrigation under
CODEVASF in the São Francisco valley and this strongly supports
the original observations. (9)

The creation of jobs on the land, or fixar o homen a terra in
the official jargon, is the first and perhaps the most important
single goal of irrigation policy. For large sectors of the rural
population, especially those sharecroppers and small-holders who
live some distance from the valleys or other sources of water,
farming is hazardous and unpredictable even during non-drought
years. If the arrival of the winter rains, due in January or
February, is delayed by only a few weeks, this is often enough to
destroy the plantings of staple foods such as beans and manioc.
The same is true if the initial rains are not followed soon enough
by further showers, for then the crops are destroyed as they mature.
In 1975 many areas of the sertão did not receive rainfall until
March or April; supplies of staple foods were seriously endangered
and hungry farmers in the state of Rio Grande do Norte were driven
to try and ransack food stores. (10) During full-scale droughts
the magnitude of the problem is far greater, with vast flows of
peasants leaving their barren lands for the cities and work fronts.

In tacit recognition of these facts, the PPI proposals place
great emphasis on the creation of stable employment opportunities
uninfluenced by climatic vicissitudes. By 1980 it is planned to
create no less than 115,000 permanent jobs on irrigation schemes
in the Northeast, affecting a total of 350,000 people including
dependants. (11) Taken at face value, such an achievement would
without doubt help to stabilise the sertão rural population. In
practice, however, quite the opposite is true. Not only is irrigation doing little to create new, permanent jobs, but current
strategy actually displaces far more peasants from the land than
it actually absorbs on schemes, thereby exacerbating the problems
of unemployment and the rural-urban drift.

In the first place, government irrigation projects in Brazil
are highly capital-intensive and absorb little labour in relation
to the vast sums invested. Cline has estimated that it will cost
US$4,800 for each unit of labour absorbed, or over seven times
the average for Brazilian agriculture. (12) It has also been
calculated that in the Northeast it costs US$34,000 on average
to settle one family on a DNOCS scheme. (13) The cost per hectare
of Brazilian irrigation is put at US$1,450 (excluding some items
such as farm machinery and housing) (14) which is three times
the figure for irrigation in Europe and Asia. (15) DNOCS's
target of installing 22,000 families by 1980 still represents only
2.3 per cent of the projected excess rural population in the
interior by the end of the decade. By 1975 only 4 per cent of
this goal for 1980 had been met, 900 families working on twelve
projects.

Although irrigation is generating little permanent employment
on the land, its impact in the opposite direction is considerably
more marked. From three to six times the number of people are
displaced from the river valleys during the expropriations and
expulsions needed to make way for irrigation schemes than are
eventually reabsorbed into the projects. This has led to a substantial increase in rural unemployment and has given rise to much

suffering among poor farmers and their families, creating intense hostility between local populations and government agencies. River valleys in the semi-arid sertão are densely populated because historically they have offered protection from the extended dry season or the drought, even if the rivers themselves are not perennial. Cultivation of subsistence crops on dried-up river beds (agricultura de vazantes) is possible in any conditions but the most severe, thus ensuring a fairly regular food supply. Generations of land sales and inheritance have caused extensive property fragmentation, resulting in a pattern based on the intensive cultivation of small plots by minifúndistas, sharecroppers, tenant farmers and squatters. This situation characterises the areas chosen for irrigation projects; that is, valleys selected primarily because they already have stored water supplies from the reservoir-building period of anti-drought works. The effects of an ill-planned, thoughtless expropriation procedure on this type of area can be little else but disastrous.

The high social costs of irrigating heavily populated valley lands must be taken into account by any development strategy worthy of the name; but in the feasibility studies used as the basis for irrigation in the Northeast they are conspicuous if only by the almost total absence of any reference to the problem. Whether by design or out of ignorance, dislocation is a hidden cost in the PPI plans for Brazil. Three case-studies illustrate the magnitude of the problem. On DNOCS's largest project, Morada Nova in the state of Ceará, the final total of 3,000 people to be settled represents one-sixth of the original population of the area, some 18,000. On the second largest scheme, São Gonçalo in the state of Paraíba, 3,000 colonists will replace the former population of 7,000. Even on the smaller projects such as Sumé, Paraíba, at least 76 families were forced to move to make way for the current total of 26 irrigation farmers.

The methods used by DNOCS and CODEVASF to evacuate areas for project construction have been heavily criticised. On the Morada Nova scheme farmers reluctant to leave their homes watched as the bulldozers tore down their dwellings. In the lower São Francisco area of Propriá, in the state of Alagoas, peasants have been intimidated by the local police and threatened with violence if they did not leave the area when ordered to by CODEVASF. The practice of these irregularities reached such a peak in 1976 that the local bishop, Dom José Brandão, made a formal protest to the Minister of the Interior. (16) Similar tales of illegal pressures and intimidation brought to bear on a largely defenceless population are common in areas where irrigation schemes are being implemented. On the São Desiderio project run by CODEVASF in the state of Bahia, for example, farmers have been allegedly tricked into selling their land with no fuss after being given promises of irrigated plots on the new schemes as compensation, plots which were not subsequently forthcoming. Most farmers, however, left only under threat of legal or other official action. This reluctance is quite understandable in view of the fact that the area expropriated, in common with other areas taken over for irrigation, was not one of under-utilised latifúndia. On the contrary, it was one of highly productive small-holdings where a rudimentary irrigation system enabled two crops per annum of the basic foodstuffs (beans, rice and corn) to be grown. (17)

For several reasons, including ineligibility, lack of interest and hostility generated by the above-mentioned conflicts, only some 5 per cent of those families actually displaced from the humid valleys join the irrigation schemes subsequently established there. Neither DNOCS nor CODEVASF show any interest in studying what happens to those dispossessed or in making alternative provisions for their resettlement in other areas. Many of those forced off the land by irrigation schemes leave the area altogether in search of new homes and jobs, feeding the rural-urban drift and directly contradicting the stated objectives of the national plan. Others move to nearby towns to swell the slum quarters, (18) while some make do as best they can by squatting on the roadside. Other notable side-effects include a marked deterioration in the health standards of the dispossessed. This is caused by a drastic increase in the incidence of schistosomiasis, spread by the irrigation canals, as well as by a decline in the diet brought about by farmers losing their subsistence plots and having to buy food at a much higher real costs. (19) The pressure on lands surrounding project areas is also increased with the exodus, a case in point being the São Gonçalo scheme. Another side effect is that banks are reluctant to grant loans to landowners whose properties are at all in danger of being expropriated.

Another government agency faced with a similar problem is the Companhia Hidroeléctrica do Vale do São Francisco (CHESF), responsible for the giant Sobradinho dam and reservoir which, when full, will form the largest artificial lake in South America. Steps have been taken to rehouse the former urban inhabitants of the area to be flooded in new towns such as Bom Jesus da Lapa and Casa Nova, (20) but 40 per cent of the 75,000 people to be displaced by the scheme are rural in origin with no such rights. The best agricultural lands on the river banks have been taken from the peasants, frequently with no compensation or with derisory amounts given, and the farmers forced onto the drier caatinga where the soil is far less fertile and water supplies more distant and erratic. (21)

Much of the hardship induced by expropriation lies in the fact that only a handful of peasants are entitled to monetary compensation. In the sertão valleys only 30 to 40 per cent of families are landowners, and less than half of these have the legal proof of ownership necessary before they are eligible for compensation. In addition, most of the land and other resources are monopolised by a few larger landlords. Most of those entitled to something are therefore small-holders, who receive derisory amounts, averaging from a few hundred to one thousand cruzeiros (£1 = 19 cruzeiros). Most of those obliged to abandon their jobs and homes are non-landowners, who receive nothing although they may suffer considerable losses. In short, only a small proportion of the valley population affected is likely to receive sufficient compensation to enable a new life to be started elsewhere. Quite often, the recipients are precisely the larger landowners who are most likely to have other resources to which they can turn.

To be effective, any anti-drought strategy must accommodate

those sectors of the rural population who are vulnerable to
abnormally dry periods. The evidence collected from three case-
studies suggests strongly that irrigation is not performing this
function. By and large, irrigation schemes absorb farmers who have
not in the past been badly affected by the drought. Potential
drought victims, on the other hand, remain virtually untouched
by the projects on any permanent basis, although some temporary
employment may be provided on construction work or emergency fronts.
On the three projects studied only 5 per cent of colonists had
ever been badly affected by drought, that is, been forced off
their land to the city or to work on an emergency front. This is
largely because, under Brazilian law, plots must first be distributed to ex-landowners and to agricultural workers from the valleys
where land has been expropriated. In addition, DNOCS prefers to
recruit its colonists from the valley lands because selection
costs are minimised and communications easier. Farmers from the
drier caatinga are therefore strongly under-represented on irrigation schemes. In São Gonçalo, for example, sharecroppers from
the caatinga formed 63 per cent of total applicants but only
14 per cent of recruits. The high rate of applications from
sharecroppers reflects the pressing needs of this particular
rural group, the most vulnerable of all to the drought. In 1970
they formed 42 per cent of work front recruits, yet only accounted
for 7 per cent of the general occupational structure of the
sertão. (22)

As well as creating more jobs, a second and parallel objective
of government irrigation policy is to increase the incomes of
rural families. The GEIDA study envisaged, as the third goal,
the production of high-value fruits and vegetables which would
be sold on the domestic and international markets and generate
a return of US$50 million by 1980. (23) These high returns would
not only produce favourable cost-benefit ratios and justify the
heavy capital expenditure, but would also allow the incomes of
irrigation farmers to reach four times the average for the Northeast by the end of the 1970s. This would amount to US$360 per
capita as opposed to the average of US$100 per capita at 1971
values. (24) DNOCS studies confidently predict incomes for its
colonists of six times the official minimum wage, while many
other official plans make similar forecasts. (25)

Subsequent developments suggest, however, that this was a
grossly over-optimistic view. A small minority of perhaps 5 per
cent of irrigation farmers earns these high incomes. On the
three projects analysed most farmers were in debt to the co-
operatives at the end of the agricultural year. That is, the
incomes obtained by the farmers from the sale of their crops, which
are marketed by the project co-operative, were smaller than the
running costs incurred to produce them. Colonists do not yet have
to pay for fixed costs such as land and housing, principally
because the vast majority would simply be unable to pay if it was
required of them. On the São Gonçalo project, out of 66 farmers
who had been there for over a year 75 per cent had debts outstanding with the co-operative of between C$700 and C$14,000. A
similar situation was found on the Morada Nova scheme where, of
224 long-standing members, only 35 per cent showed a profit. The

income distributions on both projects were highly skewed. In São Gonçalo five farmers out of a total 123 earned 85 per cent of the income, while on Morada Nova four colonists out of 250 took home 27 per cent of the total income. In Sumé likewise, the top 23 per cent of farmers received 44 per cent of the income and the bottom 23 per cent got 7 per cent.

There are several reasons for this pattern of income distribution, including differences in the amount of capital possessed by new colonists, differences in the capabilities of farmers and their adaptability to irrigation techniques, variations in the amount of technical guidance given, and variations in production costs. One of the major factors affecting cultivation costs and responsible for a good deal of the income variation amongst irrigation farmers is variation in soil quality, particularly fertility affected by salinisation. In order to reduce capital costs, DNOCS decided to use already existing reservoirs for supplying irrigation water in the valleys by means of gravitational flow. One of the serious disadvantages of this decision, however, is that soil composition in these valleys is highly varied. Salinisation is said to affect 30 per cent of sertão valley lands, (26) and, in fact, large tracts had to be taken out of production on all three projects studied. As a result of the higher costs of cultivation and crop failures caused by salinisation, many colonists have incurred heavy debts. Those farmers with the heaviest debts at the end of the year were found, almost without exception, to have experienced problems of poor drainage and salinisation. The feasibility study for São Gonçalo, recognising the inherent unfairness of dividing the land into family plots, suggested instead collective cultivation of the area as one single property. (27) Their strong recommendations were, however, ignored by DNOCS.

The failure of irrigation projects to bring in the high revenue predicted for them in the feasibility studies may, to a large extent, be attributed to an unsuccessful production and marketing policy. Instead of selling luxury fruits and vegetables, irrigation schemes have been obliged to fall back on a limited range of crops which are already widely cultivated in the Northeast. Apart from the small, 26-family Sumé project, which has managed to market tomatoes fairly successfully, cotton, rice, corn, beans and bananas form the mainstay of all other schemes. These crops have virtually guaranteed markets but have no relative price advantage. Their income-earning capacity is limited, even with higher than average yields. Cotton, rice and bananas accounted for 97 per cent of total income in São Gonçalo during 1975, while on Morada Nova cotton, rice and maize brought in 82 per cent of total revenue. Traditional crops already widely cultivated in the region account for about 70 per cent of the total irrigated hectarage on government projects, according to one recent estimate. (28)

Over-optimistic projections of demand capacity by the feasibility studies appear to be one of the principle explanations for this divergence between theory and practice in the marketing of crops produced under irrigation. According to the PPI study a wide variety of non-traditional crops would be cultivated by irrigation schemes, ranging from melons, grapes and onions to sorghum and wheat. Such crops, it was predicted, would account for 84 per cent

of irrigated production on government-run projects. (29)   It
is difficult to see how such precise projections of demand capacity
could have been formulated, given the notorious inadequacy of data
on Northeastern markets.

Another factor of equal importance in explaining this discrepancy lies in the failure of DNOCS to organise farming and
marketing with the degree of sophistication necessary to make
luxury crop production viable. Private landowners have, in
contrast, been more successful in growing and selling high-value
crops at competitive rates. Grape production in the São Francisco
valley is but one example. (30) DNOCS has had almost no success
in marketing non-traditional crops. In São Gonçalo, for example,
the colonists incurred large losses when their co-operative was
obliged to sell a large onion harvest at a fraction of the expected
price because it coincided with that of a nearby, major area of
production. The small, 26-family Sumé project has managed to
market tomatoes successfully, but it is an exception to the rule.
Marketing remains largely the individual concern of each project,
there being no attempt at regional co-ordination. Potential
revenue is further reduced by the fact that schemes do not have
the facilities for processing crops, so that a large part of the
profit accrues to intermediary wholesalers and factories.

The unsatisfactory performance of irrigation projects in the
areas of employment creation, income generation and crop production
is a constant source of dissatisfaction amongst colonists. One
way in which DNOCS attempts to minimise tension and conflicts on
its schemes is by encouraging what it calls *co-operativism*. This
term is never specifically defined in the official literature but
is widely used to imply a general spirit of co-operation among
irrigation farmers. Cooperativismo also suggests that colonists
should follow unquestioningly the guidelines established by the
project administration and co-operate with it, secure in the knowledge that this course of action is in the best interests of all
concerned. At the same time, the rigidly hierarchical nature of
the organisation permits no collective expression of interests
or opinions on the part of irrigation farmers, denying them the
sharing of experiences and information essential to any form of
co-operative ethic, however loosely defined. A fundamental contradiction therefore exists between the theory and practice of
co-operativism as defined by DNOCS.

This is evident at all levels of activity on irrigation schemes
in the Northeast. From the outset the agencies try to select
candidates who show a predisposition towards co-operativism, which
appears to be a euphemism for conformity or straight acceptance
of authority. This quality is assessed and graded at the selection
stage along with sociability, receptiveness to change, and other
qualifications such as age, experience and family size. (31)
Candidates with records of political activism in the rural trade-
union movement, for example, are at a strong disadvantage. At
the production stage the system of individualised family plots
of land, combined with a rigid agricultural plan and flow of
directives from the top downwards, discourages any form of collective spirit. As soon as a colonist enters a project he is given
precise instructions on how much land he should cultivate, what

crops he must grow, what methods to apply, and to whom he must
sell his produce. Almost no room is left for individual initiative
to be exercised by farmers within official procedures; and sugges-
tions from individual colonists on how the system might be improved
are almost never invited. Lip service is paid to co-operativism
by DNOCS, but official paternalism is the order of the day.

If the sertanejo peasant has, in many ways, come off rather
badly from the introduction of irrigation, certain other groups
have prospered considerably. The main beneficiaries of government
irrigation schemes have turned out to be not the drought-hit
population of the sertão, nor even the more fortunate humid valley
inhabitants who constitute the vast majority of colonists, but
those who have never earned their living from cultivating the land.
These are, first, the members of the vast bureaucracies of the
irrigation agencies and, second, the growing number of consultancy
firms which have prospered by undertaking lucrative feasibility
studies.

Precise figures on staffing in government agencies are not
easily available, but evidence collected in the field suggests
that staffing is considerably higher than for irrigation schemes
in Europe and Africa. On two of the projects studied administrative
and auxiliary staff were almost equal in number to irrigation
farmers, and in the third the former outnumbered the latter by
three to one. This policy is, perhaps, justifiable in a region
of heavy unemployment. However, if the resources invested into
irrigation are intended to lessen the impact of the drought on
poor farmers such employment patterns make little apparent sense.

Since the late 1960s an ever-increasing number of consultancy
firms have competed for the opportunity of undertaking feasibility
studies. Firms are contracted on the basis of tenders submitted
to the Ministry of the Interior. Contracts are much sought after
and, by all accounts, very lucrative. The study for the Vaza
Barris project in the state of Bahia, for example, is reputed to
have cost the government over one million dollars. It is in the
interests of both consultant firms and irrigation agencies that the
viability of schemes be 'proven' on paper. From the consultants'
point of view favourable cost-benefit ratios justify the heavy
expense of the feasibility study. As far as the government is
concerned, a favourable study serves to justify the heavy capital
expenditure and fulfils the GEIDA precondition that all projects
should show a rate of return on capital investment of at least
10 per cent. An additional advantage for the agencies is that if
the economic viability of irrigation can be demonstrated on paper
first, the flow of federal funds will be guaranteed and the organisations' survival assured, at least in the forseeable future.

This eagerness to assure the world that irrigation is an economically workable proposition in the Northeast has led to fundamental anomalies in the programme. The most obvious example is
the marketing failure on irrigation projects, resulting in far
lower income-earning capacity for colonists than predicted in the
feasibility studies. Another lies in the enormous social and
economic costs of displacing thousands of valley farmers from their
homes and jobs, costs which are never taken into account in the
crude cost-benefit calculations of consultancy firms.

Government irrigation schemes in the Brazilian Northeast have, then, done very little to alleviate the hardships of the drought-affected peasantry. If anything, poverty and rural-urban migration have been exacerbated. Yet despite the particular criticisms levelled against irrigation above, anti-drought measures to date have, in a broader and more fundamental sense, been ineffective because they treat the drought problem as one of water supply. In fact the problem is far more complex, and closely related with the whole phenomenon of economic marginality in the sertão. Problems usually attributed to the drought, such as poverty, famine, malnutrition, unemployment and migration, are a basic part of everyday life in the Northeast regardless of whether or not there is a drought. These phenomena can be observed in every dry season; every year is a drought year in the sertão. Rainfall shortages merely exacerbate these basic conditions, producing dramatic newspaper headlines. Unfortunately the drought provides a ready-made excuse for politicians, who have a vested interest in obscuring the basic causes of poverty by attributing it to climatic rather than human causes.

Any effective anti-drought strategy must tackle the problem of economic marginality on a broader front, providing groups such as sharecroppers and small-holders who are particularly vulnerable to climatic vicissitudes with the means that will enable them to build up their resources. This would improve their economic strength and provide stability in all but the most serious of droughts. These measures would increase farmers' incomes by providing a combination of improved farming technology, small farmer credit, better marketing facilities, and land redistribution in selected areas.

In order to break the vicious circle of poverty and dependence of the peasant on non-institutional credit (provided by landlords and merchants) a system of agricultural loans to small producers, especially non-landowners, is urgently needed in the Northeast. Borrowing during normal years in the sertão, and even in drought years when the government provides emergency credit, is heavily monopolised by larger landowners whose resources in the form of cattle offer security to the banks. A system of loans tailored specifically to meet the more modest yet equally critical needs of small farmers could help to provide greater economic security for large sectors of the rural population. Another major bottleneck for the small producer is at the marketing stage, which is dominated by a chain of landlords and intermediaries that absorbs 60 to 70 per cent of the retail value of crops bought from peasant producers. The organisation of large-scale co-operatives would undoubtedly help to break this monopoly and ensure that the farmer with few resources received a fairer return for his labours.

Redistribution of under-utilised land in key areas of the sertão to small producers could help to provide more security for landless labourers vulnerable to the whims of landlords. The potential benefits of such a policy have been suggested for areas where labour is particularly concentrated. (32) However, the government's record on land purchases for peasant farmers is not encouraging. The only step taken so far in this direction came with the PROTERRA programme, which was designed to redistribute land to small and medium-sized producers through a system of subsidised credits. Unfortunately, nearly all of this credit was used for large cattle and sugar estates as well as for non-agricultural, speculative investment. Landless workers are ineligible because they lack the necessary guarantees for the banks, while small landowners are often effectively ignored for the same reason. By 1976 only 75 land titles had been redistributed to small landowners in the entire Northeast. (33) Under SUDENE's 34/18 fiscal incentive scheme also, 90 per cent of loans to agriculture have been used to set up large-scale livestock enterprises of 35,000 hectares and more. (34) This policy creates more unemployment because cattle raising tends to displace labour from the land which it takes over, and many thousands of peasants are summarily evicted from their homes in the process.

Agricultural development policy has not, therefore, favoured the small, weaker farmers most at risk from the drought. The latest official measure designed to rectify this imbalance is the so-called Projeto Sertanejo (Programa Especial de Apoyo ao Desenvolvimento da Região Semi-Árida do Nordeste) inaugurated in August 1976. The basic idea is to improve agricultural technology and employment opportunities in selected areas of the sertão which are adversely affected by drought and population pressure. A series of *development nuclei* are to be established, each covering an area of 280,000 hectares, and the properties which comprise them would be provided with financial and technical assistance to improve crop and livestock production. It is calculated that 100,000 properties would be included in the plan, generating 450,000 jobs during the 1970s. (35)

One of the greatest potential obstacles to the scheme's having any substantial impact on the drought is that existing DNOCS irrigation projects will form the nuclei, thus further concentrating resources in already privileged areas. Another major disadvantage is that there is no provision whatsoever for the redistribution of property either to small landowners or to landless agricultural workers. In the sertão population is concentrated heavily on minifúndia and, because of the intense pressure on their limited resources, it is these properties which are particularly badly hit by droughts. In 1970, for example, farms of under 10 hectares provided 86 per cent of work front recruits although they represent only 4 per cent of the total area under cultivation. (36) If peasants are genuinely to be encouraged to stay in the countryside rather than migrate to the cities, the only way to relieve this pressure is by redistributing areas of underutilised farmland to those in need. As the plan stands, there is every likelihood that resources made available from the Projeto Sertanejo will become monopolised by large landowners with wealth and connections, those who are least likely to suffer during drought years.

Anti-drought strategy in the Northeast will be centred around government irrigation schemes for the forseeable future. Irrigation currently absorbs two-thirds of government spending on agriculture in the region. (37) From an official point of view it certainly offers considerable advantages over the politically more controversial policy areas of land redistribution, small

farmer credit and the formation of co-operatives. Irrigation
tampers only marginally with local power structures, and a large
government bureaucracy is provided with stable employment where
there might otherwise be none. Furthermore, the verdant pastures
of irrigation schemes offer a refreshing visual contrast to the
semi-arid caatinga and appear to justify the presentation of
projects to the world as shining examples of agricultural progress.
While the beneficiaries of these policies are clearly visible, the
victims of so-called 'development' are forgotten as an embarrassing
inconvenience to planners. It is probable, despite the vast sums
of money invested in irrigation, that the everyday problems of
poverty, famine and unemployment which are made worse periodically
by the drought, will remain indefinitely with the Northeast. A
major reason for this lies in the inescapable conclusion that
irrigation in its present form is irrelevant to the needs of the
rural poor.

NOTES

1   DNOCS, *Frentes de Servico* (Fortaleza, 1971), pp.57-8.
2   *Jornal do Brasil*, 29 July 1976.
3   *Diario de Pernambuco*, 16 June 1976.
4   RAUL BARBOSA, *A Sêca de 1958* (Fortaleza, 1958), p.5.
5   A.O. HIRSCHMAN, *Journeys Towards Progress* (20th Century
    Fund, New York, 1963).
6   GEIDA, *Programa Plurianual de Irrigação (PPI)*, vol. 1,
    pp.16, 51 and table 4-8, (Brasilia, 1971).
7   DNOCS, *Irrigação* (pamphlet), (Fortaleza, 1975).
8   GEIDA, op.cit., vol. 1, pp.10-18.
9   The three case-studies were: (1) Sumé, Paraíba: 260 hectares
    of irrigated land, with 26 families. (2) São Gonçalo, Paraíba:
    600 irrigated hectares, with 123 families. (3) Morada Nova,
    Ceará: DNOCS's largest project and showpiece, it had 1,100
    hectares of irrigated lands for 253 families in 1975. The
    three projects together account for 20 per cent of the total
    area irrigated by DNOCS and 45 per cent of the total number
    of families absorbed. For the CODEVASF information, see
    A.L. HALL, *Drought and Irrigation in North-East Brazil*, PhD
    thesis, University of Glasgow, 1976.
10 *Diario de Pernambuco*, 25 and 28 April 1975.
11 GEIDA, PPI, op.cit., vol. 1, pp.8-9, and vol. 3, Annex 8,
    p.15.
12 W.R. CLINE, Análise de Custo-Beneficio de Projetos de Irrigação
    no Nordeste, *Pesquisa e Planejamento Econômico*, 2 (2),
    December 1972, p.259.
13 JORGE COELHO, *Considerações em Torno do Programa de Agricultura
    Irrigada na Zona Semi-Árida do Nordeste* (CETREINO, Recife,
    1975).
14 W.R. CLINE, *Irrigation Projects in Brazil's Northeast; Case
    Studies in Social Cost-Benefit Analysis* (IPEA, Rio de Janeiro,
    1971, revised 1972), p.21.
15 COLIN CLARK, *The Economics of Irrigation* (2nd edition, Pergamon
    Press, 1970), pp.62-71.

16 *Estado de São Paulo*, 15 September 1976.
17 A Situação Criada pela Implantação do Projeto de Irrigação
    São Desiderio, *Cadernos do CEAS*, 44, pp.46, 51.
18 This was a feature of the three case-study projects and has
    been observed in other areas. See CEAS, op.cit., p.44.
19 Ibid., p.45.
20 It has been alleged, however, that these rehousing arrange-
    ments were only planned after intense pressure from the World
    Bank on the Brazilian government.
21 *Visão*, 3 May 1976; and PAULO MARCONI, Sobradinho: um orgulho
    nacional?, *Cadernos do CEAS*, 45, September - October 1976.
22 CLOVIS CAVALCANTI and DIRCEU PESSOA, *Caráter e Efeitos da
    Sêca Nordestina de 1970* (SUDENE/SIRAC, Recife, 1973), table
    5-6, p.111; and Agricultural Census, 1970.
23 GEIDA, PPI, vol. 1, tables 4-11, 3-5, pp.9, 33.
24 Ibid., vol. 3, Annex 18, p.18.
25 JOSE LINS ALBUQUERQUE, *Sobre Irrigação em Regiões Subdesenvol-
    vidas* (DNOCS, Fortaleza, 1971), p.14.
26 COELHO, op.cit.
27 HIDROSERVICE, *Recuperação Hidroagrícola da Bacia de Irrigação
    de São Gonçalo: Relatorio Final - Carta de Apresentação*, and
    vol. 9, p.85 (São Paulo, 1971).
28 COELHO, op.cit., p.38.
29 GEIDA, PPI, vol. 2, Annex 3, p.4.
30 *Visão*, Report, 22 December 1975.
31 DNOCS, *Seleção de Agricultores: Fichas Para Classificação de
    Candidatos* (DNOCS, Fortaleza, 1975).
32 GEORGE F. PATRICK, Efeitos de Programas Alternativas do
    Governo Sobre a Agricultura do Nordeste, *Pesquisa e Planejamento
    Econômico*, 4 February 1974, pp.76-8.
33 HELVECIO DORNAS, *O Processo da Reforma Agraria na Região
    Nordeste* (SUDENE/DAA, Recife, 1975); and *Latin America*, IX,
    43, 31 October 1976.
34 SUDENE, *Projetos Agro-Industriais e Agro-Pecuarios Approvados:
    Situação até junho de 1974* (Recife, 1974).
35 *O Povo*, 22 August 1976.
36 CAVALCANTI and PESSOA, op.cit., p.114; and Agricultural
    Census, 1970.
37 *Cadernos do CEAS*, 44, 1976.

Chapter 9

STATE AND SOCIETY IN NORTHEASTERN BRAZIL: SUDENE AND THE ROLE OF REGIONAL PLANNING

Francisco de Oliveira

This article is concerned with the emergence of the Superintendencia do Desenvolvimento do Nordeste (SUDENE), the large federal
aid agency established in Northeast Brazil in 1959. (1) Some
introductory remarks are necessary to outline the politico-
economic background in the Brazilian Northeast at the moment of
the planned intervention of the central government in the late
1950s; these remarks will also indicate the main methodological
lines of the study. Section 2 deals in more detail with the
relationship between the creation of SUDENE and the political
conflicts and alliances in the Northeast during the post-war
period. Section 3 analyses SUDENE's policies, and the strong
American influence in the formulation of those policies. Section
4 finally looks into the sonsequences of federal intervention in
the region.

1 INTRODUCTION

The political arena in the Northeast in this century has been
characterised by the opposition between the sugar cane bourgeoisie
on one hand, and the cotton and cattle raising oligarchy on the
other. The local institutions of the state, however, were traditionally dominated by the latter, and federal intervention through
the Departamento Nacional de Obras Contra as Secas (DNOCS) has
since the 1920s reinforced their oligarchic power. DNOCS had
concentrated on the building of dams (açudes) and drilling of
wells for irrigation, and on the building of non-paved roads.
Most of the dams and wells were located in the lands of cattle-
raising farmers, and their effect on crops was limited to some
subsistence cultures serving the local labour force. The roads,
in their turn, could theoretically serve all kinds of purpose,
but in practice benefited only the cotton economy: in fact, cotton
was the only product of the Northeast hinterland to be sold outside the region in significant volume. Another aspect of DNOCS
activities was the creation of 'labour fronts' for the building of
roads and dams in periods of severe drought. Wages in the labour
fronts were often paid in kind, wage goods being bought by the

DNOCS from the landowners at a high price. Applicants recommended by the coroneis (the landowners) were given priority in the fronts, which thus became the object of clientelistic practices. Payments to fictitious workers or even funds for non-existent works, made available by the DNOCS, were also appropriated by the local oligarchy, which had, in effect, complete control of the government agency in the region.

The sugar cane bourgeoisie was in a weaker position. They were in a state of decadence caused by two main factors. Struggling for survival, this bourgeoisie resorted, in the first place, to non-capitalist forms of defence against the cyclical crises, the most important of which was the development of an extensive economy of subsistence during the slump. A substantial part of the wage goods were, thus, produced by the workers themselves; this eliminated pressures for expansion through higher yields and, since all available land was already under cultivation, capital accumulation failed to take place. That is the basic reason for the weakness of the Northeastern bourgeoisie. The second reason, affecting the sugar cane sector in particular, was the state intervention through the Instituto do Alcool e do Açucar (IAA). The IAA determined the yearly production quotas for each region and for each productive unit within each region; it also established national minimum prices guaranteed by the government. Since productivity in the plantations (if not in the usinas) was higher in the Centre-South than in the Northeast, such policies led to the expansion of production in the Centre-South and to the protection and perpetuation of archaic relations of production in the Northeast.

The weakness of the bourgeoisie in the Northeast produced some notable political consequences. Unlike the situation at the federal level, the oligarchic hold on the state remained unchallenged. Political power presented a clear class content, and the relations between the state and the subordinated classes were devoid of the ambiguities of the populist regime at the national level. With the exception of a brief period in the late 1950s, the subordinated classes did not join a populist alliance with the bourgeoisie, as in other parts of the country; their opposition to the dominant classes tended, therefore, to be more open and direct than in the Centre-South.

Within the complex system of relations of production in the sugar cane region the workers fought the capitalist class as proletarians (for wages) and as semi-peasants (for land, and for the elimination of the semi-compulsory forms of labour such as the cambão, an exchange of labour for usufruct of land). Two related processes exacerbated these social conflicts in the Northeast during the post-war period. In the first place, the decadence of the bourgeoisie was accompanied by the expansion of non-capitalist relations of production and by the corresponding impoverishment of the semi-peasants in the sugar cane region. Second, the semi-peasants on the fringes of that region faced an increasing competition from the Centre-South in the markets of food staples and cotton, being therefore compelled to increase production in order to maintain their real earnings. Both developments led to the multiplication of subsistence plots producing marketable surpluses within the limits imposed by the land tenure structure, and to the

rise of the land rent; in this context, stronger pressures for
the expulsion of the semi-peasants from the land and for the
intensification of semi-compulsory labour brought social conflict
to a point of high tension. It was the disruption of the pax
agraria in the Northeast, provoked by both the local politico-
economic situation and by the economic expansion of the Centre-
South into that area.

The creation of SUDENE, or the introduction of regional planning
coupled with federal financing of industrial investment in the
Northeast, inaugurated a new and decisive stage in the process
of economic integration of the region into the national capitalist
system. The new stage was characterised not only by a new form
of economic expansion of the Centre-South based on direct industrial investment, but also by the transformation of the very structure of the state in the region. This latter point requires some
further observations.

The state in Brazil played the decisive role as agent of the
process of centralisation of capital promoted by the Centre-South.
Since the 1930s until the mid-1960s capitalism in the country grew
continuously on the basis of industrial development. This period
was characterised by the internal realisation of internally created
value, and this explains why the degree of openness of the
Brazilian economy, as measured by the coefficients of imports and
exports, decreased throughout the period and reached, by the end
of the 1960s, an extremely low level. An increasing internal
realisation of value accompanied by high rates of growth would
not be possible without the simultaneous development of internal
financing of the economy. State intervention, specially in the
financial sphere, played a crucial role in the process, by centralising a substantial part of the existing money-capital in the
form of taxes and reallocating it according to the new correlation
of forces determined by the rise of monopoly capital. (2) Such a
process would transform, in its turn, the character of the state
in the country. Capital centralisation turns the mode of production of commodities into a full mode of production of surplus
value. The nature of productive and unproductive labour is changed
by the same token, and the very nature of the state and its relations with all social classes is modified. The production of
certain commodities and services could not from then on be seen
as the result of a technical division of labour whereby the state
would transfer goods to the private sector; such productions will
be continued by virtue of their technical characteristics, but
they will now be incorporated into a social division of labour;
i.e., to the relations of generation and appropriation of value.
The non-profitable utilisation of the surplus appropriated by
the state becomes impossible: public funds will cease to finance
inefficient activities, and state-owned enterprises, operating
previously at a loss, will be turned into profitable units. The
systematic deficit in public enterprises characterised a process
through which public income was turned into goods and services;
in the new situation, public income will be turned into surplus
value.

The public financing of big and rentable capital from the
Centre-South in the Northeast was just an aspect of this new

character of the state's economic activity; in the end, planning
turned out to be an attempt to quantify costs and benefits at the
macro-economic level, and served to justify government policies
by making them appear as the rational product of a neutral technocracy. This article is an attempt to describe how the development
of the *new state* in the Northeast was affected by the political
processes described in the previous paragraphs, and to analyse the
impact of the government intervention in terms of its economic
and political consequences upon that region.

To say that the capitalist expansion from the Centre-South can
be regarded as one of the general causes of the creation of SUDENE
does not imply that SUDENE was a necessity from the moment the
unequal development in the various parts of the country gave origin
to different economic-political regions. Nothing would be more
alien to the intentions of this paper. If it is true that the
creation of SUDENE cannot be understood without retrospective
understanding, it is also necessary to consider the concrete conditions under which value has been created in Brazil. No blind
determinism could help in formulating a pre-vision of what would
occur later on. That is why it is necessary now to investigate
more recent developments, which, determined by an historical heri-
tage, have led to a *planned* state intervention. And even taking
into account the specificities of capitalist expansion in Brazil,
no prediction could be formulated; for, under certain historical
situations, under-developed regions can persist in countries where
capitalist relations of production are fully developed. The specific questions to be tentatively answered here, therefore, will
be: why was SUDENE created at that particular moment, and what
was the political context in which it operated during its early
years?

A final word on the question of method: regional planning is
not regarded here as an instrument created and operated by an
independent technocracy for the reduction of *regional imbalances*,
but as a moment of the process of regional division of labour
brought about by capital accumulation at a national level; it
fostered the gradual capitalistic homogenisation of the Brazilian
economic space. The regional imbalances approach, adopted by
SUDENE itself and by all planning documents in Brazil, starts
off from a static picture of the region; such a picture is compared with the situation in other regions and the differences
are treated as *deviations*. The focus is on the results of
differential developments, not on the processes leading to different regional situations. Despite its structuralist guise,
the regional imbalances approach is basically neo-classical in
its analytical framework: to take just one example, the question
of unemployment in the Northeast is analysed in terms of distorted
or irrational production functions, despite the structuralist
considerations surrounding the argument. As a matter of fact,
whatever its rhetoric, regional planning for the Northeast has
since the beginning been aimed at the expansion of oligopolistic
corporations from the Centre-South in the region: this was, and
still is, the obvious objective of the powerful system of fiscal
incentives operated by SUDENE. The result of such a policy was,
with the capitalisation of the regional economy, the further aggra-
vation of the regional imbalances.

2   DECADENCE OF THE INDUSTRIAL BOURGEOISIE OF THE NORTHEAST, THE
    END OF THE PAX AGRARIA AND RISE OF THE POPULAR MOVEMENTS:
    THE MENACE TO BOURGEOIS HEGEMONY AT THE NATIONAL LEVEL

The most salient feature in the Northeast in the post-war period
was a gradual and steady rise of what we would like to call, in
general, the popular forces. These popular forces were made up
by semi-peasants, small-holders, sharecroppers and arrendatarios,
whose most conspicuous organisation was the Peasant Leagues, but
who were also represented by various organisations within the union
movement, including the church. The most relevant political
characteristic of this mobilisation, however, was that it was
largely independent, and against the coroneis, sugar planters and
mill owners. For the first time in the social and political history
of the Northeast, the rural masses emerged as an autonomous political factor, and could not be mistaken as a captive electorate.
Of course, one could not assess the political emergence of the
rural masses by electoral criteria; in fact, in spite of their
growing significance, the national and local parliamentary representation of the rural dominated classes remained very weak.
    The other fundamental political element of the popular forces
was the proletariat, urban and rural. The proletariat had not
emerged as an autonomous political force in the 1950s. It existed
long before, and its opposition to the bourgeoisie was traditional
in the political history of the Northeast, mainly in Pernambuco.
As non-capitalist relations of production were reproduced by the
bourgeoisie at the fringes of the sugar sector, part of the labour-
force became quasi-peasant; but such development did not change the
proletarian character of the labour force. The novelty in the
1950s was the new kind of relationship between the urban and rural
proletariat on the one hand and all other dominant and dominated
classes on the other. As the proletariat joined with the agrarian
dominated classes, it gave the popular movement the unprecedented
force which it knew in the 1950s and early 1960s. As to the
relationship between the proletarian and dominant classes during
the period 1945-64, this underwent the following changes:
    (a) Between 1945 and 1950, the proletariat appeared as an
independent class through a working-class party, the Communist
Party; it interfered autonomously at the regional level and established national links with the working class of the whole country,
mainly of the Centre-South.
    (b) From 1950 to 1958, the proletariat merged itself into a
coalition led by the rural oligarchy (cotton planters and cattle
raisers), fighting the local bourgeoisie, despite the existence
of an anti-oligarchic populist coalition at the national level.
    (c) In the following period (1958-61), the proletariat changed
its political partner: it joined forces with the local industrial
bourgeoisie, led by Governor Cid Sampaio in Pernambuco. In that
coalition, the industrial bourgeoisie seemed to be the leading
partner; in reality, the proletariat's strength equalled that of
the industrial bourgeoisie.
    (d) From 1961 to 1964, the proletariat led, for the first time,
the political coalition which this time, strangely enough, brought
the cotton-cattle sectors of the oligarchy under the lead of the
working class.

It should be noticed that such developments were not homogeneous throughout the Northeast. But since the state of Pernambuco is the political epicentre of the Northeast, those changes which took place in Pernambuco prefigured to a certain extent the political process in other states. In other parts of the Northeast, however, the changes described above are not so neat as in Pernambuco, and did not develop along the same lines. In some other states - as in Ceará, for instance, the most oligarchic of them all - an alliance between local political groups and national political forces was gradually established; the focal point of politics in Ceará started moving from the PSD to the PTB. Such a shift expressed an alliance of the national bourgeoisie with the agrarian oligarchy of Ceará, as the latter moved to its dissolution. Party denominations matter here less than the general sense of the process. In another period, the UDN took over, but the process developed along the same lines: the seizure of the local power by an extension of the national bourgeoisie of the Centre-South.

In Rio Grande do Norte, things followed the same pattern; the splitting of the UDN in to two wings, led by Dinarte Mariz and Aluisio Alves, was induced by the penetration of the bourgeoisie of the Centre-South. Dinarte Mariz represented the cotton-cattle oligarchy, whereas Alves's populism expressed the penetration of the national-bourgeois state. In Bahia, shifting political coalitions accounted not only for the development of class struggle at the local level, but also for the growing influence of the Centre-South. In the period under analysis the alternation of the PSD and the UDN in the local government, and the rise of the PTB just before 1964, indicated the end of the oligarchic hegemony and the prevalence of Centre-South capitalist interest as represented locally by the strong state-owned industrial sector. (3)

What should be retained from the previous considerations is that, except for very short periods, a populist situation has never fully asserted itself in the Northeast. To say that Miguel Arraes represented populism in Pernambuco would be misleading. In fact, it would be the formal labelling of a movement, or class conflict, whose structural foundation is completely different from that of the Centre-South. The government of Arraes did not include the local industrial bourgeoisie, and the support of a big industrialist such as José E. de Moraes did not change its political nature. The participation of E. de Moraes as a representative of a large, industrial group of the Centre-South rather constituted an attempt to block the rise of the urban and rural proletariat, together with the rest of the dominated rural classes. Arraes himself was opposed not only to the local industrial bourgeoisie, but also, and more generally, to the bourgeoisie that, from the Centre-South, was extending its hegemony over the whole country.

The coalition of popular forces led by Arraes and Julião was characterised by its opposition to the growing hegemony of the industrial bourgeoisie. In this sense, it went beyond populism. But the decline of the local bourgeoisie and the dissolution of the pax agraria in the Northeast appeared to the leading sectors of the bourgeoisie at the national level as a threat to its hegemony. This should not be over-estimated, however; in fact, the rise of the popular forces reached its climax when the populist pact in the Centre-South started breaking down, as the relationships between the state, the industrial-financial bourgeoisie (both national and international) and the proletariat became less ambiguous. Here lies the historical reason for the defeat of the popular forces: they were unable to challenge the forces unleashed by monopoly capitalism, that succeeded in winning over an essential element of the state apparatus, the Armed Forces. We are not arguing that the bourgeoisie had history on its side, nor that the revolutionary attempt should be lamented. For it represented a qualitative change in the history of class struggle in Brazil, and its meaning has not yet become fully apparent. It put an end to an era of mystification; all social and political agents would exhibit, from then on, their true colours.

In what sense was the popular coalition in the Northeast opposed to the international-associated bourgeoisie of the Centre-South? Is it a political metaphor, suggested by an ex-post observation of post-1964 events? The reconstruction of the past in the light of our knowledge of subsequent events is, of course, a necessary démarche; still, it is a reconstruction, and not an invention. The antagonism between the popular coalition in the Northeast and the industrial bourgeoisie of the Centre-South - the latter bidding for national hegemony - will firstly emerge over the issue of the role of the state. The popular forces were not able to get hold of the state apparatus; they were only nominally in the government. That prevented the final dissolution of the ambiguity of the state; but the popular pressures laid bare its capitalist character.

More generally, the antagonism between political forces was closely related to the forms and conditions of capital accumulation in the country. The growing political action of the peasant and semi-peasant masses, as well as of the urban workers, collided with the oligopolistic expansion from the Centre-South; and that took place at the very core of the process of centralisation of capital. The penetration of commodities produced in the Centre-South, followed by investments from that region (which preceded the creation of SUDENE), destroyed the regional economy, both agricultural and industrial. Such destruction allowed for a differential accumulation, or over-accumulation, based on the seizure of the Northeast market and on the setting up of modern industries which benefited from a higher organic composition of capital and from a lower cost of reproduction of the labour force in the Northeast. Trying to oppose this course of events, the popular forces in the Northeast, urban and rural, would claim for the strict compliance with civil law on rights of property and of the labour legislation, specially in relation to the correct payment of minimum wages. It is true that these regulations had, in the 1930s, served the process of accumulation; however, as the powers of monopolisation advanced, they were to be used against it. The importance of this point is manifested in the fact that minimum wages were kept lower in the Northeast than elsewhere, even after the dominance of the Centre-South had been completely established as a consequence of fiscal incentives provided by SUDENE.

The creation of SUDENE, representing the planned intervention
of the state in the Northeast, was the immediate result of class
conflict which in that part of the country took the form of
regional conflicts, or of regional imbalances. The industrial
bourgeoisie, in the process of establishing its supremacy, had
no choice: the popular classes of the Northeast had to be curbed.
In a situation where bourgeois populism was declining, however, a
direct attack could lead to the national unification of the popular
movement. The subjugation of the local bourgeoisie had therefore
to come first. SUDENE was precisely the instrument of that
indirect assault, suggested by Furtado in the opening of his book
Dialetica do Desenvolvimento with Liddell Hart's phrase 'avoid the
frontal attack'. (4) SUDENE carried out the quick destruction of
the regional economy of the Northeast, within the framework of
the national process of national economic integration promoted
by the Centre-South. It is true that such powers of integration
would develop in any event, but without SUDENE it would have been
slower, and the Northeast could have remained for many years a
sort of Brazilian Ireland. Nevertheless, it was precisely the
speed of the process which determined the planned character of
state intervention.

The link between the creation of SUDENE and class antagonism
in the country is manifested in the ideological arguments of the
time. In parliamentary debates as well as in plans, projects and
programmes of the new organ, the final justification of SUDENE
was presented in terms of *national security*. Furtado's conference
in the ISEB, published later under the title *O Operaçao Nordeste*,
and his famous document *Uma Política de Desenvolvimento Econômico
para o Nordeste* are both good examples of that argument. (5) They
emphasise the threat to national unity represented by the deepening
of disequilibria between the Northeast and the Centre-South. (6)
In *O Operaçao Nordeste* Furtado maintained that national unity would
be mainly threatened by the antagonism between the working class
of the Centre-South and immigrants from the Northeast, such antagonism being caused by the depressing effects on wages of the
excessive supply of Northeastern manpower. (7) The real threat,
however, - and this is behind Furtado's argument - was that the
conflict between the working class and the bourgeoisie was exacerbated by a large labour surplus, which included, incidentally, as
many workers from Minas Gerais as from the Northeast. Curiously,
but not contradictorily, development plans for the Northeast made
it clear that abundant manpower in the region was a prerequisite
for industrial expansion, since regional wage differentials would
function as a powerful incentive to new investments in the area.

The antagonistic character of class struggle in the Northeast
and the threat it represented to the 'national unity and security'
was reiterated in subsequent documents of SUDENE. In *Projetos a
presentados aõ Governo da República Alemã* explicit mention is made
of the disruption of the pax agraria in the area:

Growing demographic pressures in the Northeast ... have generated
very serious social and political problems, which may be described as follows: (a) general feeling of dissatisfaction; (b)
appearance of resentment against more developed areas in the
country; (c) creation of peasant associations aimed at the
immediate solution of the land problem. (8)

The associations mentioned in the text - the Peasant Leagues - precede the creation of SUDENE, and are a component of the political context in which SUDENE emerged. The document is concerned about the peasants in the Northeast having become independent political agents, liberated from the coroneis and from the voto de cabresto. The same concern is expressed in another document arguing in favour of SUDENE's autarchic nature and autonomy within the federal administrative system: 'It is therefore certain that such (regional) economic inequality, in a large country such as Brazil, could lead to the formation of antagonistic regional groups, threatening "National Unity"'. (9) This passage was not written during the hot ideological debate which preceded the creation of SUDENE; it was signed by SUDENE itself, and carried its authority. The document, incidentally, was approved by the Attorney General, and the autarchic character of SUDENE, which the original law had not made clear, was confirmed.

The 'Nation', in the passages quoted above, was the bourgeois nation; and the required unity was the unity which should emerge from the expansion of the Centre-South. In fact, to justify such expansion by stressing poverty in the Northeast was not convincing; poverty was nothing new in the region. Moreover, various SUDENE documents emphasised that the identity of the regional economy could be preserved: quite to the contrary, its strategy tended to dissolve it.

3 THE NEW STATE IN THE NORTHEAST: THE SUDENE

The executive bill creating SUDENE was approved by the National Congress and became Law No. 3692 of 15 December 1959, after having gone through various amendments. The parliamentary debates on the bill reflected the reactions of the various social classes, in the Northeast and outside it, to the new federal policy for the region. The parliamentary processing of the Bill has been admirably described by Amelia Cohn in her study *Crise Regional e Planejamento*; the minutes of debates in the two houses during 1959 contain invaluable material for the understanding of the subject.

Many observers of Brazilian politics are surprised that SUDENE was opposed by Northeast congressmen, with the exception of those closely linked to the Northeastern bourgeoisie, and supported by those of the Centre-South. The mystery disappears, however, when the class conflicts in the region and the effects of the capitalist expansion in Brazil are considered.

Before the congressional vote in the SUDENE law, the executive had created by decree the Conselho de Desenvolvimento do Nordeste (CODENO), a sort of pre-SUDENE, responsible for the elaboration of the SUDENE bill. CODENO was composed of governors of the nine Northeastern states, and representatives of the ministries; its executive secretary was appointed by the President of the Republic. The Deliberative Council (Conselho Deliberativo) of SUDENE was similarly structured, which led some people to talk about a 'new federalism'; in fact, by reinforcing the central executive power such organisation meant the weakening of the federative principle.

SUDENE had been created as an instrument of planned intervention, aimed at the overcoming of inter-regional class conflict and at the promotion of capitalist expansion of the Centre-South. These are not post facto conclusions; the objectives of the whole project were made quite clear from the beginning, though its success could not be taken for granted at its early stages. Among other things, SUDENE had the power of creating mixed enterprises, involving union, state and even private capital. Such power was unprecedented within the political administrative framework of the country. The Brazilian state should become a producer in the Northeast, but enterprises could be set up in practically every sector of activity; indeed, a series of investments were made ranging from water supply services to industrial ventures such as USIBA steelworks (Usinas Siderurgicas da Bahia). That was the first time the state played such a role in the region. That is why it played it without the ambiguities of the producer state in the Centre-South.

SUDENE could also allow imports of industrial and agricultural equipment at privileged exchange rates (câmbio de custo), after consultation with SUMOC (predecessors of the Central Bank) over those cases which could negatively affect the balance of payments; it could recommend tariff exemption for the importation of equipment, participating, for this reason, in the Tariff Policies Council (Conselho de Politica Aduaneira). Law 3692, which created SUDENE, totally exempted from payment of income tax all new firms processing local raw materials, and partially exempted those which were already doing that. Taken as a whole, the economic advantages granted by SUDENE legislation constitute a mechanism whereby that part of the total surplus value appropriated by the state in the form of taxes was transformed into capital. In other words, the objective was to turn a substantial part of the national wealth appropriated by the state into prerequisites of monopoly expansion in the Northeast, with the assistance of the counterpart of such an expansion: the monopoly state.

In abstract, the project did not necessarily collide with the interests of the local bourgeoisie; in practice, however, the internationally-associated bourgeoisie of the Centre-South took the lion's share, by virtue of higher organic composition of capital, greater production and higher rates of profit. The weakness of local capital was such as to make difficult its reproduction under the new circumstances; the fiscal exemptions granted to them just put off their bankruptcy, except for those regional groups which were already integrated into the international associated sector and had expanded their operations beyond the regional boundaries. One could mention, among the latter, the industrial and financial Baptista da Silva group, the Bezerra de Mello group, owner of industries in the Centre-South involved in nation-wide hotels, the Lundgren group, owner of the big national chain of cloth retailers (Casas Pernambucanas), the Mariani Bittencourt group, controlling the Banco da Bahia, and the Calmon de Sá group, owner of the Banco Economico da Bahia.

SUDENE's strategy could be seen as a brilliant example of how to avoid the frontal attack. It is important, however, to bear in mind the concrete conditions under which such a strategy was carried out; the military language expressed, in fact, a political

situation involving regional and national class conflicts, as
well as the relationship between the state and society in the
country. Instead of tackling directly the conditions of reproduction of the agrarian economy in the region, the SUDENE proposals started off from a supposed economic impracticability of
the semi-arid region; that was a means of flanking the agrarian
conflict. The problem of the sugar economy was formulated in
terms of an inadequacy between good quality natural resources and
the existing technical division of labour, avoiding thereby any
reference to the social conflicts at the core of the sugar sector.
The migratory flux towards the Centre-South was treated either
from the point of view of the economic inadequacies of the semi-
arid region, or from that of a false conflict between migrants and
workers of the receiving area; this way of dealing with the problem
dodged the issue of class conflict in the capitalist centres of
the Centre-South. SUDENE also emphasised the *swelling* of the
coastal cities of the Northeast and the related question of urban
under-employment, avoiding any reflection on the real nature of
such phenomena. Its main cause should be looked for in the process
of division of labour at the national level promoted by the industrial expansion of the Centre-South.

What was the objective of SUDENE's thrust? It was to remove
the cotton and cattle oligarchy from the state in the Northeast.
Such an objective interested, for completely different reasons,
all social forces in the region; i.e., the popular classes, the
local industrial bourgeoisie, the international associated bourgeoisie, and the popular classes of the Centre-South. SUDENE
could, therefore, attach to such an operation a socially *neutral*
character; in so far as the removal of the oligarchy was accompanied by local investment by private firms of the surplus appropriated by the state, the inevitable result could only be the
transfer of power to the internationally-associated bourgeoisie
of the Centre-South.

Given its objectives, SUDENE could not follow a clear-cut course.
In fact, the popular forces would, at a certain moment, make their
influence felt in the anti-oligarchic coalition which supported it.
From its creation in 1959 to the approval of the first Plano
Diretor in 1961, SUDENE was affected by the shifting alliances
involving the social forces which supported it and even those
which opposed it. This process of alignment and realignment can
be analysed in three non-chronological moments. In a first moment,
the local industrial bourgeoisie and the internationally-associated
bourgeoisie closed ranks with the cotton and cattle oligarchy when
researches on the viability of the semi-arid region threatened the
structure of land tenure. In a second moment, the local industrial
bourgeoisie collided with the internationally-associated bourgeoisie when it became clear that the latter would be the exclusive
beneficiaries of SUDENE's policies. Finally, as a consequence of
the local bourgeois opposition to those policies, SUDENE had to
count more and more on popular support in order to destroy its
main enemy, the *old* state, embodied in the DNOCS, and implement
the integration of the Northeast into the national economy. This
third moment is illustrated by public meetings in which the popular
forces petitioned for the approval of the first Plano Diretor.

The seizure of the state in the Northeast by monopoly capital did not automatically follow from the creation of SUDENE, nor from the functioning of the system of fiscal advantages in its original form. The nature of planning in the region was also affected by social movement; SUDENE's intervention remained irresolute as long as class conflicts were not solved. The dominance of the Centre-South in the Northeast was, in fact, made possible by a provision of the law approving the first Plano Diretor whereby income tax deductions were granted to firms investing in the Northeast, proportionate to their investments. It is worth mentioning that article 34 of the Law No. 3959, which provided for such deductions, had been proposed by Gileno de Carli, a Northeast congressman associated with the sugar industry and President of the Instituto do Alcool e do Açuacar. Carli took the idea from similar policies conceived for the Italian Mezzogiorno, and thereby introduced one of the missing instruments for the financing of monopoly capital: the almost complete transformation of the surplus appropriated by the state into capital. Obviously, the instrument benefited the expanding monopoly capital, since the higher the amount of taxes to be paid, the higher would be the deduction. Through the regulation of Law No 3959 and in the law of the second Plano Diretor, the SUDENE tried to concentrate all resources thus generated in a general investment fund (FIDENE, Fundo de Desenvolvimento do Nordeste) for the financing of projects approved by SUDENE itself. Subscription to this general fund, however, was, according to the law, just an option, the other possibility being direct investment in industrial enterprises. Not surprisingly, investors preferred the second alternative, and FIDENE eventually became extinct.

SUDENE's consistent portrayal of the Northeast as a 'problem region', as 'the poorest area of the Western Hemisphere', and as a 'threat to national unity' must also be seen in the light of the American politics at the time. Kennedy's external 'new frontier', the Alliance for Progress, represented a new style of international relations, adapted to the new stage of inter-imperialist as well as capitalist-socialist block competition. The Americans had already long since turned their attentive eyes to the region. A documentary film made by American ABC Television entitled *The Troubled Land* focused on the political emergence of the agrarian dominated classes in 1959, under the leadership of the Peasant Leagues. This documentary pretended to stand by the peasants and rural workers, as it mentioned the violence committed by the coroneis and senhores de engenho; a well-known politician, industrialist and landowner, appeared in close-up pointing a gun at some unseen target, obviously the peasants. The film also showed a mutirão led by the Peasant Leagues, in which Francisco Julião appeared in person. The clear message was that the peasants and rural workers of the Northeast were on the verge of occupying the land.

In the first months of Kennedy's administration, a host of observers, including an unknown Mr Henry Kissinger, visited the Northeast. In July 1961, after consultations with the American Embassy in Brazil, the White House invited Celso Furtado to Washington in order to examine the problems afflicting the region

with President Kennedy himself, and to discuss Alliance for Progress
financial aid to regional development as defined by SUDENE's
projects and programmes.   In few other moments in the history of
Brazilian-American relations has imperialist interference in
internal affairs been more impudent.   The self-esteem of some
important characters, the will to preserve the mystique of Kennedy's
period, and the present amiable relations between the two countries
have so far impeded the complete disclosure and denunciation of
that interference.   Part of the truth has come out in Roett's *The
Politics of Foreign Aid*, and Joseph A. Page's *The Revolution that
Never Was*, but these studies have not broken with the Alliance for
Progress's rhetoric, and ascribe the failure of the association
between Furtado's SUDENE and US aid to some superficial causes
such as the adoption of different criteria for the definition of
investment priorities, or linguistic difficulties.

   As a result of these talks, a team of the Alliance for Progress
arrived in the Northeast at the end of 1961; it was headed by
Merwin Bohan, ex-ambassador and a member of the old Joint (Brazil-
US) Commission.   The team's conclusions were published in a document called Northeast Team Survey Report, which came out at the
beginning of 1962 in English and Portuguese.   The original version
of this document, best known as the Bohan Report, is quoted in
the present study; (10) it contained such direct and open recommendations to curb the Peasant Leagues Movement that it could not
be accepted by the Brazilian government.

   A second version was then prepared, with corrections and
deletions suggested by the government; this version was then incorporated into the programme of the Alliance for Progress.   Although
a direct mention of the Peasant Leagues in the correlation of
forces in the Northeast was avoided, the basic content of the
document remained the same.   The first part of the recommendation
made by the Bohan team envisaged a crash programme of an assis-
tencialist nature, whose stated objective was to neutralise the
Peasant Leagues and to undermine the political leadership of the
emerging popular movement.   The short-sighted scope of the American
policy-makers was somewhat broadened in the second part of the
document, where programmes and projects of economic development
were formally suggested.   In reality, this second part of the Bohan
Report proposed the demographic draining of the Northeast in order
to reduce pressures which, in the cities as well as in the countryside, now took political forms.   This was compounded by a programme of public works, whose immediacy and assistencialism were
patent. (11)   This programme was also aimed at the setting up of
a road network allowing for major military operations against the
popular movement whenever necessary.   The Americans neither trusted
SUDENE, nor the Brazilian government, so they tried to boycott
SUDENE's plans.   Indeed, all the programmes concerned however
slightly with real issues of Northeast development were either
mentioned with extreme caution or straightforwardly discarded by
the Bohan Report.   Examples of this are the Report's recommendation
that the socio-economic structure of the sugar cane region should
not be touched, and that the capacity of the Paulo Afonso hydro-
electrical plant should not be increased. (12)   It is not difficult
to see what was behind those propositions: on the one hand, the

Americans were not interested in antagonising the local industrial bourgeoisie; on the other, they were not keen on fortifying a state-owned enterprise controlled by unsympathetic political forces.

US aid in the Northeast attempted in effect to undermine SUDENE's authority by offering direct aid to those state governments considered to be politically opposed to the popular movement. The first deal of this kind was made with the government of Cid Sampaio in Pernambuco, when the Northeast Agreement itself had still not been put into effect. The second involved the government of Aluísio Alves of Rio Grande do Norte; this deal was sanctioned by President Goulart, whose myopic political tactics consisted of weakening his left wing, represented in the Northeast by Miguel Arraes; and SUDENE had to swallow it. The American Consulate in Recife grew to the magnitude of an embassy, comprising more than eleven consuls and a legion of officials, including CIA people disguised as Peace Corps agents and even technical and diplomatic personnel. In fact, apart from the activities related to the so-called Northeast Agreement, the American government launched various parallel programmes such as that of CLUSA, whose objective was to infiltrate rural unions controlled by the church. CLUSA was, in reality, a CIA organisation, as revealed by Joseph A. Page in his book quoted above.

The undermining of SUDENE's authority was a strategic operation by US aid and the Alliance for Progress. SUDENE's role itself was still undefined and in a situation where government intervention through its regional agency depended more and more on popular backing in the Northeast. Page and Riordan Roett have put forward the naive view that the disrupting action of US aid prevented the eclosion of a 'revolution without violence' and helped to preserve the status quo by reinforcing the rural oligarchic power, including that of the sugar cane bourgeoisie. In reality, US aid's intervention broke the status quo and contributed toward the consolidation of bourgeois hegemony at the national level under the aegis of international and mainly American capital; the Bohan Report itself had already made clear that the *Northeast problem* would only be solved by the complete integration of the region to the national economy. (13)

The Bohan Report's firm stand for the capitalist integration of the Northeast did not lack a machiavellian aspect. It publicly associated SUDENE with imperialism, though in a sort of conflictive relationship. As a consequence, SUDENE lost part of the popular support required for the unambiguous adoption of programmes reflecting the popular aspirations; thereafter, the complete control of the agency by the international and associated bourgeoisie of the Centre-South would depend exclusively on the solution of the conflict at the national level. When the populist regime reached its final stage, the opposition of the popular forces in the Northeast to SUDENE was irremediable, as a consequence of the agency's complete surrender to imperialist and national associated interests. Indeed, SUDENE itself had withdrawn from the proposal of the second *Plano Diretor*, which included a provision that only one hundred per cent national firms could enjoy fiscal deductions for investment in the region.

The government of Miguel Arraes in Pernambuco denounced the US
aid agreements for educational projects (the first of the *crash
projects* mentioned above) signed by his predecessor, Cid Sampaio.
Arraes argued that a state in the Brazilian federation was not
entitled to get into such kinds of deal with a foreign government.
One of US aid's objectives, as shown earlier, was to weaken SUDENE's
position; despite this, SUDENE preferred not to take part in the
argument, adopting in this the same tactics as Goulart, who sought
to dissociate himself from the popular forces on his left. The
agency, moreover, helped US aid to dismantle the peasant associations. It took part, for instance, in the highly demagogic visit
by Robert Kennedy to the Engenho Galileía (sugar plantation and
mill) which was the symbol of the Peasant Leagues. In this visit,
Kennedy gave the peasants a power generator; when he asked one of
the peasant leaders of Galileía, however, what he would regard
as the best possible gift, the reply was: 'the withdrawal of the
police from Engenho Galileía'. SUDENE also sponsored the so-called
Tiriri Project, whereby the Engenho Tiriri, in the south of Pernambuco, was rented to a peasant co-operative; the project was
intended to present, through its demonstration effects, an alternative to the Leagues and Unions, and at the same time to protect
the land tenure structure in the zona da mata. Finally, SUDENE
strongly backed the colonisation project of the Alto Turi in
Maranhão, despite abundant evidence of its unviability; the real
objective of the project, in fact, was to reduce the pressure on
the land in the region, exercised by politically independent rural
workers. All this illustrates SUDENE's removal from the popular
camp and surrender to the emerging capitalist forces.

4 THE SUDENE AND THE PLANNING OF THE HEGEMONIC EXPANSION OF
   MONOPOLY CAPITAL

All elements of the regional and national class struggle were cast
together in the 1964 crisis, and the outcome of the conflict in
the Northeast was determined by the growing acuteness of the political divisions at the capitalist centre and by the intervention
of the Armed Forces. Regional planning, as a consequence, acquired
then its definitive character. As this article has tried to show,
the origins of the non-spontaneous process of state intervention
in the region can only be explained, on the one hand, by two types
of contradiction; those within the Northeastern economy, and
those between the Northeastern economy and that of the Centre-
South; and, on the other hand, by the different class conflicts
emerging from these contradictions. Nothing was predetermined,
however, with regard to the historical role of SUDENE; that is
why its evolution has been related, in this study, to the various
political situations arising from changes in the correlation of
forces, and from the successive realignments of the social representations. One can think, ex hypothesi, that if the class conflict in the Centre-South had not reached the point it did, the
outcome of the struggle in the Norhteast could have been other
than it was. Such speculation cannot be pushed too far, because
the situation in the Northeast contributed, in its turn, to the

sharpening of political conflict in the Centre-South. In any event, post-1964 SUDENE reflects more the political watershed at the national level than the outcome of the regional conflicts.

Through the system of fiscal incentives (known as the 'system of 34/18'), SUDENE inaugurated one of the most effective devices for the financing of monopoly expansion in Brazil. It is not fortuitous that the trick of the fiscal incentives should be copied by various government agencies operating in other regions or sectors; this is, in fact, essentially linked to the reproduction of monopoly capital in the country. The incentives have first been extended to the Amazon region, to fishing, reforestation and tourism. Later on, they have been orientated to the financing of exports, programmed obsolescence, and various other fields; as a whole, the fiscal incentives system constitutes a powerful mechanism whereby the entire national wealth is transformed into the condition of capitalist reproduction. Thus, the increasing conjunction of the state and the internationally-associated bourgeoisie was to a certain extent prefigured by SUDENE. In this sense, the agency was the forerunner of the authoritarian state; it announced the end of a period of ambiguous relations between the state and bourgeoisie, which would thereon come so close together that they would appear to be the same thing. Correspondingly, the limits between state and civil society would be apparently blurred.

In the area of the transfer of the hegemony of the internationally-associated bourgeoisie from the Centre-South to the Northeast, the results of the industrialisation carried out under the aegis of 34/18 are perfectly well known. The principal economic groups of the Centre-South transferred themselves to the Northeast, implanting factories and productive units which ensured the monopolistic homogenisation of national economic space, even when, in some cases, they operated with spare capacity, and even when they represented a duplication of production that, from a marginalist point of view, could be more economic in the Centre-South. Even when the results of the industrialisation programme left much to be desired from the point of view of employment creation, or deviated from the labour-intensive pattern envisaged by SUDENE at the beginning, it is undeniable that the Northeast was completely integrated into the national economy. There is no sense, then, in continuing to speak of regional economies in Brazil, and the fact that SUDENE itself continues to play the same old tune merely results in the discrediting of the regional planning agency, which incidentally has ceased to have any sense of *planning*. (14)

It is a different matter to think that the problems of the people of the Northeast, of its peasants and of its workers, have been resolved. The 'resolution' of regional and even national class conflicts has been achieved by the dismantling of the political forces of these classes, by repression. From here, it can be seen that the resolution (this time not in quotation marks) of the questions linked to the raising of the standard of living of the labouring classes of the Northeast is now undoubtedly linked to the destiny of the whole of the Brazilian working class. It is for this reason that we have argued earlier in this article that the 'assault on heaven' represented by the challenge thrown out at the bourgeoisie by the labouring classes of the Northeast and of Brazil should not be lamented. It has been a landmark in the socio-political history of the country; regional specificities no longer exist, and the form in which the monopolistic state resolved class conflict at that particular conjuncture of Brazilian history has consequences that cannot be minimised. The insistence of the SUDENE bureaucracy, impregnated perhaps with nostalgia and certainly clothed with the best intentions, is, in continuing to posit the problems of the Northeast as *regional*, now historically reactionary; it only serves to oil the wheels of monopoly capital.

As for the industrial bourgeoisie of the Northeast, it has paid a price that it could not have dreamed of. And its existence is 'irrepetible desde siempos y para siempre', to use the admirable words of Gabriel García Márquez. In the movement of concentration and centralisation of capital in Brazil, and in the particular form imparted to it by the planning of SUDENE, there is no place for it. The few regional economic groups that survived managed to do so because they raised themselves to the same level as the big monopoly groups of the national economy. And to some extent they were already moving to this position at the time of the creation of SUDENE; the tax advantages administered by it served them equally as mechanisms for concentrating and centralising capital. The rest of the industrial bourgeoisie of the Northeast was irreparably thrown into the dustbin of history. Dies irae.

The agrarian cotton- and cattle-raising oligarchy of the Northeast, which had controlled the state for so long, and which thought for a moment that it had won in 1964, survived only to be able to write its own epitaph. It survives only because in truth almost all of Brazilian agriculture is still a vast area of primitive accumulation; but the movements of capital concentration will end up reaching it as well. This is the meaning of the recent expansions of capitalism in the countryside in the Centre-South, especially in São Paulo, Rio Grande do Sul and Parana. De te fabula narratur. Some of its members survive as spectres, phantoms who now speak because they have been transformed into state functionaries. This survival, this transformation into state functionaries, is truly a sign of its complete dissolution in the future.

At its limit, the expansion of monopoly capitalism in Brazil points to the dissolution of the regions as special and differentiated areas of production and appropriation of value. Certainly, sectoral differences will persist, but no one can truthfully say that the reproduction of Rhodia's capital in the Northeast (to take an example) is different from the reproduction of Rhodia's capital in São Paulo. This movement coincides with, and in fact constitutes the basis of, the centralisation of power in Brazil at the level of the Federal Executive, and it is certainly one of the main ingredients of the permanent institutional impasse that the Brazilian political regime is living through. The other vital ingredient, of a more profound character, is the openly exploitative relation that the regime is able to maintain with the subordinated classes, with the workers of the countryside and of the cities, and with the peasants and semi-peasants in all parts of the country.

NOTES

1 The bibliography on SUDENE is not large. Among the books and
   articles on the subject, it is worth mentioning: JOSEPH A. PAGE,
   The Revolution that Never Was: Northeast Brazil 1955-1964
   (Grasman Publishers, New York, 1972) and RIORDAN ROETT, *The
   Politics of Foreign Aid in the Brazilian Northeast* (Vanderbilt
   University Press, Nashville, 1972). These two books focus on
   the American policies for the Northeast. The MPhil thesis of
   A. COHN, *Crise Regional e Planejamento* (Universidade de São
   Paulo, 1972) analyses the political aspects of the creation
   of SUDENE. SUDENE's performance is assessed in K. CAIO
   KOCK-WESER, *La SUDENE, Doce Años de Planificación para el
   Desarrollo en el Nordeste Brasileiro* (Instituto Latino-
   americano de Investigaciones Sociales (ILDIS), Santiago de
   Chile, 1973). CELSO FURTADO, *Social Reconstruction in Societies
   Dominated by Traditional Groups*, is a document presented to
   the Social Planning Conference in Puerto Rico, 1966; the
   author analyses the conflict between the objectives of SUDENE
   and the interests of the conservative forces in the Northeast.
   ANTONIO BARROS DE CASTRO, O Desenvolvimento Recente do
   Nordeste, in *7 Ensaios sobre a Economia Brasileira* (Forense
   Editora, Rio de Janeiro, 1972) contains an analysis of
   BDENE's policies in the light of the recent development of
   Brazilian and Northeastern economics. FRANCISCO DE OLIVEIRA
   and HENRI-PHILIPPE REICHSTUL, Mudanças na Divisão Inter-regional
   do Trabalho no Brasil, in *Estudos CEBRAP 4* (Editora Brasileira
   de Ciencias, São Paulo, 1973) examine the effects of the
   policies of fiscal incentives on the industrial structure,
   and the tendencies towards capital centralisation in the
   region. The emergence of SUDENE in the context of capitalist
   expansion in Brazil was studied by OCTAVIO IANNI in As Origens
   Políticas da SUDENE, in *Revista Mexicana de Sociologia*, No. 4,
   October - December 1971, Mexico. Another analysis of the
   process of industrialisation promoted by fiscal incentives
   and its relations with capital accumulation at the national
   level can be found in RAIMUNDO MOREIRA, *El Proceso Industrial
   en el Nordeste Brasileiro y el Proceso de Acumulación de
   Capital a Escala Nacional en la Decada del 60* (Instituto
   Torcuato de Tell, Centro de Estudios Urbanos y Regionales,
   Buenos Aires, 1975). Also important, though written at an
   early stage and therefore lacking historical perspective:
   ALBERT O. HIRSCHMAN, *Journeys Toward Progress* (The Twentieth
   Century Fund, New York, 1963); also by the same author,
   Desenvolvimento Industrial Brasileiro e o Mecanismo de Crédito
   Fiscal do Artigo 34/18, in *Revista Brasileira de Economia*, 21
   (4), (Dec. 1967, Rio de Janeiro); STEPHEN H. ROBOCK, *Brazil's
   Developing Northeast: A Study of Regional Planning and Foreign
   Aid* (Brookings Institution, Washington, 1963).
2 A brief remark on the theory of the economic role of the state
   can elucidate our position. The pertinent question here is
   this: what is the state in monopoly capitalism? All available
   answers seem insufficient. The most common Marxist interpretation holds that the state is a kind of crutch; it tries to

counteract the tendency of the rate of profit to fall. Rudolf
Hilferding contended that financial capital gradually became
separated from real capital. In our view, such separation has
not occurred; it is neither necessary nor possible, since it
would reduce the rate of profit itself. It seems to us that
the state in monopoly capitalism is financial capital itself;
as such it performs the transformation of the whole monetary
resources of the country into money capital, and avoids the
economically dangerous concentration of financial means in
private hands.

3   Various articles analyse the electoral results in most of the
Northeastern States during the period 1945-64. Most of them,
however, miss the social conflicts underlying the electoral
process. See, for instance, F.F. CASTRO, A Campanha Eleitoral
de 1958 no Piauí, in *Revista Brasileira de Estudos Políticos*,
8 (Belo Horizonte, April 1960); GLAUCIO D. DILLON SOARES, El
Sistema Electoral y Representación de los Grupos Sociales en
Brasil, in *Revista Latino Americana de Ciencia Política*, FLACSO
2 (1), (April 1971, Santiago de Chile); A.F. MONTENEGRO,
Tentativa de Interpretação das Eleições de 1958 no Ceará, in
Revista Brasileira de Estudos Políticos, op.cit.; NELSON DE
SANZA SAMPAIO, Eleições Bahianas, in *Revista Brasileira de
Estudos Políticos*, op.cit.; GLAUCIO VEIGA, et al., Geografia
Eleitoral de Pernambuco, in *Revista Brasileira de Estudos
Políticos*, op.cit.; AMELIA COHN, Crise Regional e Planejamento,
op.cit., in footnote (1).

4   CELSO FURTADO, *Dialética do Desenvolvimento* (Editora Fundo
de Cultura, Rio de Janeiro, 1964) and *Teoria e Política do
Desenvolvimento Económico* (Editora Nacional, São Paulo, 1969).

5   CELSO FURTADO, *A Operação Nordeste* (ISEB, Rio de Janeiro,
1959). The document *Uma Política de Desenvolvimento Económico
para o Nordeste*, (GTDN, Departamento de Imprensa Nacional,
Rio de Janeiro, 1959) is widely believed to have been written
by Celso Furtado. The GTDN is the basic document for the
creation of SUDENE.

6   *Uma Política de Desenvolvimento*, op.cit., p.8.

7   FURTADO, *A Operação Nordeste*, op.cit., pp.14-16.

8   SUDENE: *Boletim Económico*, vol. 1, No. 1, 1962.

9   FERNANDO HENRIQUE MENEZES DE OLIVEIRA, ZENALDO BARBOSA ROCHA,
MÁRCIO ROBEIRO MACIEL and JOSÉ DE MELO GOMES, A Natureza
Juidica da SUDENE, in SUDENE, *Boletim Económico*, vol. 1,
No. 1, 1962.

10 From the Bohan Report:
    How could the rural worker know that there is a possibility
    of social change and progress without any resort to vio-
    lence? ... When (they) have a problem ... they go to the
    Leagues for help. Apart from their revolutionary doctrine,
    the Leagues' most alluring services are sympathetic advice
    and quasi-juridical assistance to the workers. In reality,
    the Leagues do very little for the peasant in the tribunals,
    and turn their failures into supplementary evidence that
    a drastic change of the social order is required. But the
    worker, like a beaten dog, is impressed by the sympathy
    with which he is treated, and joins the Leagues. (Relatório

da Missão ao Nordeste do Brasil, Anexo I, Programa a Curto
Prazo. Centros de Trabalho Aliança para Progresso. Original
version in Portuguese, typewritten.)

(To avoid the workers' claims being dealt with exclusively
by the Leagues) we are proposing in our short-run programme
that our centres should be set up in the sugar cane region
and also in some urban areas where the Leagues have been
more active.

Apart from these short-run measures, (we should also tackle)
the more basic problem, which is to assist the anti-
communist elements among the rural and industrial workers
in the formation of stable labour organizations. This is
the only way of fighting Castro and other communist influences upon this quite volatile segment of society (sic).
One of the most promising efforts in this direction was
undertaken by the Catholic Church. In Rio Grande do Norte,
five Unions, comprising 28 municípios, were created under
the leadership of Dom Eugenio Salles and his Serviço de
Assistencia Rural (SAR). (Relatório da Missão ao Nordeste
do Brasil, op.cit., Anexo II, Programa a Longo Prazo.)

11   The Bogan Report recommended (in Part I, Melhoramento do
Aproveitamento de Recursos Materiaia. Condições de Vida Rural
e Operta de Alimentos para o Nordeste, 6. Fixacas das Popu-
lações Ruralis) that 1,500,000 Northeastern families should
find new job opportunities in other regions in the short run,
plus 10,000 yearly. 'The families who prefer to stay in the
region', continues the Report, 'should leave their present
communities'.

12   The Bohan Report, op.cit., Anexo II. Programa a Longo Prazo.
C. Energia Elétrica.

13   'As stated above, the solution for the Northeast problem is
a tighter integration of this region with the rest of the
country, which is fast expanding'. (Bohan Report, op.cit.,
B. O Programa Quinquenal de Desenvolvimento.)

14   For an assessment of these results, see DE OLIVEIRA and
REICHSTUL, op.cit., and MOREIRA, op.cit.

For Product Safety Concerns and Information please contact our EU representative GPSR@taylorandfrancis.com
Taylor & Francis Verlag GmbH, Kaufingerstraße 24, 80331 München, Germany